Semiotic Analysis a Policy

MW00577126

Semiotic Analysis and Public Policy evaluates several key areas of public policy that are dependent on narrative, naming, sign, and branding to create meaning. Semiotic analysis, drawing on the work of Saussure, Peirce, and others, allows for creation of a case-oriented model of brand versus product, and of medium compared with message.

Using a critical Habermasian lens, Atkinson convincingly exposes approaches focusing too heavily on instrumentality and rhetoric that claims a resolution of complex societal dilemmas. Rooted in the literature on public policy and semiotics, Atkinson creates an opportunity to delve more fully into the creation of narratives and meaning in policy, and the origins and maintenance of public programs. Evaluation of such programs shows various levels of disconnect between popular understanding of public considerations, political outcomes, and what results from the administrative/regulatory process in support of the law.

This book will be of interest for scholars and researchers of public policy, policy analysis, public administration, public management, and policy implementation.

Christopher L. Atkinson is Assistant Professor in the Public Administration program at the University of West Florida in Pensacola, Florida, USA. He serves as contributing faculty in the doctoral program at Walden University and has taught courses in the School of Public Administration at Florida Atlantic University, Boca Raton, Florida, and at Unity College, Unity, Maine. He received his PhD from Florida Atlantic University, and BA and MPA degrees from George Washington University in Washington, DC. His research interests include public management and policy studies, public budgeting and procurement, regulation, and emergency management.

Routledge Studies in Governance and Public Policy

For more information about this series, please visit: https://www.routledge.com/Routledge-Studies-in-Governance-and-Public-Policy/book-series/GPP

Semiotic Analysis and Public Policy

Connecting Theory and Practice

Christopher L. Atkinson

Routledge
Taylor & Francis Group

NEW YORK AND LONDON

First published 2019
by Routledge
52 Vanderbilt Avenue, New York, NY 10017

and by Routledge
2 Park Square, Milton Park, Abingdon, Oxon, OX14 4RN

First issued in paperback 2020

Routledge is an imprint of the Taylor & Francis Group, an informa business

© 2019 Taylor & Francis

Library of Congress Cataloging-in-Publication Data
Names: Atkinson, Christopher L., editor.
Title: Semiotic analysis and public policy : connecting theory and practice / edited by Christopher Atkinson.
Description: New York, NY : Routledge, 2019. |
Series: Routledge studies in governance and public policy ; 34 |
Includes bibliographical references and index.
Identifiers: LCCN 2018056893 (print) |
LCCN 2019004012 (ebook) | ISBN 9781351205993 (Master) |
ISBN 9781351205986 (Adobe) | ISBN 9781351205962 (ePub3) |
ISBN 9781351205979 (Mobi) | ISBN 9780815383475 (hbk) |
ISBN 9781351205993 (ebk)
Subjects: LCSH: Policy sciences—Case studies. | Political planning—Case studies. | Semiotics—Political aspects—Case studies.
Classification: LCC H97 (ebook) | LCC H97 .S46 2019 (print) |
DDC 320.601/4—dc23
LC record available at https://lccn.loc.gov/2018056893

ISBN 13: 978-0-367-67169-3 (pbk)
ISBN 13: 978-0-8153-8347-5 (hbk)

Typeset in Times New Roman
by codeMantra

To Debra Atkinson, my mom, for her work ethic,
&
To Janet Smith, my grandmother, retired postmaster of
St. David, Illinois, USA, and exemplar of public service.

Contents

List of Figures

List of Tables

Preface

The Words Fail Us

Christopher L. Atkinson

In the introductory editorial of a 2018 issue of Public Administration Review (PAR), Jeremy Hall and R. Paul Battaglio lamented recent US federal government dismissals of evidence- and science-based budgeting and policy. "This was shocking to those of us who believe in professional public management and support practices, policies, and management approaches that are evidence-informed or evidence-based" (Hall & Battaglio, 2018, p. 181). They went on to warn of how the term 'evidence-based' could be employed symbolically in an environment characterized by voters motivated by values and beliefs – that using the term in this way might *game the system*, appealing to bias. They claimed that the PAR "plays a central role in this debate...in transferring knowledge to practitioners on the front line who can make immediate use of our findings across all levels of government and international boundaries" (p. 182).

Hall and Battaglio are surely correct about the use of terms in symbolic ways. Throwing the net wide, public administration includes a host of disciplines, touching social and natural sciences. Meaning and seeking after knowledge can get lost amid the political context, where beliefs might be as important as facts in determining an outcome.

Public practitioners are busier than ever throughout the world, with government increasingly expected to do more with less under often-hostile political and practical circumstances. While I read PAR and generally enjoy the articles, the assertion of PAR's central role is overconfident, if taken as the voice of public administration as an academic discipline. It is a sound question whether most frontline practitioners read PAR, or most academic work in public administration or its related disciplines for that matter. One might be able to make a case for the membership in the American Society for Public Administration (ASPA) as beneficial for a government job, because of ASPA's valuable practitioner-oriented webinars on program evaluation, human resources, and other career-oriented concerns. Most public administrators work outside a context when they have the luxury of time to read academic journals, even if journals were written precisely to their interest and potential use.

I was once asked by a student how they should bring theory into the public workplace. I measured my words: Bring it in carefully, because the modern public workplace is busy and performance is essential to survival. Public-sector leadership is ideology-driven and aware of how symbols might trump evidence. It seems as though the academy is sometimes not aware of this, given its tendency to maintain a steady focus on production of work that is, sorry to write, irrelevant to most practitioners.

The more the academy asserts its relevance, the more practice might be tempted to waive off public administration as a discipline, let alone a profession. It is more important than ever before that administrators, and the field's academics, not talk down or be seen as speaking in a condescending way to the public. It is essential that there be an increase in recognition that the reality of public administration's work is, for the public espousing it, their *reality*, whether positive or negative. The public is (mostly) outside of its government and suspicious of it; it needs to be welcomed back in. The separation between practice and research in the academy is real, and possibly widening. There is a question of priority: Closed theory-space that excludes and limits participation, or open theory-space, less constrained, comfortable with debate, and able to address and possibly even include opposing voices? (Abel, 2017).

For the public's part, people have plenty of reasons to question and doubt policy and programs; in the name of a supposed systematic, objective orientation, programs sweep in, supposedly offering tremendous improvements benefiting all concerned, only to leave questionable processes and outcomes in their wake. Science is misunderstood; its potential errors are not taken into account. The rigors of method and pretensions to objectivity do not stand up to practical application in the real world, across the spectrum of human experience. The concern with "true, objective knowledge" ignores the idea that interpretation is required to make sense of data; facts are derived as a consequence of both the person considering and the consideration. There is a need to balance the philosophical and methodological in policy studies, and to have respect for both; perception and theory guide development of what is construed to be fact – data themselves do not create facts or truths, or even lead to understanding, which is a better goal (Alvesson & Sköldberg, 2018).

The potential success told in narrative ultimately outweighs the practicality of implementation, at least initially, and in the minds of many not well acquainted with a public program. The story of potential success in a program is not even a pure description of what is likely, because the telling of the story is wrapped up in the self-reflexivity of the storyteller (Kim, 2016). We may be receiving not only the intent for a program, but also what the sender of the message feels about the client community, whether they understand the community well at all, or how confident the policymaker is in the solution being offered. Through stories, as Kim notes (2016), we are also reminded that there is more than one way to look at a situation.

Public administration's best role is to *host* this discourse and engage the public with integrity and attention to the consequence of the public's viewpoint. If public officials are good subject matter experts, that is one aspect of the work, but interacting and communicating with the public in a fruitful way *is the primary work*. What's more, it is a privilege.

Barring constructive interaction, segments of the public and leadership in the public sector may display a certain conceit, and speak with supposed authority about matters which they know little. Public administrators may do the same thing, in a public forum, and have their lack of understanding demonstrated to them by members of the public who know better. About government, the public may charge corruption or incompetence, and still suggest the presence of vast conspiracies, of a sort that would require near-perfect knowledge and timing from both individuals and institutions. Sometimes, when government fails to work, it is not because there was any intent or calculation at all. When we are incompetent, we are sometimes unable to figure that out; still, citizens may be blissfully unaware of the folly of their reasoning or assertions about public matters, especially when the assumptions come from a place of misunderstanding. Of course, there are times when the intent is for programs to fail, and program failure is not incompetence so much as is willful nonfeasance or negligence that does serve specific interests other than those of a program's intended clients. It is important to be critical enough in regular evaluations of public matters to know the difference; in any case, there is wisdom in foregoing a position of superiority, because we may not be entitled to it.

The assumptions being made about public bureaucracy – that public employees as a group are incompetent or worse – are especially foolish, in light of the fact that the public employs these people. These comments come from an uninformed place. By taking such an accusatorial view of public employees, based on unappised, biased, and self-interested rhetoric from elected officials or media outlets, the public is generally taking a pass on its truest, best role: participating, fully informed and constructively, in the public sphere. For some, high-placed concepts of civic-mindedness were swapped out for consumerism and individual pursuits, and service in the public interest for government-as-product or entitlement. Too many assumptions are made about the validity of constructs in the public sphere, as if willful ignorance were a badge of honor. Not only is the public manipulated – it might even be happy about it, with the assumption that the surface action – a favored candidate winning, or a crooked figure eliminated – has much at all to do with their individual lives. Rather than focusing on our pressing challenges as a society, the public may participate in fashioning others' ego-driven stories of conquest, and views of attaining the 'public interest,' like extras in a reality television show. When these activities come to naught, the public demands action, change, reform, or even revenge. But this is a poor excuse for public involvement, and by that time, the opportunity for intervention and correction has passed.

How did we get here? Can we hope for something better, or are we stuck with tribal brutishness, accusations of incompetence and ill-informed claims of superiority, and huge scores of people who need and deserve better service from their government, and frankly, from their society as a whole?

Public policy has been defined as "the study of government decisions and actions designed to deal with a matter of public concern" and are "**purposive** courses of action devised in response to a **perceived problem**" (Cochran & Malone, 2014, p. 3, *emphasis mine*). Policies are expressions of the will of the people, passed through an often-elaborate system of interpretation, and are expressions of how society and its government are changing to serve the public. Because this dynamic takes place in a public setting, the policies and programs may be taken to be representative of the public on some level, in the sense that public policy is not only about government choice in action but also about choosing among options, some that are more ethical or appropriate than others. The line between market values and morality perhaps has become blurred (Cochran & Malone, 2014). Absent individual efforts, the natural road to intervention in the public sphere has been through policy and institution of public programs.

While people become less engaged in certain respects, such as attending live public meetings of governing bodies, they have become more active online, through social networks and other virtual venues. While new forms of airing grievances are always welcome, it is questionable whether this participation amounts to much, when not accompanied by other forms of action. Where society could focus on obligations it has, the discussion too often rests on rights to one's apathy and the place of individuals, each utterly alone on millions of islands connected by smartphones. Meanwhile, the world of public policy moves forward, sometimes referring largely to itself, or to illustrations of a need to return to times long gone, in favored ideations of problems and their solutions. Meanwhile, much public work is being done, but for what ends?

Instrumental rationality and the legal tradition cannot hope to save us without help, even if society hinges largely on means and goals; as Habermas suggested, technology has become an ideology of its own, able to conceal hidden agendas, rather than serving as means to an end (Alvesson & Sköldberg, 2018). Rather than being a vehicle for accomplishing important public ends, the law may be obliging in concealing the real intent behind inscrutable, unapproachable language and process. Administrators may cover their actions with technological blather. It is a structuralist position that there are expectations of how law and policy are structured, to be considered the law. It is possible within this structure to bury intent. The image painted by law is not a mirror of the actual world; rather, it references "concepts in our mind" (Tyson, 2006, p. 214). The more we have structured the world in the form of legal frameworks, definitions, and the like, the more we might feel confident that the world created via the law is stable and unchanging, even if its basis is weak and lacking coherence with an actual, lived experience. Our experience of the world in policy is directed in some sense by how words are used in law – it is a mediation, and decisions are made for us about what we see or do not see. What law 'tells' us through such portrayals is accomplished via a system of rules, structures, and rudiments, and emphasis, and the presence or absence of certain facets, becomes very important to uncovering meaning (Tyson, 2006).

These are difficult times, and leadership is conspicuously absent in many instances; it may be that people want power without the responsibility. If "leaders think that they are special, that ordinary rules do not apply for them, and that followers should be expected to do as the leader says, not as the leader does" (Price, 2006, p. 1), where does this leave public policy in practice, obligations of the process and its implementers to the public, and any expectations the public may reasonably have for involvement in the public sphere? Actions of leaders may be attributable to their "belief and knowledge" rather than simple selfishness (Price, 2006, p. 1). Leaders in the public sector may not even fully comprehend what is expected of them from an ethical standpoint; a lack of knowledge and belief in one's base of understanding and need to act may lead to decisions that are not in the public interest, but because the leader is simply not aware, the decision's power to achieve positive change is fettered (Price, 2006). Attributing broad, near-total knowledge of the policy environment and the information needed to make decisions with full understanding to leaders is, on the face of it, absurd.

But, this is not a text that seeks to identify villains. Hopefully, leaders do the best with what they have, given their bounded rationality; the monochrome portrayal of people as entirely good or bad, for purposes of advancing policy beliefs, serves only to push differing sides further apart. As the level of leadership increases, so does the potential for leaders to lose the detail of the operation, and to act in a way that they feel is justified, even though others viewing such interactions may have an entirely different view. If leaders have no interest in carefully exploring data and analyses, and reviewing competing narratives, then the chance for maladministration is even higher.

The place of public administration is all the more important when we take stock of the realities of public-sector leadership. The public at-large might settle for agreeing with a leader, absent sufficient information by which to make an informed decision, simply because the individual seems nice, or is seen as a successful person. There is no real critical evaluation of policy positions or potential of same for attainment, most of the time.

What might make these times more difficult than others is the immediacy of response, the polarization of thought and the gap between sides in debates, and the need to tell stories, replete with heroes, villains, victims, all tied together with a happy ending to fit within the confines accorded by the 24/7 media cycle, reality or not. This holds at least until the next big story comes along. Critical insight, and attention to the use of signs, symbols, and myths, has never been more necessary to maintain coherence in the public sphere. People need to talk and move forward with one another, and to create more appropriate, tolerant, and inviting contexts. The need for faux-naïvety (Hair, 2011) and hiding of intellectual ability, to avoid harsh interaction with public stubbornness, similarly must end.

For many, there exists a need for "perpetuation of the past and serving the ends of an evanescent order" (Wellmer, 1974, p. 11), and challenges to this worldview, including critical theory, are thus met with disapproval. There is potential for liberation from this preferred path, but one must realize that the control on the collective viewpoint is more or less total, from an early age. One's acquisition of language, as Wellmer observed, is a training in social life that shapes how one sees reality, and constructs it. Not only are most unaware of the nature of this imposition from a critical standpoint, but they also do not interpret the meaning of what is going on around them, the communication exchanges, systems, and process, in any more than a cursory manner. It is a game, but many involved with this game are not aware that a game is being played. The supposed objectiveness of our daily reality is nothing of the sort; there is a domination of the masses, but it is not experienced as coercion as much as it is not experienced at all. We may not feel repressed by this system, so have no interest in being saved from it. Because there is little consciousness, patterns of reason can remain inflexible; if only through a bit more emphasis on instrumental rationality, we can achieve a just society (Wellmer, 1974). One answers the impossible with the farcical. Even in closely analyzing a scenario, there is a risk that a depiction of reality, socially constructed, is a mere fabrication, lacking the detail and nuance of the actual circumstance (Alvesson & Sköldberg, 2018).

The concern with staying within or rebuilding a traditional policy environment is that these are pretensions and artificialities, not unlike the rebuilding of a historical environment (Jackson, 1980). Recent interpretations may not result in the 'original landscape' or even an approximation, and are not the 'image of creation' (Jackson, 1980, p. 101). What is especially worrisome is that desired outcomes are anachronistic – a return to a halcyon period might be viewed as a return to the 'bad-old days' of prejudice or misunderstanding. It is as much 'what' with a policy as 'when.' There is nothing particularly sacred about any of it. Policies are tied to their historical present, created in the now as they are interpreted, even as they are, like the things the Smithsonian collects, bits and pieces of a vernacular past – considered and possibly cherished alongside the trappings of their contexts (Jackson, 1980). What might be otherwise considered a string of questionable assumptions and decisions makes more sense when considered in context. In reality, people want both: sentimentalization and a return to a Golden Age, and government and policies that make sense for today. Hand-crafted, on-trend, artisanal public administration; government-as-product, citizen-as-consumer, all imagined to work better with fewer resources and increasing demands, with convenient bureaucratic scapegoats when programs fail to achieve their objectives. When, if ever, is it something real?

There is not a set of generic ideas that allow comfort, upon which we may all agree. As a result, we may not remain within a false space of comfort, where competing ideas are not voiced, and those that disagree are not afforded the opportunity to share their views. The more attention one pays to protesting the right of others to speak, the more attention might be paid to the offending party and their words. Instead of an opportunity to disagree, society is becoming more inclined to trade discourse for opportunities to voice rage that is sometimes ill-informed, sometimes ineffectual against prevailing societal trends. The result can be that the potential for engagement from passionate participants in a discourse, which should be encouraged, is torn asunder by entropy. Instead of engaging ideas individually and offering individual voice, there is a sense that a shortcut is good enough – if the loudest voices in the room believe a certain concept, then it might be true more or less, and supporting it certainly is more appropriate than doing nothing, or allowing nonsensical, disagreeable, or appalling speech to be aired at all.

Symbols are paramount. Jung addressed this concern: "it is folly to dismiss [cultural symbols] because...they seem to be absurd or irrelevant. They are important constituents of our mental makeup and vital forces in the building up of human society, and...cannot be eradicated without serious loss. Where they are repressed...their specific energy disappears...with unaccountable consequences" (Jung, 1968, p. 83). What makes more sense is to attack ideas that give one discomfort on their merits, and argue against them forcefully with evidence. Debates become about performance of emotion and the power of the affront to one's sensibilities as a statement, and symbol itself, valid or not. This is dangerous because it reduces the opportunity for a robust, engaging public sphere, and because critical thinking is absent, revenge-taking may substitute for disagreement and growth. There are too many problems that require the public's cooperation and engagement, to move toward and achieve solutions.

The answer we seek probably does not lie on the periphery, either right or left. The public should be thinking for itself, and not be lulled into the idea that capitalism, conservatism, or progressivism have it 'all figured out' for us. What power has figured out is an ability to perpetuate itself and use people toward the ends of those in power. The public is prone to distortions, due to communication failures and intentional obfuscation, and is regularly and predictably distracted by pseudo-events. "By harboring, nourishing, and even enlarging our extravagant expectations we create the demand for the illusions with which we deceive ourselves. And which we pay others to make to deceive us" (Boorstin, 1992, p. 5).

When it comes to measures taken to reform programs, it is the programs themselves that are expected to carry out reforms, by and large. Bureaucratic organizations are resilient and meet such challenges fairly well but we should not be so unmindful of the cumulative impact of such "reformist" agendas over time, particularly those based in ideological notions of the failure of government to achieve efficiency or effectiveness. It is worth considering that public-sector employees do a commendable job carrying out the public's business as a general rule, and this is true even when their efforts are compared with those of the private sector (Caiden, 2001). This may lead us to the idea that "reform" and trashing of the public sector for political points in election cycles serves exactly that purpose, and worse, the damage such activity inflicts upon the public sector is doubtless ruinous over the long term, both to careerists in public service and to those who may consider a career in government.

However, the text of policy in its law form might be illusory, bearing little if any resemblance to the reality of the problem or issue its creation is intended to address. It could be vague, seeking after the expertise and detailed understanding of the other, in administration, to effect some sense of comprehension to the concern in play. This imperfect construct in the public sphere seeks to impersonate and then modify a caricature version of reality, though the body politics fails to understand well enough all players and machinations in place to actually achieve much of anything, most of the time. Because the system is not actually based so much upon the closeness of fit between policy and reality or accomplishment in outcomes, but rather on stability and creating the right conditions for operation of markets, the lack of movement makes little difference. The disconnect is hardly noticeable: "Government itself had become too big, had taken too much upon itself as insurer and guarantor of economy and society, manager of natural and human resources, and sponsor of intellectual and cultural talent…beyond its…capacity to realize" (Caiden, 2001, p. 655).

Our desire for progress is in some aspect how we are getting stuck; it is a priority inversion – where a low priority item takes over our resources, taking away from the larger task in context. The fact is, the small aspects are important, and how larger aims are achieved. A policy is often constrained by precedent. Efforts to achieve 'effectiveness' fail because there is too much attention to the efficiency of certain components. Those components can be fine-tuned, with not much benefit to the effectiveness of the system. Further, there is a tendency to want to address the one most important factor, even when the problem at hand might have a multi-factor cause, and necessitate a more complex design in terms of solution (Christian & Griffiths, 2016). The need for the simple, quick-hit answer is popular in politics because it can make someone appear a genius, but real resolution is more often with the details overlooked in an oversimplified model.

This book engages instances of regulation, policy, and public constructs through semiotics and lenses of critical theory. It was written with both academics and practitioners in mind. I began writing this book with the general concept that **words fail us** (a play on Murray Edelman's 1977 book titled *Political language: Words that succeed and policies that fail*). The prescriptions and pronouncements alone do not accomplish the difficult work of government or of engaging the complexity of the public sphere, even though they might accomplish a connotative, vision-forming, and branding task (Berger, 2019). Rhetoric does not build bridges between groups or heal wounds; rhetoric is self-interested, and through its efforts to persuade, creates winners and losers, heroes and villains, and stories that are as serviceable, if not more saleable to mass audiences for constituting reality, as indicators of social change. The words do not have to accomplish anything other than to create belief and spur desired actions that lead either directly to processes that produce preferred policy options, or become a self-referential validation for such action. Even in the presence of considerable scientific evidence, symbols and stories may capture the public's imagination, driving citizens from the cold, dismal world of reality into a place where everything is possible, where they are important, and perhaps most vitally, where they were absolutely right all along. This fantasy can be made real by decisive action in some identified area – made possible through laws, executive statements, program design and implementation, empanelment of blue-ribbon committees, and the like. The more one locks into a preferred way of thinking, the more the rest of the world, with its differing opinions and interpretations, seems to fall away.

The purpose is to examine why accomplishment in policy is sometimes arguable or absent, even in instances of grandiose policy pronouncement and celebration of great social-political effect. A further intent is to encourage readers to take time to engage policy rhetoric and the instruments of policy critically, to identify the breakdowns between thought and action that jeopardize not only the success of intended policy schemes, but also the trust placed in government institutions by the public. When people are caught up in a public role with the possibility of reform for its own sake, or in dismantling institutional structures for the purpose of doing that, without fully understanding original purpose and practical use, would-be change agents are engaging in behavior that is self-serving and harms the public interest. It is not only unfair to prey upon the unfamiliarity of the public on a policy issue, it is wrong. This is so even if the intended outcome is supposedly, in the mind of the acting official, in the public interest. Ideology and statements of broad positive intent are means that belie cold facts to the contrary. The public may believe that altruism informs official behavior, but likely a primary driver is the attaining and keeping of power, or achievement of private benefit; the two do not need to be mutually exclusive, but differences in problem definition create public programs that could be doomed to failure. If one evaluates statements and text on their own, as self-referencing objects, and then in context, as part of the legal tradition, or larger policy discussion, one may find divides that demand discussion. The statement of policy may not align with the outcome, and the simple fact of the matter is that this is because it does not have to, to accomplish the intended policy ends. Still, "officials bear the responsibility for turning goals into realities – without them, policies remain only promises" (Riggs, 2001, p. vii). Promises are not enough.

I am asking questions and viewing cases in which some in authority positions have no interest. I have no illusions about the value of this volume or its inherent worth, other than to hope that it will contribute to the larger literature, extend understanding, and lead to more discussions and debate. Any role I have as critic of program and process is intended to invite discourse, and to offset this seeming natural tendency to welcome into public policy debates only those that already agree with pre-determined notions. I consider the passage and announcement of policies and programs, lacking appropriate subsequent implementation and review, or the disconnect between stated intent and implementation, as pervasive deviations (Avesson & Sköldberg, 2018) in the public sector. I recognize, though, that the systems that supposedly exist to serve such programs might exist for other reasons – individual ego aggrandizement and wealth-creation, for example – and so intent might well be a serviceable cover for perpetuating an all-too-common public lie.

For policy students, the cases in this book might be taken as a warning to avoid assuming much about intent from public pronouncements, and about the need to follow the logic of how a program is supposed to achieve stated goals, and whether any success achieved is measurable. Where knowledge and interest exists, citizens should be involved in public policy processes; where interest and knowledge are lacking, society must do a better job of addressing that, even if it means that leaders may find it more difficult to engage in self-serving policy behaviors toward scripted outcomes. People are not only entitled to involvement – they are entitled to liberation and to lead their own way out from constraint. They are entitled in the public space to not be customers in a self-service checkout line; they are allowed to be burdened with the difficulty of thinking about public matters and the potential that they have been misled by their understanding of policy processes.

References

Abel, C. (2017). The varieties of theory and their roles in public administration. *Public Administration Quarterly, 41*(4), 670–694.

Alvesson, M., & Sköldberg, K. (2018). *Reflexive methodology: New vistas for qualitative research*, 3rd edition. London: Sage Publications.

Berger, A. A. (2019). *Media analysis techniques*, 6th edition. Thousand Oaks, CA: Sage Publications.

Boorstin, D. J. (1992, orig. 1962). *The image: A guide to pseudo-events in America.* New York: Vintage.

Caiden, G. E. (2001). Administrative reform. In A. Farazmand (Ed.), *Handbook of comparative and development public administration, 2nd edition, revised and expanded, 655–667.* New York: Marcel Dekker.

Christian, B., & Griffiths, T. (2016). *Algorithms to live by: The computer science of human decisions.* New York: Henry Holt.

Cochran, C. L., & Malone, E. F. (2014). *Public policy: Perspectives and choices,* 5th edition. Boulder, CO: Lynne Rienner.

Edelman, M. (1977). *Political language: Words that succeed and policies that fail.* New York: Academic Press.

Hair, R. (2011). 'Local color': Ronald Johnson, Charles Ives, and America. *Comparative American Studies, 9*(2), 131–145.

Hall, J. L., & Battaglio, R. P. (2018). Research, evidence, and decision making: Charting PAR's role in evidence-based management. *Public Administration Review, 78*(2), 181–182.

Jackson, J. B. (1980). *The necessity for ruins and other topics.* Amherst: University of Massachusetts Press.

Jung, C. J. (1968). Approaching the unconscious. In C. J. Jung & M. von Franz (Eds.), *Man and his symbols, 1–94.* New York: Dell.

Kim, J. (2016). *Understanding narrative inquiry: The crafting and analysis of stories as research.* Thousand Oaks, CA: Sage Publications.

Price, T. L. (2006). *Understanding ethical failures in leadership.* New York: Cambridge University Press.

Riggs, F. W. (2001). Prologue. In A. Farazmand (Ed.), *Handbook of comparative and development public administration, 2nd edition, revised and expanded, vii–viii.* New York: Marcel Dekker.

Tyson, L. (2006). *Critical theory today: A user-friendly guide*, 2nd edition. New York: Routledge.

Wellmer, A. (1974). *Critical theory of society (J. Cumming, Trans).* New York: Seabury.

Acknowledgments

I am grateful to Natalja Mortensen, Senior Acquisitions Editor and her team at Routledge, for the opportunity to pursue this book project. Without them, this book would not be possible. Thanks to anonymous reviewers who provided excellent critique and valuable advice in the book's commissioning stage. I also offer my appreciation to the staff at codeMantra for their editing work.

Special thanks to my wife Allison and my children for their patience and encouragement. I could not have completed this project without their support.

Professor Joseph Woelfel (University at Buffalo, The State University of New York) provided me a copy of the CATPAC software, which I have used here to analyze communication in Thailand energy policy and sustainable development. Thanks to *Public Integrity* for permission to use two previously published articles, here presented in updated form; both are copyright © the American Society for Public Administration, www.aspnet.org, reprinted by permission of Taylor & Francis Ltd, http:// www.tandfonline.com on behalf of the American Society for Public Administration:

- Christopher L. Atkinson (2015). New York City's conflicts of interest law: Compliance versus ethical capacity. *Public Integrity, 17*(3), 227–241.
- Christopher L. Atkinson (2016). Symbol and substance in local government workforce development: First source hiring programs. *Public Integrity, 19*(4), 374–393.

I presented a draft of Chapter 8, on reforming the Affordable Care Act, at the Southeastern Conference for Public Administration (SECoPA) in Birmingham, Alabama, in September 2018. I am obliged for the opportunity to present, as well as the feedback received.

Great thanks to Professors Ali Farazmand, Cliff McCue, and Alka Sapat at Florida Atlantic University in Boca Raton, for being such tremendous mentors as I have worked toward an academic career. Thanks to my new colleagues at the University of West Florida in Pensacola, who have provided me a welcoming scholarly home. Thanks to Ms. Cheryl Roberts for discussions about the use of social networking and implications for policy, and Dr. Steven Tinsley for our discussions about symbolic use of language in an economic development context. Thanks to Broward County, Florida government, for offering formative career opportunities. Best regards to students in my courses past and present: fair winds and following seas.

With a project of this scope, errors of commission or omission may have occurred – those errors are mine with apology given in advance.

CLA, 9/30/2018

1 Introduction

Public policy is value-laden, contested territory; its processes and results are seldom objective, and frequently the actors involved cannot even agree on the nature of the policy problem in question, let alone a firm definition sufficient for construction of a program with clear evaluation criteria. When official actors do agree, the outcomes may be decidedly different from what is claimed in the language of politics and policy. There is a need to comprehend the actions of policy analysts, politicians, and other actors as they encounter the policy process; this work of communication within the policy process bears a product – whether a law, program, regulation, or form – and this may have considerable bearing on the public interest. To the extent that public rhetoric has a claim on reflecting some concept of the public interest, it is valid to challenge not only the policies themselves, but also the definitions of problems and the very rhetoric that results in policy action. Even as people seek to achieve some reasoned conclusion, there are abstract shortcuts made. Symbol sometimes acts as a proxy for meaningful involvement. What is acceptable in terms of policy may result in very little of practical import, when the story of policy, its process, and seeking to serve the public interest is itself a moving discourse with value of its own (Fischer & Gottweis, 2012).

When a concept is thought of as universally revered, there is a possibility for ambiguity in policy design and implementation, and in how one may evaluate the success of policy endeavors. There is genuine danger in becoming captivated by the possibility of helping an affected group, without understanding the group's context or what group members need to be successful. If there is hubris in public policy, it may have an abode in policy where a rich diversity of publics of varying needs and means are painted with the broad brush of 'the people,' and common forms of help, thought to assist in achieving presumed goals or meeting needs, may have little to do with reality. What is needed is considered and frequent attention to the connections between intent, symbol, outcome, and the potential for manipulation in policy; this attention is not just from policy analysts and academics, but from those who work in policy and encounter it as consumers.

In political discourse, the importance of economic growth, fairness in the justice system, environmental stewardship, and public health are longstanding norms with considerable shared approval. Calls for responsibility and clarity also figure heavily in politics and public policy – administrators as well as elected officials have a need to be accountable, or at least be seen as accountable, in their public semblances. The role, if not myth, of accountability and transparency span and even transcend partisan politics and administrative notions of efficiency and effectiveness. Well-intentioned, nonspecific policy, created through an elaborate, misunderstood system of agenda setting and access, has great value, but the nature of that value is not always well understood.

Brown noted that "contemporary bureaucracies favor the 'objectivity' of instrumental rationality to the 'subjectivity' of moral commitment...rationality thereby becomes the ideological catchword for the mystification of a curtailed individual participation in public affairs and for the parallel political dominance of existing elites" (2005, p. 161). The stated goals of public policy may be abstract, in some cases, but are possibly useful in their vagueness. It is then all the more important that pause be given to the great weight afforded such abstractions – in popular culture, policy, and society broadly. Semiotics, the science of signs, affords such opportunity for fruitful exploration – to understand how a fascination with instrumental rationality might not save policy from its own hubris, to uncover underlying assumptions, and to lay bare conventional wisdom for what it is.

This introductory chapter first considers the notion of failure in public policy. The public sphere and the idea of instrumentality are then discussed, followed by a connecting of values and instrumentality in policy. Because public policy centers on legitimacy and consent, these aspects are featured next. Having set a foundation in relevant critical literature, the chapter shifts to semiotics and public policy – specifically focusing on metaphor, symbol, and implications for government's role. The plan of the book finishes out this chapter.

On Failure in Public Policy

This is a book about failure, in the sense that it touches on issues related to the "neglect or omission of expected or required action" (Stevenson & Waite, 2011, p. 511). In a larger sense, its chapters explore the widening gulf between what is expected and what is realized in public policy – between image or reality-building, and consequence to the public benefit. There has been an unacceptable erosion in trust in the public sphere. The ceaseless chipping away at the public sector's project of legitimation has resulted not in reform and improvement, but a triumph of image and appearance over broad obligations.

Evaluation in the public sector is often misunderstood. Because the public already is predisposed to distrust government efforts, for right or wrong reasons, the tendency is to believe government has somehow botched its efforts, even when it is doing a reasonably good job. Government is necessary – it has the capacity to influence through its coercive power, cajoling the public into doing what it should be doing; while this limits individual freedom, it constrains individual behavior so that others' rights may be maintained (Hacker & Pierson, 2016). Yet, government is approached cynically by the public; the public is apathetic to becoming more involved in the public sphere, and it would appear that they have a good reason for their apathy. Gilens and Page (2014) found that policies that are supported by the affluent become law; the influence of average citizens on such outcomes is practically nil, and business groups are, expectedly, most dominant. Where lower- and middle-income groups support policies that become law, it is where that would have happened anyway. What might look like failure, or triumph, is not that at all – it could just be a matter of perspective.

It is not a secret that some with influential power would just as soon have a clearing out of the public sphere, in favor of monied interests, including supporting schemes where voting rights would equal levels of taxation, and those with no resources would have no voice at all. The public at large is reduced largely to being "mad as hell" on Election Day (Hacker & Pierson, 2016, p. 341). Many lack a strong understanding of public policy, but, given the above – what would be the point of learning and engaging in public discourse if it did not matter? Whether government or policy failed depends on how one defines failure, and it simply has not mattered what most people think about that. Being 'mad as hell' – against incumbents, major media outlets, being ignored, losing jobs because of suboptimal trade deals, or a litany of other reasons – is impotent, useless rage. It accomplishes nothing because decisions to be made, even if they give voice to the rage, almost never benefit the people sustaining the anger. Policy likely worked, and exactly as planned – just for someone else. Citizens should not need to be livid to want to become involved with government and policy; involvement should matter.

While many do not care about *how* government works, they care very much about what it does. People know that they need certain services from government, like a passport for instance, and from a pragmatic perspective want that assistance (Berger & Luckmann, 1966). They do not necessarily worry about the processes, or the levels of review and authority, or the checks and balances that ensure fairness and accuracy, or of the care and concern devoted to monitoring and reporting of performance. Levels of knowledge differ between citizens and public administration practitioners. Even within public administration, there are ranks of knowledge and emphases of expertise. Where we work frequently with some particular material or issue, we may be expected to be more comfortable with discussion and use of the substance. The rest of it – the sum total of the constructed reality of the world, and its accompanying public policy universe – perhaps does not even enter our minds.

Out in the hostile flame of the public space, personal opinions of all sorts have become a proxy for bad behavior and warrant for the use of governmental might as a blunt instrument. The ego of individual actors within the political system has been allowed, or perhaps invited, to speak once, simply, and for all about fiendishly complex topics, despite the fact that they may not be well prepared for the conversation. Debate and discourse are regularly, prematurely concluded in the interest of some supposed but nonexistent consensus. Trust in individual knowledge in public policy circles, as actors seek to put their stamp upon the government, may know no bounds. A bystander might suppose that belief is as good as fact, when political interests can challenge science with a simple retort: "Can you prove that 100%?" – knowing that science simply does not work that way. Science denial efforts have gained prominence (Strauss, 2017) as knowledge that confronts identity is rejected (Krauss, 2015). Doubt, science's best friend, is sacrilege in politics; doubt loses elections – it looks suspiciously like failure.

It is no wonder that the public is confused, though it is out of fashion to admit puzzlement. Internet search capacity is taken for wisdom far too regularly. Appeals to persuasion are frequent; power, in the public sphere and elsewhere, is entwined with rhetoric, and specifically the ability to cause a stir and drive the news cycle. These rhetorical appeals can take the form of rich imagery and thick use of symbols, to create and refine a preferred reality for those perceiving such communications. Meanwhile, discourse in the public sphere might be described as hollow or inane (Branstetter, 2011). Facts need not necessarily have anything to do with the exchange. There is an apparent divergence between the ability of actors in the public sphere to create beautiful pictures of desirable futures, and the capacity to turn those pictures into reality. The actual translation and implementation can be particularly unpleasant, fraught with unintended consequences, or simply result in an inability to attain the desired result. A policy hubris and attendant ego – a gritty belief in the power of the individual to effect change – runs time and again into the seeming permanence of wicked policy problems. Oversimplified policy definitions and soundbites, unsurprisingly, prove ineffective at changing policy reality, but are effective in the public discourse. People will vote for candidates who seem to understand their frustrations and particular worldview, respect or appear to respect them, and show concern for how truly awful it is to feel ignored for so long; the appeal to authenticity in an age of inauthenticity is real. The motivation may be little more than that (Lindsay, 2017).

The Public Sphere and Instrumentality

Is there truth to the idea that those in the public sector have the will to engage in solving a public policy problem, and to follow rules of communication so that discourse is understandable, so that decision-making is rational? Is this effort sincere? (Kemp, 1985). Is there a genuine effort to encourage "learning, participation, and self-determination" (Forester, 1985b, p. 203). Or, are there efforts to intentionally mystify the public? We may be driven to ask (and will ask throughout the course of this book): Does the current emphasis on instrumentality in public policy undermine the values it purports to uphold?

The work of Jürgen Habermas on legitimation in the public sphere is instructive for this discussion of sign, symbol, and public policy. As Habermas defined it, the public sphere is

> a realm of social life in which something approaching public opinion can be formed...[where citizens can] confer in an unrestricted fashion – that is, with the guarantee of freedom of assembly and association and the freedom to express and publish their opinions – about matters of general interest.
>
> (Quoted in Held, 1980, p. 260)

There is little discussion of whether the public opinion, once developed, would have a hearing with government or if government should do anything specific with it. The creation of a collective public opinion contrasts with how government works most of the time. Government solves technical problems with instrumental solutions. It is not regularly a builder of shared vision. It may occasionally find itself acting in a capture capacity to secure rights for the building of private-sector wealth. Sometimes it is the keeper of the rules, hopefully to lower transaction costs in a manner that benefits society broadly. Administration, in particular, has a tendency to hide behind masks of objectivity, when policies themselves are not objectively developed.

Society is marked by its attention to process and instrumentality. Rationality has been extended to all corners of the living of one's life. This shift has transcended values in many instances (Held, 1980). Even where discourse is values-oriented – in public rhetoric for example – the tools of the trade for implementation and administration remain in instrumentality. This is a fundamental break and is a constraint upon the public sphere in practice: Intent, voiced in a normative frame, does not necessarily equal written law, and this, in turn, does not necessarily yield measurable objective fact in output or outcome. Yet, administration relies upon instrumentality as a source of its legitimacy, in prized form as technical expertise: unapproachable, unyielding, and sphinxlike. Administrators are holders of a supposed objective rationality, and given this, there is little reason for the public to follow up on what is arguably one of its greatest obligations: to hold government to account. If the public cannot hold government to account, thinking critically about the policies introduced, programs offered, and outcomes created, then we have little reason to believe that the public's contribution to active discussion or deliberation will be consequential.

It is worth contemplating that the intent of the public sphere to provide for a venue aimed at deliberative democracy, in the interest of the ultimate legitimacy of political and administrative forces that serve as government, has been damaged due to distortion of reality in public discourse. These distortions may be either unintentional or systematic; they serve to cloud discourse, undermining freedom and attainment of active deliberation by the public in the public sphere. Culture itself is infused with preferred ideology. There has been a placement of individual needs first, before those of the collective, and yet, individuals within this system are no less functionary as economic mechanisms serving elite interests than they ever were (Held, 1980). The divide between elite classes and everyone else has grown, and the public imagination, at least in the US, centers on the hope that this gap will not only be reduced but fully transcended (Freeland, 2011). Institutions have not succeeded in reducing the gap; governmental institutions might be broadening this break. Instead of being part of society as individuals with the ability to become self-actualized, today's workers are still primarily tied in identity to jobs and functions. They are their jobs as far as society is concerned. Processes that install them in society insulate them from the processes of government and governance, as those routines are handled by others. The rationalization and instrumentalization of society leave little understanding for most people about the public sphere, of which they should rightly be a part, nor the information they require to become involved and to be good fellow stewards of the ship of state.

As Habermas suggested, the goal of instrumentalization and power centralization can be to extend power, exclude along demographic lines, promote the illusion that government can easily solve complex societal dilemmas, and restrict involvement in the public sphere as a general matter. Programs can exist strictly to render legitimacy to government, without any consideration of actual performance (Forester, 1985b). We might end up with "distortions of pretense, misrepresentation, dependency-creation, and ideology...with immobilizing depoliticizing, and subtly but effectively disabling consequences" (Forester, 1985b, p. 204). We lose out on "politically unobstructed discussion and common sense" and instead accept unaccountable and exclusionary government as legitimate. This poor result comes from ignorance and distrust, and ignorance and distrust fuel acceptance of such an end as conclusive.

Even with its belief in technical solutions to problems, government must admit that it cannot guarantee progress, however defined. Crises of rationality and legitimacy occur when government appeals to competing interests and fails to meet demands. Legitimacy of the enterprise can be withdrawn. With classes taking advantage of one another, and more appeals being made to disparate ends of the class spectrum, it becomes more difficult for government to hold on its own legitimacy (Held, 1980) – meeting expectations for a large enough group of 'the public' without them ever becoming involved in a considerable way. Since it increasingly cannot succeed, failure becomes normalized.

As much as public administration has historically prided itself on its role as a source of technical subject matter expertise, this role has been more and more loathed by a public sick of being told what it does not understand. Public administration might be thought to be hiding behind its intelligence, accosted by politicians currying favor from the electorate, and unable to address real-world issues at street level. Even if the public does not understand, the time has probably come that the public will no longer allow for that to be a reason for non-action. Still, considering that "public business ought to be the business of the public" (O'Neill, 1985, p. 63), the public is either uninvolved or, when they seek to become involved, their involvement is seen as something of an affront to elites. Attempts at involvement may be met with apathy, unctuous appeals to listening, or half-hearted thanks for comments. For its part, instead of being a means to allow citizens to play a needed and vital role in the public sphere, "education, like the mass media and ultimately the market, is part of an organized system to subvert the critical powers of insight and imagination" (Misgeld, 1985, p. 80).

In public policy, statements are made about what constitutes a problem and how society might best respond to it. For a moment, at least, there is a relationship between the person reading or hearing about the problem and the proposed policy, and something of an invitation to consider the issue from a given standpoint. However, as matters are formalized in public discourse and eventually law, they become more settled. There is less room to debate what is settled, from the perspective of a citizen. The problem is as it has been defined. The solution has a stamp of authority, having been worked through by government in its technical-instrumental capacity. What would be the point of discussing it further? This perhaps engenders cynicism in an already-withdrawn public, when problems are defined errantly, solutions fail to accomplish expected results, or practices result in unanticipated, and deleterious consequences. The myth that instrumental approaches by a team of experts are here to help resolve a problem is challenged. The ability for government to transform political rhetoric into "rational authority" (Kemp, 1985, p. 182) through design and implementation of a program is impaired.

Connecting Values and Instrumental Rationality

Governmental institutions have values that are ethical and normative as a result of the people within them, their leaders, and the society around them. We depend upon civil servants to be fair and honest, and to treat the public with civility. However, if they are not also in some sense business-like, with attention to the bottom line and defensive of their positions, they may find themselves ousted in a power grab (West & Davis, 2011).

Bainbridge emphasized that the importance of law to modernity rests in the "continuing maintenance of order and certainty" (2006, p. 157). While law and the legitimacy of the state are closely linked, law as a signifier has shifted from the rule of law to a vague concept of quest to protect varying conceptions of justice (Bainbridge, 2006), which might mean many different things to diverse people at distinct times. While the rule of law is a sturdy basis for reason and action, a wobbly impression of justice can act as a strong justification for action even if widespread agreement on the particular meaning does not exist in a given instance.

The counterfeiting of truth in politics makes public communication much more like marketing to consumers, with voting power more like buying a product. Efforts to involve the public have occasionally seemed limited to agitation, which, unlike propaganda, might use the same term repeatedly (Bove, 2014), to drive home a point and whip the crowd into a frenzy. It is more difficult to involve the public in deliberative democracy, and it is clear enough that the political benefit of the public's involvement, while most likely not their full consent to govern, can be had through agitation. This allows the machinery of governmentality to continue to turn, even if not necessarily in the public interest, because government itself might know that it does not possess the ability to solve the problems. "If you cannot change a situation, the next best thing is to make it look as if you are" (Bove, 2014, p. 122).

Following this thinking, "complexity is simplified into operating procedures and performance measures. These components substitute, in turn, for desired outcomes. Thus, partnership stands for good governance; passive public consultation exercises stand for substantive democracy; competition stands for efficiency and so on" (West & Davis, 2011, p. 233). There is arguably too much attention to instrumental matters, such as the scheduling and timing of deliberations about processes, and not enough time spent on review of the outcomes of such processes (Swindal, 1994). Public officials have the responsibility to check to ensure that program outcomes match expectations, and that those program expectations match broader societal expectations (Koivisto, 2014). The system should not reflect only processes or values, but both of these.

The language of government and law has long been a battlefield, prone to violent display. It can be reasonably stated that this language is not colorful by accident or for its own sake. There is purpose in such image-making. It has been offered that describing state functions in combative language is common; because word choice is not a value-free matter, and use of certain terminology has ideological trappings, such language does not describe the world as much as actively make it. Boshoff wrote that "the law is a system of signs that turns reality into speech, but...also turns speech into reality" (2013, p. 426); extending this thought, "language does not reflect reality, it does not even distort reality; it creates reality" (p. 433). The language of law, policy, and the products of the public sphere as a whole are not 'neutral' – and we should not accept them as neutral, merely reflective of whatever baggage we have brought to the discussion ourselves. These artifacts are flushed with efforts to make not only meaning in a context-specific way, but to effect a reality upon the environment and circumstance to those listening. This may be a valid, legitimate effort to make meaning with common elements of truth, or it may be an evasive effort that purports to be something that it is not, for all manner of goals that undermine liberty and freedom, both individually and societally.

Legitimacy and Consent

Legitimacy was defined by Suchman as a "generalized perception or assumption that the actions of an entity are desirable, proper, or appropriate within some socially constructed system of norms, values, beliefs, and definitions" (1995, p. 574). "Legitimacy is not a commodity to be possessed or exchanged but a condition reflecting cultural alignment, normative support, or consonance with relevant rules or laws" (Scott, 1995, p. 45). In administrative context, legitimacy rests with three ideals: "the rule of law, sound public policy, and democracy" (Arkush, 2012, p. 611). John Locke wrote that "all peaceful beginnings of government have been laid in the consent of the people" (1690), and the giving of this consent is associated with care on the part of government in supporting those ideals. Pauker emphasized: "What is actually legitimate in a well-developed, advanced society is the rule of law – the mechanisms, the procedures that have been established to govern it" (1973, p. 3).

"Public servants must attend to law, community values, political norms, professional standards, and citizen interests" (Denhardt & Denhardt, 2000, p. 554). However, "[administrative agencies'] preoccupation with the low arts of organizational survival blinds them to the brighter angels of their nature" (Rohr, 1986, p. 182). When public administration loses sight of its larger cause for being, its actions may serve only to "legitimize existing structures of rationality and power" (Denhardt & Denhardt, 1979, p. 114), "leaving people who desperately need to play a role in the public sphere out of the discussion and uninvolved, and the larger goal of a democratic and representative government, at best, a fiction useful for its narrative value" (Atkinson, 2017).

A major question undergirding the consideration of symbol in public policy is the gaining of consent. Increasingly, citizens have been seen as consumers by governments, as if they are using public services as any other commodity or product, and neglecting the essential nature of the interaction between people and government that is part of the maintenance of a healthy public sphere (Forester, 1985a). It might be agreed that communication has become increasingly distorted, but it is worth asking: To what purpose or end has it become distorted, in particular interests and generally? What might be the long-term effect of allowing such societal dynamics to continue unchecked? What are benefits, if any, of turning away from this approach to governance, in terms of not only improved communication but also improvements in citizenship as well?

The importance of image has been greatly enhanced, from commodification and marketing in consumer sectors to the shaping of ideals and political preferences in the public sphere. Reality might be termed effaced by cultural shift, relying upon circular cultural references and ultimately forming representations and simulacra, indicative of a hyperreality as suggested by Baudrillard (Corazza, Scagnelli, & Mio, 2017). As the shift moves from ideas to images, the focus becomes more heavily weighted against a public capable of critical judgment. Politics are thin, and discussion is weak (Simon, 2000). Instead of acting as an engaged citizenry, the public is likely to 'consume programs' like commodities, disrupting the potential for citizenship behaviors.

Szerszynski (2002) suggested that environmental protests were heavily dependent on images – "connotative meanings and visual rhetorics" – rather than "the narrow definition of fact and analysis" (pp. 54–55). Legitimacy does not stem as much from the validity of a claim as it does from a demonstrator's earnestness and apparent level of commitment to their cause. The symbolic nature of protest is ritualized in many instances, in the guise of David taking on a Goliath of one form or another, and the weak but righteous defeating the powerful (Cohen, 2008). The specific players matter little in the grand scheme of the narrative as it plays out because the protests themselves have become ritualized, with various actors playing roles with scripts that have precise expectations. Protecting one tree is protection of all trees, or saving one river is safeguarding of all water, in a feat of synecdoche. The ritualization and use of symbols might be taken as cultivation of a mythos of organization. None of this is unique to environmentalism, as these constructs and tendencies find resonance in other public organizations, public policy endeavors, and the public sphere. The use of symbols – to elaborate and summarize belief – can be quite effective in extending a preferred theme or construct of an organization, but institutional aptitude in this respect limits discourse and questioning of validity (Szerszynski, 2002).

What might the public define as good? As with the problem of defining what constitutes a problem suitable for public sector-based solutions, defining what constitutes doing good in the public sector is also difficult. It might be reasonably expected that certain aspects of 'good' include "requirements of transparency, openness, the rule of law, democracy, participation, and accountability" (Koivisto, 2014, p. 592). We might take these at face value, even though it is probably useful to consider first why they too are so readily taken as good. There are other questions to ask: Is good government merely a government doing well that which is desired by the majority of the public? Is serving the desire of the majority that voted enough? What about the strange netherworld of Electoral College and popular vote comparisons in the US? What if such public policy outcomes of a government, anywhere and at any time, are fundamentally *unacceptable* or *objectionable*? Who decides what those words mean? For those sorts of reasons, which raise ethical considerations, we cannot assume efficiency and effectiveness as the only foci for public administrators. How we define problems, solutions, and success all say much about organizational culture, institutions, and society (Koivisto, 2014). Public administration has found itself engaged in a project centered on its legitimacy as a field of practice and study for some time, and intractable questions like these do not make matters easier or more soluble.

While people think little about government and the nature and use of governmental power, governmental power permeates society. When pushed to think about it, we might like to believe that the use of this power has less to do with domination, or a Foucaultian estimation of severe restriction, something to be actively resisted, and relatively more to do with liberty (Hindess, 2004). The position that government is situated to protect liberty rather than to keep order, dominating where necessary to protect the interests of a decreasing minority of those holding power within a society, becomes less defensible perhaps when signs point to priorities other than inclusiveness and participation. Endeavors toward inclusiveness within government processes would tend, on their face, to suggest some level of attention to preservation and sharing of individual entitlement to liberty and direction of government on the public's behalf. Where the tear exists between image and reality is when the image of involvement bears no effect on the outcome, and any pretension toward involvement exists simply to keep order and direct power toward an agenda of the particular.

The concept of legitimacy as individually centered, then, is not essentially important to the modern government; the point of government is to conduct "the affairs of the population in the interests of the whole" (Hindess, 2004, p. 42). This view, essential to Foucault, is central – it means that it is not just government that influences the population – many other institutions public and private also influence the conduct of society. If the public is self-directing at all, then this capacity is to be used for governmental ends. Individual liberty might exist, but it exists in a form to sustain society – not to provide for the increase or happiness of individuals, necessarily. It is, in this conception, perfectly fine if individual groups believe that government is serving them specifically or especially well, as long as the whole or collective is receiving the best deal for the common interest (Hindess, 2004).

For such reasons, the state stakes out the issues it finds most relevant or useful for its purposes. People are invited to involve themselves in the debate within this cordoned-off area, but effectively restrained from venturing beyond the identified boundaries. Even new movements are kept within the margins described by the existing social discourse, as not only government but also other institutions help reign in any legitimately free thinking inside the lifeworld. The faux lifeworld of the present, exceedingly dumbed down as it is, plays as intense real life to the public, where reality and reality TV intermingle with one another and become indistinguishable (Roberts & Crossley, 2004).

What does exist, as noted by Cohen (1995, orig. 1975), are attempts to foster equilibrium out of disorder. In such a context, legitimacy within the public enterprise is indeed a scarce resource, and politics itself is agonized with the notion of legitimacy: gaining power and creating legitimacy for those in power through the use of such power. Inasmuch as power is concerned with apportionment of values for the populace – whether or not those decisions themselves are arbitrary – this distribution is a one-way street. Politics decides what values come to the fore, and what comes to the agenda. Attempts to overturn the essential logic of the political superstructure are derailed, because all power utilization, and even the pretensions to public involvement, is strategic and by design.

With power unequally distributed, symbols, or myths, may be needed to keep the public in line with the selected program, and comfortable with the idea of acting within the established constraints. The effort may be intended to reduce the cognitive dissonance between what the public thinks it wants, with all of its individual beliefs, desires, and biases, and what it will ultimately get, meaning what the government needs the public to believe about the issue. Meaning is ascribed to symbols or myths, as may be necessary to accomplish the outcome intended by those in political power. In the end, the machinery of government, its administration, and those that act as gatekeepers, are largely unapproachable by the vast majority of the public (Cohen, 1995, orig. 1975). Where participation happens, it is ritualized, pro forma, and may have little effect on the outcome. It is entirely possible that when the goal is to maintain a stable societal narrative and quell unrest, a *Potemkin* policy structure – one just for show – would be as good as any. In an era of social networking and a virtual world of public discourse, this is a particularly important concern, especially if the public mistakenly believes that their interactions online are necessarily impactful upon a discussion and choice made in the physical world.

A problem is that power in society skews relationships between decision-makers, administrators, and citizens of various levels of involvement. There are profound differences in the population in capacity to become involved in public matters and knowledge of public issues. Disagreements exist on how public problems are defined. It could be suggested that these disagreements and disparities are used to shape belief, and maintain power and an approximation of consent to govern. Such behavior may even be commonplace, but ultimately, it undermines the legitimacy of governance. Government looks legitimate and people believe that it is legitimate, but the reality of the situation is that power is only being held because communications are so distorted, and issues and beliefs so fragmented, that the vast majority of the population knows no better. The discourse is illusory (Forester, 1985a).

Take as an example the political use of small business programs. Some small business programs, such as those that provide technical assistance, can be quite useful to small business owners by passing along information about business ownership, contracts and bidding on solicitations, marketing and using social media, and a host of other topics. Political rhetoric, though, can become narrowly focused on a group of symbolic program aspects that may have little to do with reality or what business owners need. Government policy may claim to support small businesses because they are job-producers, but policies may fail to do much because they do not target firms with the greatest chance for growth; the language of policy proposals in this area tends to center on reducing barriers or undoing regulatory red-tape. The image of certain political leaders cutting burdensome regulations and helping small businesses achieve their dreams is still visually stimulating; the voting audience can see the matter conceptually and stories about businesses and how programs will help them are saleable to a voting program desirous of change and hope. Empirical forms of evidence, or crafting solutions that may have broader benefit, are hardly the point. An evidence basis is not needed to support such programs when the existing framework has already shown to be valid for political purposes (Wapshott & Mallett, 2017).

"Elitists argue democracy simply acts as a cover for the domination of a ruling class. Pluralists counter that no such cohesive minority exists" (Bellamy, 2004, p. 21); even majorities are just coalitions of minorities, so the possibility of competitive equilibrium exists that prevents dictatorship (Bellamy, 2004). Nevertheless, the existence of competitive equilibrium or even pluralism in exerting pressure on public systems does not mean that domination of a ruling class does not exist, or that processes in a democracy do not serve as a concealment for duplicitousness. We may have reason to believe in such dominance, because even as the public sphere shows much dynamic activity, so little movement is occurring for vast segments of society that are supposedly the intended targets of these social programs. If the program is instituted for a specific purpose, it is right to challenge whether this purpose has been achieved, on behalf of the intended clients of these programs, whether the clients are underserved citizens, migrants, the environment, or any other client group the government purports to serve.

Barring that, what is lost is a chance at the legitimacy of government, in one respect, but also the chance at freedom for individuals in the larger sense. Freedom cannot be attained in an inauthentic public sphere, where truthfulness is fugitive and citizens are merely customers of a retail government. Government concerns itself with what it believes to be transparency and accountability – impressing upon the public the superiority of its instrumental might. It may be that what is not needed are endless tables of performance measurement data, which are ill-understood and mostly ignored, but a more dutiful attempt at increasing understanding.

Legitimacy is a long-term project within public administration as an academic discipline and as a career. As White and McSwain suggested, an apparent conclusory position on legitimacy is agencies

> serve as the focal point for creating (where creation is needed), and for maintaining (against the increasingly invasive and intensive impacts of technological, socio-cultural, and other types of change), the community units that form the glue, the substantive, solidarity, that must exist to hold any society together.

> (1993, p. 20)

Signification and narrative are identity-creating, and developing of the self, even if the process does not make us feel any better about the quality of our decision-making or of the paths we choose (White & McSwain, 1993). There is an increasing awareness through the immediacy of social media and other avenues of communication and mass participation that government, despite its assumed edifice of common voice, mindset, and action, is more reflective of the public at large – confused sometimes, conflicted (perhaps deeply so), though more often than not infused with a sense of motivation to serve the larger public interest, however that is being defined in that context, at that time.

Connecting Semiotics and Public Policy

A sign is "something that stands for something else," and following Saussure, is a "unity of word-object, known as a signifier with a corresponding culturally prescribed content or meaning, known as a signified" (Berger, 2010, p. 3). The view of the sign as Charles Sanders Peirce envisioned it is "first, a sign is not a thing; second, that everything can become a sign; and third, that things must act upon each other to create meaning" (Van Fleet, 2011, p. 59). Amusingly, Eco suggested that "Semiotics," the investigation and science of signs,

> is in principle the discipline studying everything which can be used in order to lie. If something cannot be used to tell a lie, conversely it cannot be used to tell the truth: it cannot in fact be used "to tell" at all.

> (1976, p. 7)

Society is composed of efforts to understand, produce, and discern the signs of others. Culture is made up of signs and provides a structure upon which a system of meaning-conveyance can function. One can examine signs and texts (as groups of signs) "to understand how the larger entity, culture, operates" (Leeds-Hurwitz, 1993, p. 17). Mikhail Bakhtin suggested that "only active understanding can apprehend the theme... all understanding is dialogical...the encounter of two texts: the already given text and the reacting text being created" (Todorov, 1984, pp. 22–23). We understand as we produce understanding (Todorov, 1984).

Beyond a footing in the literature on semiotics, this present work is rooted in the wider public policy literature, specifically the garbage can model of decision-making and the later Multiple Streams Approach (MSA). The garbage can model was based on a series of conceptual streams and assumptions for processing interactions: choices, problems, "a rate of flow of solutions," and "a stream of energy from participants" (Cohen, March, & Olsen, 1972, p. 3). This initial study suggested that decisions were most often made through oversight or flight, rather than resolution. Classical models of decision-making may fail because they depend upon rational approaches; when organizations and policy actors are burdened with complex problems and a multitude of pressures, the tendency is for options to be selected based upon "the mix of choices available at any one time, the mix of problems that have access to the organization, the mix of solutions looking for problems, and the outside demands on the decision makers" (Cohen, March, & Olsen, 1972, p. 16).

Related to the garbage can model is MSA, and its inclusion of ambiguity as a primary and defining contextual feature in the policymaking environment. The MSA framework includes three streams – problems, policies, and a political stream. The problem stream must cut through the noise of ambiguity, along with the presence of the 'right' policy and the most advantageous political environment, to open a window for policy action (Kingdon, 2003). Zahariadis (2014) notes that MSA is suitable in navigating ambiguity through its attention to manipulation related to symbol utilization. He suggests that "the process of interpretation inherent in ambiguous situations and the power of discretion enable policymakers to legitimately deviate from established norms...overlook negative experiential learning that contradicts preferred policy...or create fantasy documents...to cope with high-risk situations" (Zahariadis, 2014, p. 31). However, even though MSA is useful as metaphor for visualizing the complexity of the policy process and the strategic activities of policy entrepreneurs, it has been criticized for too much focus on policy entrepreneurs as individual actors and not enough focus on institutional arrangements (Zahariadis, 2014). There is room for additional focus on processes, language, and structure, and the choices that are made in formalizing such arrangements.

Metaphor and Symbol in Policy

Edelman proposed that "political history is an account of mass violence and of the expenditure of vast resources to cope with mythical fears and hopes...large groups of people remain quiescent under noxiously oppressive conditions" (1971, p. 1), and occasionally these burdened individuals even defend the system that keeps them down. Notably, people are more accepting of systems with occasional violent outbursts if they display what appear to be normal, passive attributes most of the time. People need comfort. If people can be comforted through manipulation, by symbols and the playing upon of emotions, then other non-public-centered plans and strategies can move forward. It might give people hope to think that government is centered on what they want – that what government does is rationally related to the desires of the broader public – but hope does not make it so. It is easier for government to create beliefs about what is possible and even what is acceptable to discuss, rather than to entertain the full range of human potential and possibility when most of that is not relevant to desired strategic ends (Edelman, 1971). Government will tell the public, through political rhetoric, what it wants or the options from which it may choose. The public will choose and adjust its perspectives as necessary to avoid dissonance in thought and belief, even if there is no benefit to the options or even in deciding one way or the other.

In policy, words and actions are therefore purpose-driven: Short statements with open meaning are effectively small containers with outsized content; even one word (for example, *change*) can mean everything to a voting public. Narratives of objectivity and efficiency (Farmer, 1995) are means of control, and sometimes are pretensions that appeal to various underserved communities without actually representing their interests or improving their prospects.

Certain words and combinations of words, placed in public context, are taken as signs of credibility or validity for policy functions. As Evans suggested, metaphors hold great value in creation of meaning generally (2015), echoing Kingdon (2003) and they hold value in policy circles as well. There is a universality to some policy metaphors – this makes them easily grasped by a large segment of the population (people that vote), and these people are likely to support these metaphors because they sound like concepts that evoke certain beliefs and feelings that are consonant with their experiences.

Kingdon suggested that symbols in policy act "as reinforcement for something already taking place and as something that rather powerfully focuses attention, rather than as a prime mover in agenda setting" (2003, p. 97). Stone (2012) also raised the value of symbols in public policy, identifying stories, synecdoche, and metaphor as devices used in politics in the construction of problems. She noted ambiguity as the chief characteristic of symbols and made a generally positive argument for the place of ambiguous symbols in political rhetoric, which "enable the transformation of individual intentions and actions into collective results and purposes" (2012, p. 178). While Stone noted that coalitions built upon ambiguity may fall apart as inner conflicts come to the fore later in policy processes, she nevertheless suggested that because symbols can convert personal preferences into shared actions, people can become unified by their ideals through symbols. At the same time, Stone allowed that symbols "exist outside the realm of the practical and the real" and "allow us to believe we are authors of our own destiny" (2012, p. 182).

In reviewing Stone's outline of the functional purposes of ambiguity and strategies for its use, it might be troubling that symbol is so readily taken as given and strategically valuable for political purposes, groundless though it often is, free to play in meaning and definition with little apparent demand for a firmer foundation. Stone wrote that "by portraying a decision one way in press releases, speeches, preambles, or surrounding language, yet executing it in another, leaders can perform the political magic of making two different decisions at once" (2012, p. 181). The statement may be true taking a cynical view, but there is danger in comfort with such relativism. Such political magic might be more commonly referred to as lying. Popular agreement with a vague symbol may incite political action, but the players in such popular uprisings might be assenting to the symbol, however they have individually authored it, and not necessarily to the resulting policy. The work done in the name of the public writ large, based on the use/abuse of symbol, might be based upon a *false* consent of the people – a consent not freely given – because the people failed to understand the resulting policy or the actual intent of the official actors. An art of this sort to public policy might be akin to a confidence game. Words and phrases in the public sphere might not be best lazily left as expedient ideographs to extend political fortunes. While symbols might present a chance for people to write themselves into a policy story, the only narrative that matters is the one yielding formalized policy, and made law.

How a public figure uses a metaphor, in political rhetoric, for example, says much about what was originally meant by the speaker and the intended influence upon the hearing public, in terms of manipulation – it may say decidedly less about the possible policy outcome or what may come of any enacted policy, once implemented. Rhetoric has been suggested to be interpretive as well as productive, and it is intended to be persuasive (Selzer, 2004); rhetoric tells where politics would like the policy to go and also how politics defines the issue. The creation of the policy concept is one matter, the program derived from the concept is another, and the two may have little to do with one another.

Further, the policy concept's loud birth may be enough for political purposes in the public sphere. The existence of the concept, having served certain purposes, may yield most of the intended results, making policy implementation and evaluation irrelevant to political purposes. To the public, the feelings and beliefs are real, after all, and that is real enough. What is worse, the people involved in the public sphere have, either through commission or omission, agreed on the state of things and the nature of discourse as participants in it. Reality, constructed as it is, and any meaning existing in the system, has been devised by those present. If it is consistent over time and does not work, it has failed the public for no good reason, even if it is relatively simple to point to individual reasons for inaction, or reification of systems that do not achieve positive social change.

Kingdon (2003) included in his classic text on MSA a section on origins for policy initiatives, but found that "origins of initiatives does not make for very complete theory about agenda setting or alternative specification...[because] (1) ideas can come from anywhere; (2) tracing origins involves one in an infinite regress; and (3) nobody leads anybody else" (p. 71). This paper does not necessarily seek to trace the origin of an idea, mostly because ideas can become distorted, or mutated and recombined (Kingdon, 2003). Rather, the origin of the idea is less important than the *intent* of law and policy, something that can be discerned as it becomes formalized in law and procedure, and how the intent and its foundational rhetoric and the resultant policy environment and its outcomes may become increasingly estranged from one another. It is suggested here that it is at least possible to know what was originally intended in policy and how the consequential policy differs. Analysts may be able to separate the symbol from a formalized policy as a sign from its signified, through use of the materials of the policy itself, where official actors retain control of the products and deducing social/political construction is not the primary consideration. Areas of public policy are heavily dependent on narrative, naming, sign, and branding to create meaning – these are interpretive turns. Refusing to take the value of public policies as given, we may become more aware of the purely symbolic benefit to such programs and, setting it aside, arrive at a deeper understanding of what is a disturbing break between the sometimes smug brashness of policy, in announcement, proclamation, formalization, and the bricolage of administrative rulemaking, and outcomes, or lack thereof.

Semiotics and the Role of Government

In describing privacy being sacrificed to increasing public space, Leeds-Hurwitz offered the model of parlorization, where certain expressive fine 'appointments' of the traditional parlor tell others "what we would have others think of us, while real personal and individual content is devalued and displaced, shoved behind the scenes" (1993, p. xxvi). In applying this to the public sphere, discourse about public policy and values, down to the agenda process itself, may be a form of parlorization, where society's statements of policy are meant symbolically, to express what we want others to know and believe about us, even though the parlor may bear little resemblance to the rest of the house.

What can be done to identify the source of meaning in political rhetoric, and the varied lives of symbol that supply the laboratory of public policy? Is it possible to discern authenticity? Methodologically, Krebs and Jackson cautioned that scholars should "avoid centering causal accounts on unanswerable questions about actors' true motives and to focus instead on what actors say, in what contexts, and to what audiences" (2007, p. 36). One might propose a conceptual model of semiotic analysis for public policy connecting reference, symbol, and referent. This application to policy to policy is fashioned after Eco's 1976 model; while the policy applications have been left as generic issues, it is clear enough how a misalignment between symbol and reference can occur. This is not to suggest that a symbol cannot be meaningful, but from a public policy perspective, outcomes might be reasonably expected from programs after the warm glow of successful passage of law has worn off (Figure 1.1).

Methodological approaches associated with the semiotic analysis are myriad. Here, as an exploratory effort for applications in public policy, it is possible to focus on three basic levels of interaction within the public sphere: the alignment between legislative intent, enacted program, and program outcomes or lack thereof; the connection between enacting authority, administrative code, and official guidance; and the agreement between political rhetoric and program language. Among all the cases reviewed, there is an initial effort to answer a basic research question: Does the current emphasis on instrumentality in public policy undermine the values it purports to uphold? As corollary items to this question, does this analysis suggest a general trend toward invalid truth claims in public policy in the cases studied, in stated intent compared with performance,

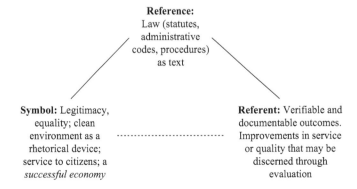

Figure 1.1 Reference, symbol, and referent (after Eco, 1976, p. 59).
Source: Created by C.A., based upon Eco, 1976.

for example? If there are invalid truth claims, which group(s) benefit(s) from such claims?

The cases explored in this book are unified in philosophical and methodological orientation toward the semiotic view – in uncovering hidden meaning in word use in policy. The illustrative and critical case analyses have the intent of moving beyond observation of phenomena to at least an initial application that is explanatory and possibly even predictive of behaviors and outcomes observed in public policy situations (Holton & Walsh, 2017).

The Plan of the Book

Chapter 2 follows with a further theoretical discussion of the relationship between sign and signified in public policy, with particular focus on this relationship in the guise of law. Chapter 3 is an illustrative case, reviewing an enforcement action under the US Federal Food, Drug, and Cosmetic Act and addressing a breakdown between intent and outcome in implementation of policy. Chapter 4 focuses on a conceptual example – green public procurement – through the use of a Greimas square to uncover values associated with such policies. Chapter 5 provides an analysis of the literature on public-sector ethics programs and pursues a critical understanding of the break between the topic in theory and practice. What ethical aspects are emphasized by government codes and training, and what do such programs suggest about the understanding that exists between government and the public?

Chapter 6 analyzes workforce development programs, including those that engage in activities to spur interviewing/hiring of hard-to-hire or disadvantaged individuals. There is potential for community benefit in such programs, but ambiguity in detailing expectations and program processes might lead to underwhelming results, even though passage or existence of the program might be enough for advocate groups. Chapter 7 examines the immigration laws of Germany. Of particular interest is the 2016 Integration Act, in the context of the previous action to encourage immigration due to declining population, and its motto "Support and demand." This is a fervently contested area of policy inquiry, and semiotic analysis is especially appropriate to increase understanding of denotations, connotations, and construction of systems of meaning upon which immigration structures are built.

Chapter 8 considers, through a sentiment analysis of tweets, the reform of the Patient Protection and Affordable Care Act (P. L. 111–148), often referred to in the popular press as the Affordable Care Act, ACA, or *Obamacare*. This contentious policy debate is of tremendous importance to many Americans, who are torn by political allegiances and the reality of skyrocketing medical costs. Chapter 9 looks at the term "sustainability" in an applied context, exploring energy policy in Thailand and implications for reification of the term. Imprecision in the term's use undermines its benefit to society in policy terms. Finally, Chapter 10 concludes the book; case analyses challenge pervasive thinking in public policy, where appearance, symbol, and data are given as a substitute for outcome orientation. Attention is paid to the idea of deliberative democracy – bringing the book full circle to the separation between what is possible in the public sphere, and what is accessible to the public.

References

Arkush, D. (2012). Democracy and administrative legitimacy. *Wake Forest Law Review, 47*, 611–629.

Atkinson, C. L. (2017). Legitimacy in public administration. In A. Farazmand (Ed.), *Global encyclopedia of public administration, public policy, and governance*. Springer. doi:10.1007/978-3-319-31816-5_1134-1.

Bainbridge, J. (2006). Lawyers, justice and the state. *Griffith Law Review, 15*(1), 153–176.

Bellamy, R. (2004). Developments in pluralist and elite approaches. In K. Nash & A. Scott (Eds.), *The Blackwell companion to political sociology, 17–28*. Malden, MA: Blackwell.

Berger, A. A. (2010). *The objects of affection: Semiotics and consumer culture.* New York: Palgrave Macmillan.

Berger, P. L., & Luckmann, T. (1966). *The social construction of reality: A treatise in the sociology of knowledge.* Garden City, NY: Anchor.

Boshoff, A. (2013). Law and its rhetoric of violence. *International Journal for the Semiotics of Law, 26*, 425–437.

Bove, A. (2014). For whose benefit? Fear and loathing in the welfare state. *Journal of Political Marketing, 13*, 108–126.

Branstetter, J. (2011). Bridging the divide: Normatively anchored, problem-driven research in political communication. *French Politics, 9*(2), 182–199.

Brown, R. H. (2005). *Culture, capitalism, and democracy in the new America.* New Haven, CT: Yale.

Cohen, A. P. (1995, orig. 1975). *The management of myths: The politics of legitimation in a Newfoundland community.* St. John's: Memorial University of Newfoundland.

Cohen, E. H. (2008). Symbols of disapora Jewish identity: An international survey and multi-dimensional analysis. *Religion, 38*(4), 293–304.

Cohen, M. D., March, J. G., & Olsen, J. P. (1972). A garbage can model of organizational choice. *Administrative Science Quarterly, 17*(1), 1–25.

Corazza, L., Scagnelli, S. D., & Mio, C. (2017). Simulacra and sustainability disclosure: Analysis of the interpretive models of creating shared value. *Corporate Social Responsibility and Environmental Management, 24*, 414–434.

Denhardt, R. B., & Denhardt, J. V. (2000). The new public service: Serving rather than steering. *Public Administration Review, 60*(6), 549–559.

Denhardt, R. B., & Denhardt, K. G. (1979). Public administration and the critique of domination. *Administration & Society, 11*(1), 107–120.

Eco, U. (1976). *A theory of semiotics.* Bloomington, IN: Indiana University Press.

Edelman, M. (1971). *Politics as symbolic action: Mass arousal and quiescence.* New York: Academic Press.

Evans, V. (2015). *The crucible of language: How language and mind create meaning.* Cambridge, UK: Cambridge University Press.

Farmer, D. J. (1995). *The language of public administration: Bureaucracy, modernity, and postmodernity.* Tuscaloosa, AL: University of Alabama Press.

Fischer, F., & Gottweis, H. (2012). Introduction: The argumentative turn revisited. In F. Fischer & H. Gottweis (Eds.), *The argumentative turn revisited: Public policy as communicative practice, 1–30.* Durham, NC: Duke University Press.

Forester, J. (1985a). Introduction: The applied turn in contemporary critical theory. In J. Forester (Ed.), *Critical theory and public life, ix–xix.* Cambridge: MIT Press.

Forester, J. (1985b). Critical theory and planning practice. In J. Forester (Ed.), *Critical theory and public life, 202–227.* Cambridge: MIT Press.

Freeland, C. (2011). The rise of the new global elite. *The Atlantic.* Retrieved from https://www.theatlantic.com/magazine/archive/2011/01/the-rise-of-the-new-global-elite/308343/.

Gilens, M., & Page, B. I. (2014). Testing theories of American politics: Elites, interest groups, and average citizens. *Perspective on Politics, 12*(3), 564–581.

Hacker, J. S., & Pierson, P. (2016). *American amnesia: How the war on government led us to forget what made America prosper.* New York: Simon & Schuster.

Held, D. (1980). *Introduction to critical theory: Horkheimer to Habermas.* Berkeley: University of California Press.

Hindess, B. (2004). Power, government, politics. In K. Nash & A. Scott (Eds.), *The Blackwell companion to political sociology, 40–48.* Malden, MA: Blackwell.

Holton, J. A., & Walsh, I. (2017). *Classic grounded theory: Applications with qualitative and quantitative data.* Thousand Oaks, CA: Sage Publications.

Kemp, R. (1985). Planning, public hearings, and the politics of discourse. In J. Forester (Ed.), *Critical theory and public life, 177–201.* Cambridge: MIT Press.

Kingdon, J. W. (2003). *Agendas, alternatives, and public policies,* 2nd edition. New York: Longman.

Koivisto, I. (2014). Varieties of good governance: A suggestion of discursive plurality. *International Journal for the Semiotics of Law, 27,* 587–611.

Krauss, L. M. (2015). Teaching doubt. *The New Yorker.* Retrieved from http://www.newyorker.com/news/news-desk/teaching-doubt.

Krebs, R. R., & Jackson, P. T. (2007). Twisting tongues and twisting arms: The power of political rhetoric. *European Journal of International Relations, 13*(1), 35–66.

Leeds-Hurwitz, W. (1993). *Semiotics and communication: Signs, codes, cultures.* Hillsdale, NJ: Lawrence Erlbaum Associates.

Lindsay, C. (2017, February 5). Quora question: How is Trump the populist savior of the working class? *Newsweek.* Retrieved from http://www.newsweek.com/quora-question-heart-why-trump-divides-us-551491.

Locke, J. (1690). The second treatise of government. Retrieved from https://www.gutenberg.org/files/7370/7370-h/7370-h.htm.

Misgeld, D. (1985). Education and cultural invasion: Critical social theory, education as instruction, and the "pedagogy of the oppressed." In J. Forester (Ed.), *Critical theory and public life 77–118.* Cambridge: MIT Press.

O'Neill, J. (1985). Decolonization and the ideal speech community: Some issues in the theory and practice of communicative competence. In J. Forester (Ed.), *Critical theory and public life, 57–76.* Cambridge: MIT Press.

Pauker, G. J. (1973). *Sources of instability in developing countries*. Santa Monica, CA: Rand Corporation.

Roberts, J. M., & Crossley, N. (2004). Introduction. In N. Crossley & J. M. Roberts (Eds.), *After Habermas: New perspectives on the public sphere*. Oxford: Blackwell.

Rohr, J. A. (1986). *To run a constitution: The legitimacy of the administrative state*. Lawrence, KS: University Press of Kansas.

Scott, W. R. (1995). *Institutions and organizations*. Thousand Oaks, CA: Sage Publications.

Selzer, J. (2009, orig. 2004). Rhetorical analysis: Understanding how texts persuade readers. In C. Bazerman & P. Prior (Eds.), *What writing does and how it does it: An introduction to analyzing texts and textual practices, 279–308*. New York: Routledge.

Simon, J. (2000). Ideology, imagology, and critical thought: The impoverishment of politics. *Journal of Political Ideologies, 5*(1), 81–103.

Stevenson, A., & Waite, M. (Eds.). (2011). *Concise Oxford english dictionary*. Oxford: Oxford University Press.

Stone, D. (2012). *Policy paradox: The art of political decision making*, 3rd edition. New York: Norton.

Strauss, V. (2017, February 5). An 'alternative facts' South Dakota bill sparks fears for science in the Trump era. *The Washington Post* (online). Retrieved from https://www.washingtonpost.com/news/answer-sheet/wp/2017/02/05/an-alternative-facts-south-dakota-bill-sparks-fears-for-science-education-in-the-trump-era/?utm_term=.b29e940adc87.

Suchman, M. C. (1995). Managing legitimacy: Strategic and institutional approaches. *The Academy of Management Review, 20*(3), 571–610.

Swindal, J. (1994). The problem of problematization in discourse ethics. *Philosophy & Social Criticism, 20*(3), 1–18.

Szerszynski, B. (2002). Ecological rites: Ritual action in environmental protest events. *Theory, Culture & Society, 19*(3), 51–69.

Todorov, T. (1984). *Mikhail Bakhtin: The dialogical principle (W. Godzich, Trans.)*. Minneapolis: University of Minnesota Press.

Van Fleet, P. (2011). Tarski, Peirce and truth-correspondence in law: Can semiotic truth-analysis adequately describe legal discourse? In J. M. Broekman & F. J. Mootz III (Eds.), *The semiotics of law in legal education, 57–76*. Dordrecht: Springer.

Wapshott, R., & Mallett, O. (2017). Small and medium-sized enterprise policy; Designed to fail? *Environment and Planning C: Politics and Space*. doi:10.1177/2399654417719288.

West, K., & Davis, P. (2011). What is the public value of government action? Towards a (new) pragmatic approach to values questions in public endeavours. *Public Administration, 89*(2), 226–241.

White, O. F., & McSwain, C. J. (1993). The semiotic way of knowing and public administration. *Administrative Theory & Praxis, 15*(1), 18–35.

Zahariadis, N. (2014). Ambiguity and multiple streams. In P. A. Sabatier & C. M. Weible (Eds.), *Theories of the policy process*, 3rd edition. Boulder, CO: Westview.

2 Semiotic Analysis and Public Policy
Theory and Practice

In public policy circles, discussion of semiotics is infrequent. The term has a variety of definitions; this does not assist it in its approachability or readiness for use and application. If we hope to understand communication in public settings, it might be worthwhile to study semiotic applications, to gain insight into the making of meaning, and reality, within an increasingly complex and diverse public environment. The paucity of discussion about semiotics is unjustified; semiotics can help "us learn about ourselves and others and how we make and convey meanings" (Leeds-Hurwitz, 1993, p. 12).

On a basic level, the word 'semiotics' means "everything that can be taken as a sign" (Eco, 1976, p. 7). It could also mean "anything that 'stands for' something else" or a study of a "sign system," where signs are "words, images, sounds, gestures and objects" (Chandler, 2007, p. 2). A more formal definition comes from Ferdinand de Saussure, who wrote that semiotics is "a science which studies the role of signs as part of social life" (Saussure, in Chandler, 2007, pp. 2–3). Charles Sanders Peirce, considered the co-founder of semiotics, defined the term as "the quasi-necessary, or formal, doctrine of signs" and specifically an engagement of the character of these signs (Peirce, in Chandler, 2007, p. 3).

Semiotics is useful; it uncovers a system of rules that help create meaning in a system of signs (signifiers, the words we use to describe) and the thing-in-itself (signified, the object, or the concept). Through rules, the attempt is made to come to some common understanding of abstractions in the words used by society, which seek to create meaning, and which are heavily imbued with overtone and nuance that might be understood, taken for granted, or taken to have a given meaning, when the actual or intended meaning is dissimilar. The use of signs is part of how people communicate with one another and is dependent on the context of the use. The words themselves do not create meaning – rather, those apprehending the words, voicing them, hearing and understanding their message, are invested in the prospect of creating meaning. If we are not engaged in this exchange, we would merely be consuming the meaning created by others (Chandler, 2007).

Signs do not have any value of their own. As noted above, their use is what gives signs meaning. The relationship between signifiers and the signified is arbitrary. This is immediately applicable to policy. Policy seeks to define the world in words that are chosen – definitions of problems developed through processes, evidencing particular worldviews. When policymakers do this they seek to fix reality in a certain respect so that matters are closed and debates are done – the sense of arbitrariness between the words and the concept, between the problem and the solution, is reduced or at least appears moderated. Policy behaves differently than most other forms of communication, then, where "the relation between the signifier and its signified is not a matter of individual choice" (Chandler, 2007, p. 27). Policy *might well have started* as the choice of an individual, and through various means of communication and control of message, the relationship between signifier and signified might actually have become fixed, in a manner different than it would have been otherwise, due to the actions of an individual. Even if arbitrary, there is great power in this fixing of sign relationship.

While there has been attention in the literature to semiotics, and to public policy, there is a need for additional discussion on the useful link between semiotic analysis and public policy. This chapter explores application of semiotic analysis to public policy. First, the chapter offers a consideration of semiotics historically and generally. The connection of semiotics to public policy and law is then discussed.

Historical Foundations

General linguistics is concerned with the "science of language...concerned with human language as a universal and recognizable part of human behaviour and of the human faculties" (Robins, 1971, pp. 1–2). Within linguistics is semantics, the "study of meaning" (p. 19), where "meanings of utterances may relate to the whole world of the actual and potential experiences of the speakers" (p. 18). As linguists seek to understand the making of meaning, they take up context as part of communication – nonverbal actions are part of communication, and the cause of communication and its effect are also worth noticing (Robins, 1971).

Socrates took up the idea of private meaning in *Cratylus*; as Harris and Taylor suggest, private meaning, even when it battles with common sense, "validates...as many private languages as there are individuals... [making] nonsense of our normal understanding of the difference between truth and falsehood" (1989, p. 5). A word used could mean whatever we wish it to mean, and it becomes difficult to establish truth or false in meaning claims; we are left with a relative correctness. Speaking, and indeed naming of actions or even concepts, is an act, and in order for the action to be 'accomplished successfully,' the action and use must be proper. Language is both functional and rational, or it cannot do its work of representing reality. While this work spends time caught up in sounds, it does relate the question of whether the name effectively relates back to the "thing named" (Harris & Taylor, 1989, p. 17). The point of such inquiry is whether truth can be regarded at all if it is illusory; through word usage, language is used more or less correctly and properly, as long as private meaning and languages do not, in effect, supplant truth.

Aristotle followed with a plainly stated, basic theory of language, thus: "Words spoken are symbols or signs of affections or impressions of the soul; written words are the signs of words spoken" (Aristotle, *De Interpretatione I*, in Harris & Taylor, 1989, p. 21). Aristotle pointed out that even though the speech and writing might be different, those fundamental affections are shared throughout humanity, translated into signs that become local to the individual, and made representations and symbols. Later, this push-and-pull between individual freedom, for lack of a better term, to engage meaning creatively, and the need for homogeneousness of language so that people could understand one another, continued to be a central concern. Logos implies regularity.

Hume's political theory, particularly the suggestion of the 'false religion' of enthusiasm and superstition, is instructive. By enthusiasm, it is offered that the assertion of self and assumption that there is some kind of straight affinity between governed and governing is rooted in ignorance. By superstition, frivolity requires mediation between people and unknown forces – something or someone to stand between nature and the people as an authority. Hume's work sought to reject such notions. Meaning in society is given by something above intimate relationships and attempts to make meaning – justice, for example, is an artificial construction, but because these practices are independent rules, they carry us through conflict and resist crumbling under the weight of unrest. Our collective stance on what is good becomes a social will and deviating from it serves to reinforce the obligation felt. An allegiance to this system is similarly obligatory – it is not necessarily contractual, but the governance that springs from it is then based on management of behavior and associated expectations on the part of the public, and, essentially, what is considered right, lest the government in question lose its right to govern (Haakonssen, 1993).

Kant wrote about a conviction of natural right theory, wherein there is

> an objective, timelessly valid and universally binding principle of right, which is accessible to human knowledge, which draws an irrevocable boundary between that which is right and that is which is not that obligates everyone, and which contains the criterion with the assistance of which the correctness of human actions can be judged.
>
> (Kersting, 1992, p. 344)

The implementation of this conception allows for freedom for everyone, within the external world. Innate in Kant's philosophy is a boundary-spanning world right to freedom – that a focus universally on reason would lead to global peace.

The closeness of language to reality has been a serious issue. The possibility is that much of what we consider accord between words and things could well be just a matter of arbitrary decisions that are now well worn and accepted, but not, in any case, perfect approximations and representations. Locke believed that our ideas were descended from our encounters throughout life. In the course of existence, we communicate with one another our ideas and these encounters influence our thinking and how we live our lives. Locke thought of using words as an act – a stating and then a hearing and interpreting, and if the understanding of the communicating person and the receiver is the same, then the communication is successful. Locke also took note of non-correlative ideas – where there is no 'thing' to relate as an object for communication – just thoughts and representations unto themselves (Harris & Taylor, 1989).

Locke also aligned the personal will and communication – the utterance is an act, and the speaker is choosing, based on their understanding of the idea, how to convey it. Importantly, Locke included a strong component of liberty in the conveyance of ideas, in his Essay Concerning Human Understanding: "a Liberty, to make Words stand for what Ideas he pleases, that no one hath the Power to make others have the same Ideas in their Minds, that he has, when they use the same Words, that he does" (Harris & Taylor, 1989, p. 114). This liberty has a potential conflict with responsibility, particularly in the language of the public sphere, and notably where leaders are uttering words without regard to their eventual interpretation, or with the thought that misinterpretation might occur and might actually be helpful to a cause or certain ends. Simple ideas about objects are less cumbersome, certainly, than public policy, where significant disagreements can arise on even the definitions of parts of a complex puzzle, let alone the response of governments and actions to be taken.

It is difficult, as Locke suggested, to separate opinion, perception, will, and belief (Harris & Taylor, 1989), particularly when many statements are made metaphorically, and where absolute certainty of the receiver's interpretation – of alignment with the intended message – may not even matter. What is an especially relevant issue is how private meaning and interpretation – and liberty of utterance – translate into the public space.

While Saussure was seen as a historical linguist in his lifetime perhaps his weightiest impact has been in "describing how the structures of our social and cultural life are constituted, and the way in which once constituted they function as a system of signs" (Sanders, 2004, p. 2). Saussure first used the terms signifier and signified as two inseparable parts of the linguistic sign, and langue for language system and parole for speech (Sanders, 2004). Regarding language study, everything that reaches the lips as a result of the needs of discourse and by and individual operation is parole. Everything within an individual's brain, the stock of forms <heard> and produced and of their meaning...even when the individual is not speaking, represents what has been made official...langue.

(Saussure, in Engler, 2004, p. 57)

Parole is where the language system enters the social dynamic, while langue remains individual. The alignment of thought and sound in parole is an act that intends to convey langue, 'socially shared' as a "system of signs, each consisting of the arbitrary conjunction of an abstract concept and acoustic image" (Joseph, 2004, p. 59).

The arbitrariness of the connection between the concept being conveyed and the 'acoustic image' is of note in Saussure's conception of semiology. Even though the connection is arbitrary, it can be hard to sway the relationship that exists between sign and signified. Ultimately, what counts most in the sign system is how each signifier-signified dyad is different from all the others. The meanings given these dyad relationships might exist of their own previous definition or be the result of relative, contextual association. Saussure saw the function of meaning-making and interpretation as a human function, heavily invested in sounds, rather than the writing of words or the words themselves. The concepts (signifieds) yielded in a person's mind by parole are created when meaning is made – when words are understood. The signifier is like a container for the conceptual meaning in the signified. Even though arbitrary, the 'sign' taken together was seen by Saussure as concrete, and a real object that can be retrieved cerebrally (Joseph, 2004). Sign systems have 'value' in Saussure's view, but value does not equal meaning. The value in this model derives from context – intrinsic worth of the words, so to speak.

Peirce included the idea of the interpretant in his semiotic triangle model. The interpretant is the creation in someone's mind (like a signified) of the relationship between an object and a representamen (signifier), with the object being only marginally related, through this creation of reality, to any object (the referent). The referent is roughly a material object or, from a policy standpoint, an outcome of a policy – something verifiable and documentable. It is worth noting that the representamen may have nothing to do with the object itself – as long as the image is created in the interpretant, then the 'thing' has been created. This allows for the possibility of one-to-one correspondence (direct correspondences between signified and signifier – an index), but also symbolic connections (signifier does not resemble the signified or object) and iconic relationships (where there is a resemblance, sharing traits, between signifier and signified, such as an imitation or a sound effect) (Chandler, 2007).

The matter of symbol is especially relevant to policy. Peirce considered symbol "a sign which refers to the object that it denotes by virtue of a law, usually an association of general ideas, which operates to cause the symbol to be interpreted as referring to that object" (Peirce, quoted in Chandler, 2007, p. 39) – so the connection is made by habit or canon. The connection may be not much more than custom. It is made more than that through conversion to the written word, when made law, and put beyond the grasp of most of the public.

Sign, Symbol, System

The sign system operates in an environment of culture that affects, and is affected by, active use of the sign system. In semiotics, it is wise to guard against the idea that the sign is the thing itself, and this is a prudent observation for policy studies. It is naïve to believe the definition of a problem in a certain way and the naming of a program actually solves the matter. Nevertheless, there is symbolic value in such action, as it sets in motion other systems, of belief, of public action and expression of sentiment, and other forms of public participation or involvement. This is a trait of policy – there is a need to define problems and the public sector is not always that good at this activity. Politics and administration are looking at different sides of the same 'problem' coin, and finding that it expresses two dissimilar versions of reality in some cases. The words used in policy are abstractions – the lack of correspondence between words themselves and readily fixed concepts is one issue, but policy processes, and the desires and behaviors of official actors and the public itself, are also to blame for any lack of alignment. All seem to believe in the words, but the words do not mean anything on their own in policy. The words fail us. They have no unchanging essence. There is no overarching agreement of interpretation, and this impacts not only public processes, but the expectations of the public, leading to failure.

Silence is the primordial void broken now and again by matters of varying levels of importance. If language is communication in extensive form, and law highly systematized, then perhaps law is an act of communicating in defiance of the void – a proclamation of the unchanging even in the face of ceaseless transformation. When one seeks to ascribe meaning to something – an object or concept – they dip into a pool of signs, and existing relationships between sign and signified, and to interpretant in context. We set about "deciphering...images in the mind" (Broekman, 2016, p. 20), even though the object or concept referenced may occasionally not exist, or be a true expression capable of being captured. Belief may nevertheless continue to be vested upon the arrangement, as signs are caught up in social meanings and representations of reality; mistrust grows from not only imprecision in the use of terms, but the use of terms in ways that do not align with use as accepted by individuals and groups. What the sign represents is a thing or idea that may not necessarily be there or exist at all; the making of meaning is a process, and the one-for-one correspondence between sign and object is not necessary for the sign to exist and function acceptably (Broekman, 2016).

For its part, the sign mediates. A symbol, on the other hand, represents, as a result of the given 'chains' of a sign. Signs may be used by force of habit; the relationship between object and sign and their interpretant is not easily broken, and seeking after the interconnections between the aspects of the triad is difficult. The process of communication itself, with the initial message, from speaker thought to what was intended, to actual message, to what the hearer heard, to how it was interpreted, to consonance or dissonance with rules for that exchange, is a textured, intricate matter. Meaning-making is purposeful and persuasive, and depends heavily on structures that already exist. There simply is not time for a speaker and listener (or audience) to agree on communication dynamics for each and every interaction. Social understanding and ability to relate to others are expected, in addition to knowledge of subject matter (Broekman, 2016). Metaphors and jokes might be used, for example, so that the speaker appears more human and approachable – credible in a way that allows for the substantive material they will relate to be accepted. The substantive material itself is, potentially, invested with considerations that will cause it to be more acceptable to the audience; notices, verbal or otherwise, that may be read as keys for the audience that the author(s) understand the readers' viewpoint and that the document is cognizant of readers' wants and needs. Failing that, a speaker or communicator may show an audience that he or she has no idea what that audience wants, or how to address those needs acceptably.

Semiotics, with an eye toward two-layered meaning – the surface communication, and deeper interaction, informed by history, social relationships and expectations, meaning – allows for analytical insight into the how of signification and meaning-making in particular instances. Lawyers and people that work with law seek to make meaning, but also to "maintain the law and follow the lines of its constitution in society" (Broekman, 2016, p. 141). Where these efforts are less forthright, the 'intertwining' of words may create pretensions to meaning. Those who work with the law would do well to consider their work as text, and like other forms of text, subject to additional interpretation well beyond their immediate work and goals, and perhaps quite separate from their own founding "goals and values" (p. 192). Roberta Kevelson, in *The Law as a System of Signs*, suggested that "The basic concepts of rights, resources, and reality take on new dimensions of meaning in correspondence with n-dimensional, infinite value judgments or truth-like beliefs which one holds" (1988, quoted in Broekman, 2016, pp. 192–193). The text may be *of* one universe of thought and satisfactory there, but be subject to many other universes of contextual small-t truth.

Barthes wrote that "we are a civilization of the written word...it appears increasingly more difficult to conceive a system of images and objects whose *signifieds* can exist independently of language" (1967, p. 10). We rely heavily on text and on meaning inherent in text but when we go to look for absolutes, they are absent; we are left to argue over meaning. "Reality has authors" and "textual representations are...[the] sites of struggle" (Chandler, 2007, p. 65). This is true in semiotics and assuredly true in the application of semiotics to law and policy. We become more used to the idea that, like Magritte's famous painting of the pipe, the image is not the thing itself. This public policy is not the solution or the answer. This law is not a program or the answer to your concerns. Do not confuse the public problem with the string of text in the authority of law. The signifier might be an empty container. The game being played may be to hide some actual process or overall strategy, through distraction.

Connecting Policy Intent and Program Outcomes

Policy attempts to resolve what it perceives as problems given certain social constructs. These social constructs are perspectival, and therefore, cannot be considered consistent for all people within a given society. The problem for policy analysis as it has defined itself is insurmountable, because the crude methods employed cannot account for these differences in social construction. Perhaps the good of policy analysis happens in spite of the analysis itself, which is grossly imperfect and perhaps even irrelevant. Beyond this surface view, an acceptable method is legitimized in one way or another by a power elite (Lyotard, 1984), and it is quite possible that certain methods providing improved results might be foregone in favor of more firmly entrenched methods. Even when policy fails, shortcomings are "not so much the fault of the analytic brain trust that created them, but deficiencies within the governmental bureaucracy asked to carry them out" (deLeon, 1999, p. 312). This might be construed as an elite ploy to retain a hold on power.

Policy analysis also has had a great basis in feelings and moral issues (Goodin, 1988, p. 71); this is possibly opposed to the cause of scientific rigor, or at the least, separate. The veneer of science has been seen by some to "legitimate policies the public would reject if it were not deluded by the mystique of science" (deHaven-Smith & Ripley, 1988, p. 97). Given its applied nature, policy analysis is tied to the outcome and the achievability of the goals it sets (deHaven-Smith & Ripley, 1988, p. 103). Depending on one's own political outlook, government can or cannot solve mankind's problems, and the methods one employs in achieving societal aims have a strong basis in ideology. Motivation and "assumptions about the polity are implicit in the design of implementation structures" (deHaven-Smith & Ripley, 1988, p. 103).

Problem definition as it exists in practice does not often progress in a natural sequence of events. The process is more apt to be a complex interrelated series of value judgments and guess-timations more closely approximating bounded rationality (Simon, 1947). Rochefort and Cobb (1993) correctly noted that

> mismatches often exist between measures of the seriousness of a problem and the level of attention devoted to it...that other factors, in addition to 'objective conditions,' could be responsible for an issue's standing...including intensity of issue advocacy, leaders' openness to the issue, and the salience of competing problems.
>
> (p. 56)

Beyond the "arbitrariness" (p. 56) of what constitutes an important problem in need of resolution, there is the "intersubjective nature of social experience and its impact both on issue initiation and policy formulation" (p. 57). Implicit in an environment of intersubjectivity is a need to act competently even as reality may shift based upon perspective.

Modalities and Possible Worlds

Philosophy is "the form of thought that asks...what determines that there is and can be truth and falsehood and whether or not we can separate" the two, and spirituality is the "search, practice, and experience through which the subject carries out the necessary transformations on himself in order to have access to the truth" (Foucault, 2005, p. 15). Part of the problem that exists in society is that understanding cannot come to most people, because they are too unwilling to risk their previously conceived notions in discourse, to engage in a search for truth and understanding that may ultimately result in their changing somehow. Perfect knowledge and understanding is an ideal and does not exist for practical purposes. We are unfulfilled because we believe that knowledge has been attained when it has not; the truth so often apprehended as the fact is subjective, and lacks the coherence that comes from having engaged with differing interpretations.

Harmony has not come to society; people are too keen to make enemies of one another, and to lord knowledge over one another. Governance suffers when people in positions of power refuse to examine themselves and their own irrationality, and see how that might adversely impact those being led. If society cares about justice so much, why is so much time in the public sphere being spent engaged in a narrowing of discourse, and in the vice of tribalism? Like Foucault's reading of Seneca's *stultitia*, lack of critical thinking allows one to be blown about with the winds of popular opinion and varying, often conflicting representations of reality. Rhetoric persuades the unrestrained mind, appealing to baser instincts. People are encouraged into thoughts, behaviors, and actions that are largely involuntary, because the outside pressures are not recognized for what they are. At the same time, our ability to recognize value in those around us is limited by susceptibility to "adornment, affectation, flattery, and illusion" (Foucault, 2005, p. 348). Such tricks are injurious – they prevent one from approaching true discourse, and from participating fully and knowledgeably in public conversation. We move further from commitment to truth, and from forming bonds based on trust (Foucault, 2005).

Even speaking a truth is tricky in today's discourse, precisely because it does involve taking such a pronounced risk. In public environments, the airing of truth may lead to chastisement of the message's sender if the truth is not wanted, or portrays a subject or topic uncomfortably. Telling the truth requires courage. There is some chance that receipt of the truth-message may end the relationship with the message's sender. For career public professionals, the airing of truth occurs in complex environments informed by political currents. Liars and flatterers might be more accepted, and rise higher through the ranks, than truth-tellers, ideals aside. However, the truth is desperately needed; as Foucault (2012) opined, "there has to be truth for the city to exist and for it to be saved. But the truth cannot be told in a political field defined by an absence of differentiation between subjects speaking" (p. 44). Everyone is, simply put, not an expert. Public administrators, as technical experts, are needed to do their jobs unobstructed, but they must absolutely be expert and competent about it. With a public that is claiming knowledge it does not have, the need is to not to receive knowledge, but to tell the supposed experts how it 'really is,' and then for those experts to simply repeat back to the public what they want to hear. Truth and courage are not only unacceptable in this view of administration – these virtues are frowned upon. And yet, administration's obligation to the truth remains.

When people endeavor to make sense of some communication through intensional logic, there can be an effort to determine the validity of the claim or counterfactual dependent on whether the consequent is implied by the antecedent. For most people, the representation is either valid or not, even though it might have considerable vagueness. The statement is a claim, and a supposition to be evaluated given the level of our willingness to follow a premise; this is dependent on how close the representation is between the antecedent and what I personally know to be probable. My view and reality could be quite different from that of others, but I would do well to recognize the existence of other possibilities, even if *unactualized* to me (Quine's term) (Lewis, 2001, orig. 1973).

In writing about possible worlds, Kripke (1980) compared the result showing from the throw of two dice, relative to all the possible states of the dice, as the actual world versus a series of possible worlds. The possible worlds of the other potentialities of the dice are "what might have been" (p. 18), or counterfactual situations. Kripke later raises the question posed by Quine about identity across all possible worlds – and suggests that "really, adequate necessary and sufficient conditions for identity which do not beg the question are very rare in any case" (p. 43).

The reason is that "a possible world is given by the descriptive conditions we associate with it...stipulated" (p. 44). The limit of our intellectual exercise in considering another possible world might be that we presume something to be true and imagine what we might do or how things might be if that were the case. A problem becomes our rigidity in setting names to things, when the concepts themselves are not inflexible – dogmatism implies precision that simply may not exist (Kripke, 1980).

Like the disbeliever in Kripke's illustration of Wittgenstein's paradox, the citizen might be tempted to look for reasons why a simple statement, such as the symbol + taken as meaning addition, based on our previous experience having seen that numerous times, might actually mean something completely different. We could conceivably "lack 'direct' access to the facts whether we mean plus or quus," even though we do know what we mean, "with a fair degree of certainty" (Kripke, 1982, p. 40). There actually is not much that is behavioral or context-based about + and its relationship to addition. But denial or skepticism can be had regardless. We may understand fully that the + symbol means addition, but it might be fun anyway to imagine what it might be like if it meant something else.

In public policy terms, it is possible for an official to feign understanding of policy, and be included in discussions with people who are fully conversant. It is akin to the feeling of reading versus actually reading – one is a pretension and the other genuine. We make a "leap in the dark" each time words are used, because the new usage is not necessarily the same as every other usage that has come before, and might be defined or fashioned in such a way to allow for "anything we may choose to do" (Kripke, 1982, p. 55). The problem with following Wittgenstein too far is that "it appears that he has shown all language, all concept formulation, to be impossible, indeed unintelligible" (Kripke, 1982, p. 62). Language and formulation do exist, and are intelligible, and often actionable, in notable ways. The language we use is intelligible because of assertion and justification. Assertion and intelligibility do not necessarily need to involve facts, or "truth conditions" (p. 86). People may take action based on the understanding they have; they are "licensed to given, without further justification, the answer that strikes [them] as natural and inevitable" (p. 88).

This language game works because, in essence, we agree to play a game, that this game informs our lives, and that we have criteria for playing the game (we know a table is a table, for example, by the attributes that make it so) (Kripke, 1982). Where matters become more complex with our agreement to play by rules of a language game is where we do not agree on the criteria for more complicated topics, such as concepts of policy, ethics/morals, the right role of government, and the like. Nevertheless, the game continues, with those that do find commonality in criteria – where assertions made are not only intelligible but justified – acting together to influence policymaking processes, and impact public outcomes in significant ways.

The rise of pseudo-problems in public policy, then, is a serious issue. Pseudo-problems can be raised as counterfactuals and be seen as having some legitimacy in that respect. The bar is low for popular acquiescence. There is seemingly a necessity in naming of problems in public policy, as Kripke (1980) noted, with proper names. The names given may have nothing to do with the actual referent; philosophically, the identity of the relationship does not necessarily follow. Just because a group of people presume something to be does not make it so, but in policy, their presumption may itself prove useful, even if based in no part on reality. Identification is contingent (Kripke, 1980), and that is perfectly fine for policy purposes.

One way of examining the polarized state of the public sphere is through the concept of a plurality of worlds. "There are ever so many ways that a world might be; and one of these many ways is the way that this world is...every way that a world could possibly be is a way that some world is," wrote David Lewis (2001, orig. 1986, p. 2). Perspectives on what is real do not have to overlap in any way for a viewpoint to be very real to an individual. Some worlds receive our attention and some do not; our attention to a particular world does not *necessarily* make it real – it is perhaps not real at all. It becomes more important then, that portrayals of reality have verisimilitude. For a truth claim, alignment with what we know to be true in our world is important for the claim to be considered valid; we believe it to be true and desire it so. Insistence on our one world of thinking may not allow much room, if any, for the potential existence of other worlds (Lewis, 2001).

The world that colors our perspective is far from absolute, but for us to be able to persist, the operating assumption is that the world is at least stable in meaning, and that one is right about one's perceptions, as long as they align with what one *knows* to be right in context. I do not mean *know* in a facetious way – from an individual's perspective, their construct of reality is exactly as valid as any other construct. It is a world unto itself, and people mostly really *are* islands of comprehension. When worldviews overlap, then some element of collective thought and action may occur. People rely upon language conventions that are mythical – the agreement is tacit and promises made by following conventions are easily broken, tied closely to alignment of interests and communication habits. "When this common sense of interest is mutually expressed and is known to both, it produces a suitable resolution and behavior" (Lewis, 1969, p. 4). In absolute terms, though, this is a rare alignment between two people, let alone between groups of individuals, or nations.

A major problem is that the world is unstable, full of error, and people especially are unstable – conspicuously because they often have full and unwarranted confidence in the quality of their decisions and the basis upon which those decisions are made (Lewis, 2001). People spend a fair amount of time arguing what is arbitrary, when perhaps arbitrariness is the rule rather than the exception; calls for interpretation and explanation are essential aspects of public policy, but these questions seek after a purely objective explanation that may not exist. Incomplete viewpoints, too, constitute the basis of decisions, and of portrayals of others, groups, circumstances and programs; official constructs are frequently limited, especially when they do not engage affected groups. Vagueness results, but it is not mistaken – it is a purposeful vagueness; it might be better to be "unproblematic," even if this means that communication is "unintelligible" (Lewis, 2001, p. 213). There is still vacillation in policy, but making a statement official, passing a law, instituting a program, all defy the underlying hesitancy.

There is a counter to the unintelligibility that goes along with possible worlds, by flipping back the idea of how people make sense of things, to considering application of common rational standards. John Searle (1998) wrote about the danger of self-deception, even given that there is a "real world that exists independently of us...[and] Our statements are typically true or false depending on whether they correspond to how things are, that is to the facts in the world" (p. 10). This is so whether or not a certain vocal percentage of the population chooses to challenge default positions of how truth may be discerned, but we nevertheless are stuck with ideas being representations of the world external to us, and thus inferior to the things themselves. We are at the mercy of the natural processes around us, even if we choose to gather together collections of ideas, wrong or otherwise, to refute that those natural processes exist.

When policymakers create policy, they consider often complex problems from the perspective of their ability to represent problem and solution in inferior forms – in legal writing and frameworks that presuppose and approximate the real world, with people and potential of untold proportion. The solutions created may fail because the basis itself is ignorant and even arrogant, sometimes willfully so. The effort may dispense with reality and attempt to put one's ideals or vision of reality upon what is actual; while the attempt to construct may fail, the attempt itself may garner enough political capital to make a difference in an election, or change the course of how power is allocated and utilized across areas of policy. We choose unintelligibility over common understanding because it allows an individual a unique path to being correct within their own viewpoint, even if they are entirely wrong. Facts may exist, but they are irrelevant if they make someone question their worldview too much on a personal level. Yet at a societal level, the facts matter very much. Intelligibility is ultimately demanded of us. It is fine to be ignorant and unintelligible, that is, until these predilections encounter the cold light of day, and the demands of interaction with an active, rational, intelligent social sphere. Absent that, ignorance and unintelligibility may persist.

To apply Searle's point (1998), no amount of evidence can win against this – if all understanding is merely a construction, then what is implied is that we are in control, when we are not. Certainty and absolutism sell well to a frightened public, but acceptance of our ignorance, on a planet that periodically rages against us, and we against it, hurtling through the inky blackness of uncaring space, does not sell well at all.

Relating Gottlob Frege, Scott Soames wrote that "the meaning of a name is not its bearer, and the meaning of a definite description is not what it denotes" (Soames, 2010, p. 9). The referent does not necessarily correspond one-for-one to the name, but perhaps to properties being described. This leaves open the possibility of symbolic logic, through "ways of thinking [about] referents, rather than the referent themselves" (p. 17). To extend the thought, "the meaning of a term is never its referent, but rather is a descriptive sense that provides necessary and sufficient conditions for determining reference" (p. 77). This thinking raises a problem of rigid designation. Our information is often incomplete and inaccurate; definitions upon which we rely are sometimes circular. Our way of thinking naturally leads us to identify differences, and in difference to note identities (Soames, 2010). The problem of the existence of counterfactuals further confounds our ability to make clear sense of problems. Because we cannot absolutely reject all possibilities, they remain open, challenging our sense of reality.

It is possible that meanings are by habit, through repetition, and not driven consciously. Echoing Foucault, Heiskala wrote that "preconscious, unconscious and rejected meanings often flow, with causal effects" (2007, pp. 261–262). At a reflective level of meaning, what is communicated by experts is not only what is, but what should be; at the constitutive level, meanings are communicated and backed by penalties, as through the writing of rules, implementation of law and programs, and enforcement practices. The various levels of understanding and system are communicated by signs and these constrain behavior, but culture and habit remain quite significant in defining signifying, meaning constructs, and actions (Heiskala, 2007).

For its part, the field of public administration is fractured between practice and theory. Academic work has been considered as collective creation of meaning, the role of norms, and how policy influences the practical circumstances encountered in communities. The eventual program that may be analyzed could represent a "consensus on meaning... [emerging] from a set of shared definitions...about past programs...the nature of individuals" and other factors (Burnier, 2005, p. 504). It has been offered that programs represent how a problem has been officially defined, but this is not necessarily so all the time. Variances in implementation, too, can cause breakages between the original intent and how a program, however constructed, actually works in practice, pretensions to administrative proficiency and instrumental rationality aside.

The resultant program might easily reflect choices made for the sake of administrative ease, long-term arguments and divisions between agencies avoided for the sake of keeping the peace in the larger institution, the preferences of the most vocal stakeholder groups, and limited knowledge and capacity of those groups, regulated industries, administrators, and political forces. The official nature of decisions is a disguise for uncertainty, and it is paid for in vagueness and lack of oversight. It is far more common than instances of technical rationality, alignment of outcome with original intent, and success in improving the lot of the public, generally.

The public administration sector, in both its practice- and theory-based incarnations, has undergone a fundamental transformation in terms of what is considered acceptable approach and process in the search for an accurate, useful portrayal of reality. Diversity and efforts to serve diverse populations have forced administration to become more mindful of particular interests and cultures and less beholden to reliance upon assumption and the *generalized reality* of a ruling elite. Nevertheless, the operating environment of the public decision-maker has become increasingly complex, often hampering the ability of the decision-maker to act rationally and appropriately in the face of thorny policy dilemmas.

As a consideration for semiotic analysis, political rhetoric gives way to legal authority and program construction, reflecting policy intent. It is hoped that policy intent is then translated into a program, with further design choices that clarify any vagueness in the legal authority, and with definitions that support those of the statute. Implementation would follow, and then an evaluative process would occur on a regular basis to provide formative evaluation for the program, with the possibility of summative evaluation to give policymakers an idea of whether their initial choice makes sense for the community.

Semiotic Analysis and Law

There is a common element to the work of Peirce and Habermas that is essential for the project of this book. Held stated it thus: "If there is a manifest discrepancy between the posited interpretation and its object, it will be uncovered as a 'gap' between actions anticipated and the actual resultant action. An interpretation fails when there is a disappointment of expectations" (1980, p. 309). Habermas suggested that disturbance of consensus was a disappointment. I would suggest that failure in the public sphere occurs from the beginning, believing that a consensus ever occurs in the first place. The public sphere is so awash with inauthenticity and an intended lack of validity in truth claims that apparent consensus situations are most probably hyperrealities, made up of language games and dependent on a distracted public. Consensus is dependent on an authentic attempt to foster deliberative democracy and achieve communication toward some shared goal. Too often, the goal of public sphere communication is the imposition of a previously selected reality upon an unsuspecting populace. Those 'preferred realities' are not in any way neutral; self-reflection and critical thought are enemies of this structure.

As Petrilli and Ponzio suggested, "Semiotics must not only describe and explain signs, it must also search for methods of inquiry and knowledge acquisition, and furthermore make proposals relative to human behavior and social programming" (2010, p. 152). Different than attempting to read the collective belief of a population in a vague way, a formalized policy exists as a closed text (Eco, 1979), inviting semiotic analysis.

"Officials bear the responsibility for turning goals into realities – without them, policies remain only promises" (Riggs, 2001, p. vii).

> Ideas don't have to be theoretically rigorous and powerful to be useful in the uncertain and confusing world of pragmatic action. Messy and imprecise semiconcepts, or concepts that do not neatly transfer into clear, sharp applications in the real world, can be useful in the hands and minds of discerning practitioners... Good theory reduces the danger of error, but it is not always available.
>
> (Siffin, 2001, p. 1)

To use Siffin's thought here, "If we lack a theoretical foundation, do we at least have a pervasive sense of order and agreement in our dealings with the subject...?" (2001, p. 3); order and agreement might be fleeting as attention shifts from the drafting of a law to implementation.

Theory and practice may be better connected in semiotic analysis, and discourse/textual analysis is helpful in terms of evaluating law. However, without context, one is left with the mistaken notion that the meaning of law is entirely divorced from its original, communicative context. Law itself is not entirely superindividual, and there is a great tradition of legal interpretation. Original construction remains important. At the time of original construction of law, and indeed as law is brought up again in various situations, implemented, and the work of resultant programs evaluated, discussions and communications occur (or not). Supporting work in administrative law and regulations exist. These provide detail to the expansive language of statute, but even these may fail to uncover the motivations, appeals to emotion, and even lies that undergird rhetoric in the public sphere, and eventually public policy. Semiotic analysis can assist with this endeavor; a discussion of methodological considerations is then imperative.

Law has a close relationship with semiotics; "law as (fundamentally a system of) meaning is only accessible through (linguistic) signs and thus [is] dependent on the process of interpreting the signs" (Engberg & Rasmussen, 2010, p. 367). Language itself is an abstract structure, but is imbued with rich contextual meaning. Considerable rhetoric and passionate pleas for governmental action often give rise to the drafting of statutes. Even where law is more dry, there are rationales for action, often structural and given to organizational proclivities, making the language of law very much of the time, place, and people at its birth. Later, law is interpreted, frequently by administrative staff members who were not present when a given law was enacted, and they too bring their cognition into the communicative mix (Engberg & Rasmussen, 2010). Further, law may also exist on the books without being put into practice or enforced.

There may not be agreement on what 'plain language' of law might mean; those interpreting the law might manipulate even plain language toward interpretations that support favored political or conceptual bases (Soboleva, 2013). Language in contracts may be read subjectively, as understood by parties to the contract, objectively, or a combination of both, with an objective view when the parties do not agree with one another (Janko, 2007). There is seldom one view on what the words of law mean and how they are to be interpreted, and this may create complexity and confusion when administrators, citizens, elected officials, and business confront law and attendant regulations. As Miller put it, "There is a grand narrative behind the rule of law. This grand narrative promises consistency, standards, and fairness to all. The problem with legal principle is that it does not accomplish those things" (2002, p. 11). Those within the venue of the law must at times speak and write specifically and peculiarly, for processes to move forward (Miller, 2002).

Language imposes "structure on our perceptions of the world" (Lee, 1992, p. 8), in addition to its effort to imitate reality. Language itself does a rather poor job in practice of mirroring anything fully; it might evoke certain aspects but an incomplete picture emerges. Much is not said because it does not have to be said; the language itself is the tip of an iceberg of awareness. When one uses language, one might be referring to an iceberg tip, in effect, but lack awareness of the entirety of that iceberg that is the lived experience that informs the thought. The language itself is borrowed, but the awareness is lost. The use may be out of context, and subject to one's own perspective. The context that was so important to the creation of the original thought, which led to the language, is simply absent, leaving the language out on its own to be used by others for their own purposes. There is an estrangement, but one is perhaps not bothered by it, or even aware of it, because the language serves a function of its own – just not necessarily the original function. What becomes important is the perspective of the person using the language, and those hearing or reading it; the meaning is constructed in the moment and actively interpreted as a function of context (Lee, 1992).

This has possibly dangerous implications for public policy study, because the legal tradition has a significant component that tends toward original construction and intent. In choosing what words to use, one is not using other possible words; the decision is constrained by under-standing, knowledge, or belief.

The language that is used can evidence a certain perspective, betray bias, or show inclinations toward given worldviews. Without being told much about writers, one can examine their writing and learn some-thing about who they are and what they think. Metaphors are nota-ble, particularly in journalism, where other groups of people can be portrayed as natural phenomena out of control, for example, or where emotions are illustrated as being under extreme pressure. The textual features show a focus for better or worse and identify where priorities exist, or what the preferred actor(s) in a conflict might be. Lee (1992) identified the term 'detention' as an official term, beholden to 'official transactions' of a governing body, lexicalized, borne of discussions amongst government officials. The word existed before its official use, but in being used officially, it takes on another level of meaning that may be seen quite differently depending on perspective, and particu-larly if one is standing against the rule, finding oneself 'in detention.' It is made a technical term, and other definitions of if, that are supported by competing narratives, are perhaps suppressed. At some point, the official meaning may be taken as given without much thought, even though the use of the term in technical respect is heavily invested in an individual ideological standpoint and the accompanying narrative. Those that are marginalized may not recognize just how unfair and ex-clusionary that term is, given its official, technical cloak. As Lee stated, "the production of text clearly has a good deal to do with the exercise of power...those that control the production of text control the operation of ideology" (1992, p. 107). How events are portrayed is important: It means the difference between an appropriate demonstration and a riot (Lee, 1992). The nature of the event and what it is called by various groups unmasks quite a lot about the event itself and those making the determination.

In keeping with the production of official language, in administra-tive circles, there is a general expectation that work will follow appro-priate formats. Work failing to follow such formats is not considered acceptable – it does not match the intended coding to be construed as official. Particularly close attention is paid to the source of authority, breadth and scope of rules and implementation, as well as policies, pro-cedures, enforcement, and remedies for non-compliance. Programs that fail to include expected aspects of technical or official language fail be-cause they lack competence of instrumentation. Lee (1992) noted how texts can reveal relevant nuances about institutional arrangements and impediments, so much can be learned from what is there, as well.

With this noted, textual production and meaning-making can be un-dermined and attacked, especially in the public sector with its propen-sity toward rhetoric and competing narratives. No matter how strong the textual production apparatus of the public sphere, a lack of credibility and legitimacy can undermine public writing of even especially high quality.

A standard way of explaining the functioning of language is that "words stand for things," and that a sentence is factual if "the arrangement of words in the sentence corresponds...to the arrangement in reality of the things that those words stand for" (Hookway, 1988, p. 8). There is concern perhaps in defining reality where the equating of words and sentences to things is less concrete; it is more difficult in that respect to discern the validity of a truth claim for a sentence describing an abstract concept. For abstract concepts, they must be made to be meaningful. Because they are disputable, the argument for this meaning or that must be more convincing, the further out the concept is from being universally understood. In seeking to communicate concepts, the sender of a message may ascribe concrete properties to inanimate objects, or overgeneralize and refer to a range of objects with the same descriptive terms (Hookway, 1988). This effort to make meaning fails, in one sense, because it leads to incorrect assumptions, but it may work fine for political purposes and accomplish partisan objectives. The nexus of statement and reality matter less in practical impact if basic terms are in dispute.

Law itself may act as sign, and even be perceived by the public to have accomplished some positive public end, without programs being implemented or policies enforced. This is due to the great rhetorical power resident in public policy purely as sign. The public sees law as having met public obligations or not; this perception is independent of whether programs based upon law have actually accomplished anything, positive or negative, when compared with the intent of the legal authority.

It is worthwhile to look at law as something other than monolithic, unchanging, and indisputable, particularly when it comes to public policy processes. It has been said that trial work involves a ritualized storytelling process (Maley & Fahey, 1991). Public policy is similar. How the public sphere chooses to define a problem – as well as create a law and program structure, implement and enforce a program, and then evaluate the results of the program compared with the original intent – is ritualized within the public sphere. Choices within the whole of the policy process are not objective choices; they are normative choices (Birkland, 2015) invested with culture and context. Further, how governments (inclusive of elected officials and administrative agencies) go about these processes does not occur in a vacuum; the reality of community and society is being shaped by these choices, as government is shaped by its context. Reality in the public sphere is constantly being created based upon definitional choices made by public institutions; the public itself may be tempted to take these decisions and definitions as given, even when the choices made seem arbitrary. The problem with arbitrariness is that it leaves out rationale. If definitional choices are based upon 'best practice,' for example, then there is a need to further evaluate what makes a practice the best option in the new context, since efficacy of process is frequently context- and actor-based.

The problem with evidence and the tendency toward its provision as a matter of bureaucratic process is that the public sometimes does not care about evidence. As Birkland wrote, "Scientific evidence is much stronger than anecdotes in understanding how and why things work the way they do. However, the results of scientific study are often controversial and unpopular, and sometimes run counter to popular expectations" (2015, p. 15). Also, politicians may not find it necessary to engage in discussions about or fully understand evidence, even if valid, when anecdotes may fully serve their intended purposes. Policy is fundamentally a human endeavor, and the decision process is such that choices are likely to be made on an emotional basis, and then backed up later with cherry-picked evidence that backs up the original choice, rather than based on a full accounting of all facts, and the perspectives of all sides. The narrowing of one's viewpoint is a survival tool, and "the results of 'scientific' policy analysis are often abandoned when other rhetorical tools seem to work better" (2015, p. 14).

While signs can help us understand policy to an extent, the real catch is far more complex than that, because as Bakhtin offered, "there is no text of texts, potential and unified" (in Todorov, 1984, p. 26). Because of this, we seek the perception or view of the other, because we cannot get beyond our own narrow view of the larger issue, or of reality generally. Can we tell much about a government from a single policy, or a single agency or program? Perhaps it depends most on the perspective of the individual telling the story, because context, interpretation, and dialogue are all essential. The text, then, of policy in its law form is necessarily illusory and bears little if any resemblance to the reality of the problem or issue its creation is intended to address. It is vague and seeks the expertise and detailed understanding of the other, in administration, to effect some sense of comprehension to the concern in play. This imperfect construct in the public sphere seeks to impersonate and then modify a caricature version of reality, though the body politic fails to understand well enough all players and machinations in place to actually achieve much of anything, most of the time.

Because the legal-rational system is not actually based so much upon the closeness of fit between policy and reality or accomplishment in outcomes, but rather on stability and creating the right conditions for operation of markets, the lack of overall movement makes little difference. "The lack of word-fact correspondence in public policy debate ceases to be revolting and instead becomes interesting" (Miller, 2002, p. 21). Quite possibly, words in policy may have moved from some correspondence with reality to "the point where words refer to little but themselves, or perhaps someone's disingenuous agenda" (p. 25). Where word definitions have always been subject to disagreement, pretense and exploitation of the public through symbols has become more pervasive as communication and discourse has grown more instantaneous and constant (Miller, 2002). This demands not only analysis of signs, meaning, and intent, but circumspection when it comes to the acceptance of public discourse, heavily reliant on symbol and grand narratives, as authentic.

Concluding Thoughts

Having noted the above, it is quite possible that legal authority has not been carried out exactly as envisioned in the enacting legislation or program language, and that this occurs commonly, more so than the precise carrying out of law that might be expected. It may even be that the original program has not been enacted to any extent at all, or that programs have taken a turn in administrative functionality that provides for fundamentally different outcomes than those originally slated for the program. Considering program outcomes, if any, in light of original intent, may provide a basis for further examination of how reference in law or administrative process is possibly removed not only from the politically desired referent but also from the original symbolic value or rhetoric that led to program passage. The chapters that follow consider case studies in light of a semiotic framework, through a variety of research viewpoints, and seek out sign and symbol, and critical disconnects that exist between intent and outcome, the crafting of law, and the practical matters of its implementation.

References

Barthes, R. (1967). *Elements of semiology (A. Lavers & C. Smith, Trans.).* New York: Hill & Wang.
Birkland, T. A. (2015, orig. 2011). *An introduction to the policy process: Theories, concepts, and models of public policy making.* Abingdon, Oxon: Routledge.
Broekman, J. M. (2016). *Meaning, narrativity, and the real: The semiotics of law in legal education IV.* Basel: Springer International Publishing.
Burnier, D. (2005). Making it meaning full: Postmodern public administration and symbolic interactionism. *Administrative Theory & Praxis, 27*(3), 498–516.
Chandler, D. (2007). *Semiotics: The basics,* 2nd edition. Abingdon, Oxon: Routledge.
deHaven-Smith, L., & Ripley, R. B. (1988). The political and theoretical foundations of public policy. In E. B. Portis & M. B. Levy (Eds.), *Handbook of political theory and policy science, 97–109.* New York: Greenwood Press.
DeLeon, P. (1999). The missing link revisited: Contemporary implementation research. *Review of Policy Research, 16*(3/4): 311–338. doi:10.1111/j.1541-1338.1999.tb00887.x.
Eco, U. (1976). *A theory of semiotics.* Bloomington: Indiana University.
Eco, U. (1979). *The role of the reader: Explorations in the semiotics of texts.* Bloomington: Indiana University.

Engberg, J., & Rasmussen, K. W. (2010). Cognition, meaning making, and legal communication. *International Journal for the Semiotics of Law, 23*, 367–371.

Engler, R. (2004). The making of the cours de linguistique générale. In C. Sanders (Ed.), *The Cambridge companion to Saussure, 47–58*. Cambridge, UK: Cambridge University Press.

Foucault, M. (2005). *The hermeneutics of the subject: Lectures at the College de France 1981–1982 (G. Burchell, Trans.)*. New York: Picador.

Foucault, M. (2012). *The courage of truth: The government of self and others II, Lectures at the College de France 1983–1984 (G. Burchell, Trans.)*. New York: Picador.

Goodin, R. E. (1988). Political theory as policy analysis – and vice versa. In E. B. Portis & M. B. Levy (Eds.), *Handbook of political theory and policy science, 63–74*. New York: Greenwood Press.

Haakonssen, K. (1993). The structure of Hume's political theory. In D. F. Norton (Ed.), *The Cambridge companion to Hume, 182–221*. Cambridge, UK: Cambridge University Press.

Harris, R., & Taylor, T. J. (1989). *Landmarks in linguistic thought: The western tradition from Socrates to Saussure*. New York: Routledge.

Heiskala, R. (2007). Economy and society: From Parsons through Habermas to semiotic institutionalism. *Social Science Information, 46*(2), 243–272.

Held, D. (1980). *Introduction to critical theory: Horkheimer to Habermas*. Berkeley: University of California Press.

Hookway, C. (1988). *Quine: Language, experience and reality*. Stanford, CA: Stanford University Press.

Janko, J. (2007). Linguistically integrated contractual interpretation: Incorporating semiotic theory of meaning-making into legal interpretation. *Rutgers Law Journal, 38*, 601–653.

Joseph, J. E. (2004). The linguistic sign. In C. Sanders (Ed.), *The Cambridge companion to Saussure, 59–75*. Cambridge, UK: Cambridge University Press.

Kersting, W. (1992). Politics, freedom, and order: Kant's political philosophy. In P. Guyer (Ed.), *The Cambridge companion to Kant, 342–366*. Cambridge, UK: Cambridge University Press.

Kripke, S. A. (1980, orig. 1972). *Naming & necessity*. Cambridge, MA: Harvard University Press.

Kripke, S. A. (1982). *Wittgenstein: On rules and private language*. Cambridge, MA: Harvard University Press.

Lee, D. (1992). *Competing discourses: Perspective and ideology in language*. London: Longman.

Leeds-Hurwitz, W. (1993). *Semiotics and communication: Signs, codes, cultures*. Hillsdale, NJ: Lawrence Erlbaum Associates.

Lewis, D. (2001, orig. 1986). *On the plurality of worlds*. Malden, MA: Blackwell.

Lewis, D. K. (1969). *Convention: A philosophical study*. Cambridge, MA: Harvard University Press.

Lyotard, J. (1984). *The postmodern condition: A report on knowledge (G. Bennington & B. Massumi, Trans.)*. Minneapolis: University of Minnesota.

Maley, Y., & Fahey, R. (1991). Presenting the evidence: Constructions of reality in court. *International Journal for the Semiotics of Law, 4*(10), 3–17.

Miller, H. T. (2002). *Postmodern public policy*. Albany: State University of New York Press.

Petrilli, S., & Ponzio, A. (2010). Semioethics. In P. Cobley (Ed.), *The Routledge companion to semiotics, 150–162*. Abingdon, Oxon: Routledge.

Riggs, F. W. (2001). Prologue. In A. Farazmand (Ed.), *Handbook of comparative and development public administration, 2nd edition, revised and expanded, vii–viii*. New York: Marcel Dekker.

Robins, R. H. (1971). *General linguistics: An introductory survey*, 2nd edition. London: Longman.

Rochefort, D. A., & Cobb, R. W. (1993). Problem definition, agenda access, and policy choice. *Policy Studies Journal, 21*(1), 56–71.

Sanders, C. (2004). Introduction: Saussure today. In C. Sanders (Ed.), *The Cambridge companion to Saussure, 1–8*. Cambridge, UK: Cambridge University Press.

Searle, J. R. (1998). *Mind, language and society: Philosophy in the real world*. New York: Basic.

Siffin, W. J. (2001). Problem of development administration. In A. Farazmand (Ed.), *Handbook of comparative and development public administration, 2nd edition, revised and expanded, 1–8*. New York: Marcel Dekker.

Simon, H. A. (1947). *Administrative behavior: A study of decision-making processes in administrative organization*. New York: Macmillan.

Soames, S. (2010). *Philosophy of language*. Princeton, NJ: Princeton University Press.

Soboleva, A. (2013). Use and misuse of language in judicial decision-making: Russian experience. *International Journal for the Semiotics of Law, 26*, 673–692.

Todorov, T. (1984). *Mikhail Bakhtin: The dialogical principle (W. Godzich, Trans.)*. Minneapolis: University of Minnesota Press.

3   On Filth

Food Regulation,
Enforcement, and Cheese

For a number of semesters, I taught regulation in the graduate public administration program as an adjunct instructor at Florida Atlantic University. In the course, I included a variety of examples and practical applications of rulemaking, administrative action, regulatory interpretation, and enforcement. The class included weighty lessons, as students began to recognize that entering into the world of public work, or remaining in such roles, takes guts – invariably and inevitably one will be wrong at times even with the best of intentions. In those moments, the test of quality public service seems to be how one responds to the error, and in providing a way forward for the people involved, the policy and agency, and the larger societal concern. The interactions of the class drove home the point of representation by those in the public service, and how essential it is for public administrators to reach out to stakeholders in policy matters, to assure that not only have stakeholders' concerns been addressed, but to afford even some small assurance that the contemplated policy will have a chance to succeed in practice.

One example that attracted significant interest from students was an effort in 2013 to prevent the importation into the US of certain French cheese, on the grounds that it was 'filthy' and 'adulterated,' a rationale officially invoked when "the article appears to consist in whole or in part of a filthy, putrid, or decomposed substance or be otherwise unfit for food," in violation of 402(a)(3), 801(a)(3). Schell, Gallo, and Cook wrote that

> Adulteration is the dilution of the quality of products through the addition of extraneous, impure or inferior ingredients, and improvements in profitability were often achieved through adulteration. Food adulteration is one of the chief characteristics of urban society, and the history of urban populations is intertwined with the history of food adulteration and the attempts to minimize it.
>
> (2012, p. 139)

Surely no one would want filthy, putrid foodstuffs visiting American shores, and the US Food and Drug Administration (FDA) is to be owed a debt of gratitude for their enforcement of the rule, banning French cheese, specifically mimolette, and preventing this material, unfit for food, from entering the mouths of unknowing Americans. Except that the above characterization is ill-informed, providing a useful example of the overexertion of technocratic expertise in areas where essential background is lacking, and where official action is nevertheless taken that abridges rights. In the instance of mimolette, overactive and ineffectual bureaucracy served no larger purpose than to prevent knowledgeable connoisseurs from enjoying a delicious cheese for a period of time, until the government apparatus got hold of its senses. The exertion of governmental potency in this case was a sham, because it served no purpose outlined in the original authority granted to the agency. The action instead uncovered an illustration of the limits of bureaucratic understanding, likely a point among countless examples where a guess was made by someone trying to do one's best, but with the result that the ideal of perfect knowledge and action by official quarters is undermined by the persistent and abject failure of people involved in writing and implementing rules and regulations.

This chapter examines the concept of filth in US FDA regulation, through the case of imported cheese refusal on the grounds of filth and adulteration, and considers the FDA's import refusal system. The research questions are: What can we learn about the FDA and government more generally from how filth is defined and enforced? Also, what do the data and processes of the import refusal system tell us about the work of this aspect of the agency, and outcomes for healthy food? Through an analysis of the data resident in the import refusal system, we can know more about what is refused and thus what was examined, the impacts on various nations of export, and make some judgments about the efficacy of the system vis-à-vis its enacting legislation. From a semiotic perspective, the term 'filth' itself was practically inscrutable from my view as a person outside the agency, so I wrote the FDA and asked them about it – they wrote back, and I share that information here. While the import refusal system is filled with data, activity tends to be reactionary, and so the system does not stand as proactively for protecting public health from harmful products as might be expected. This is not entirely the fault of the agency, but it does stray from the intent of the legislative authority. As alluded to above, efforts to gain understanding about the rationale for action behind enforcement, through inquiries direct to FDA, raised many additional questions possibly of interest for future research.

Semiotics, Rhetoric, and the Administrative Role

Semiotics seeks to present arguments that are well founded and substantiated. Through decoding, semiotic analysis interprets what is meant by a sign, in myriad forms (behavior, culture, text/language/speech) as an attempt to communicate. We may read a series of signs to understand how they interrelate and form a larger concept. An analysis may also consider the underlying dimension of the sign and its interpretation; what may seem like entertainment could actually have serious political undertones, for example, and reflect interest group perspectives and potentially even an intent to convince an audience to believe or act in a certain way. A sign may directly reflect one level of understanding, but have a deeper meaning through connotation. There is not only one meaning for the sign or system of signs – there may be many meanings, depending on how the sign and sign-system are read or interpreted; for common signs, there may be many competing explanations. The goal of the analysis, regardless, is not to express an opinion for its sake, but rather to present an argument for the interpretation of signs – how those signs fit within the larger context of culture, especially – and document the argument with evidence (Maasik & Solomon, 2012).

Semiotic analysis is not without its snares. Intent, beyond how it is identified by those originally responsible for policy and in their own words/thoughts, is itself politically and socially constructed as is much of the rest of the political sphere (Béland, 2010). Still, sign-based approaches are worth considering in analysis of public policy, particularly when there is a research question about the assumptions of policy in context, or when there is a need to better understand how public policy has come to be, often far removed from original program passage, when original intent may be difficult to discern. Approaches that consider underlying discourse are constructive in identifying incidence and utilization of "messy and imprecise semiconcepts" (Siffin, 2001, p. 1) that lie at the heart of much of public policy.

As with enacting legislation and implementing administrative code, political rhetoric might be considered a sort of policy language laboratory, where political candidates and elected officials develop language that seeks to inspire, and especially, persuade. Given that this rhetoric may be somewhat removed from the actual programs that may result from political cycles, it is worth asking whether political rhetoric in a given policy instance aligns with eventual program language, or whether the resulting program aligns with administrative interpretations, seen in the program in practice. Does the program yield expected outcomes?

The authority of bureaucracy is immense and vague, and if administrative codes and procedures are not closely aligned with a valid grant of legal authority through statute, rights may be threatened. Kerwin and Furlong wrote that "when lawsuits challenge the results of rulemaking, judges are able to evaluate the content of a rule to determine whether it is consistent with the statutes from which they derive their sole claim to authority and legitimacy" (2011, p. 34). Administrative rulemaking "was, and is, lawmaking by unelected administrative officials" (2011, p. 9). As a result, it is worth exploring how closely administrative rules and procedures align with the statutes that allow for their creation.

Specific administrative codes or procedures may "implement, interpret, or prescribe" (Kerwin & Furlong 2011, p. 5) as may be deemed necessary to bring enacted law into practice. There is great opportunity to examine statutes and accompanying administrative codes and procedures, and consider how these codes and procedures, their legal authority, and resulting discretionary interpretations, are consonant or dissonant with one another. Even where a rule is a reasonable interpretation of law, the law itself might be poorly constructed. When the law and rhetoric align, the implementation may be far less than the lofty goals set for a program. In such instances, the reference in law may not align appropriately with a desirable referent in a program objective, even if a program has considerable rhetorical or symbolic value.

Accountability as Theater

When society is a theater, as Richard Sennett observed, illusion and delusion may predominate. The players on this stage may have little invested in sentiment, as the supposed actors are simply playing roles. In government, those roles happen to be official, but they are still roles. Appearances and airs can provide cover for what is really thought and believed; the play itself is so strong, and so vibrantly presented, that it does not refer to reality as much as create it. It is self-referential. What matters is the audience believes it. Sentiment, originally a promise to achieve more for the public, may become a symbol that supplants the achievement of common benefits, in exchange for maintenance of a meager stability. Administration of public programs is not immune to such theater – it is prone as much as any aspect of public life to believe in its own value too much, as its actors and activities refer more and more inward (2017).

In this theater of society, then, calls for accountability are a common dramatic device, and an allegory for governments' inability to fully grasp and reconcile the administrative role with representation and oversight. Administration, portrayed comical in its incompetence, is a foil for the imagined policy mastery afforded elected officials; administration's reliance on technology and process becomes a tragic flaw that characteristically leads to catastrophe. We see the failings of our all-too-human public systems. There is possibly catharsis, because we can feel like we knew that a program would not work, all along. Then there is a denouement, where we forget all about it and move on to something else. The search for accountability is cyclical and unending, and the story goes on.

Kathe Callahan wrote that "accountability is at the heart of good governance" (2007, p. 125). Accountability is a herald of positive change, a harbinger of a new day coming for corrupt practices and officials, and a signal to a disaffected public that yes, the day has finally come when citizens can once again trust their government, and that all will work in tandem toward achieving the public interest. There are problems with this thinking, though – the connection between accountability and performance need not be proven to have persuasive value, and it might be more important in the political process to look like a reformer than to actually accomplish reform (Callahan, 2007). Putting too much stock in performance numbers, too, in the name of accountability ignores how little control an agency might have over its operations in context, bearing in mind a program's functions, client needs, oversight from other parts of government, and the larger economy and societal trends. Further, the public might have little patience for the minutiae of the policy craft; ideas can fail to reach the policy agenda because "people simply find the subjects intellectually boring" (Kingdon, 2003, p. 127), no matter the salience of these issues. Conveying a compelling narrative – painting protagonists and antagonists in debates as angels and devils (Shanahan, Jones, McBeth, & Lane, 2013) – might be more important than substance, even when the substance is of dire consequence. Details may fail to captivate the popular imagination. Semiotics, the science of signs, affords such opportunity to understand how a fascination with instrumental rationality might not save policy from its own hubris.

Use of certain terms and not others may signal professionalism or technical expertise; it may throw a barrier between the public and government. It may be a signal showing a delineation between an expert and the public-at-large; the use of words in policy that have little to do with actual outcomes may be a sort of ruse. Lacking use of accepted terms may show a deficiency in necessary policy capacity, even if the prevailing policy wisdom itself is flawed. There is a need, then, to speak the existing language of policy, in order to continue it or change it from within. The direction of what already exists is impactful. This special policy/regulatory language prevents those outside the process from interfering in, or possibly even understanding, the machinations of the processes within public organizations. While this may increase the stature of public officialdom in some minds, it may just as easily shortchange an important need – the reduction of barriers that exist between citizens and government, and, where needed, the giving of explanations about what is done in public agencies and why.

Quine offered, without actually recommending such an action, that removal of idioms and paraphrases and use of fully explained language might be preferable, in that misleading or confusing language may be avoided (Hookway, 1988). The use of unclear language, how unclear it is, and for what purposes, becomes a philosophical dilemma; using only words and sentences that are clear to everyone, fully accountable to a diverse population, is an ideal that is not achievable. We can accept and agree to concepts, but authors of language that seek to make everything clear to everyone will fail in that task because the receivers' ontologies are different. Seeking to understand reality is one thing, but desiring to find materials to provide evidence for one's beliefs is another, and that may not constitute a seeking after truth or anything approaching scientific means (Hookway, 1988). In public policy, some may analyze the suppositions behind rhetorical turns, and what is meant, and others (the vast majority) do not do so in any systematic way. The disputed plain of abstract statements leads to a questioned objectivity – the statement is objective to the extent that one cannot dispute it, but one may not have the knowledge or expertise to mount a contest of the validity of the statement.

It is given that cognition is allowed for within the application of law; decisions must be made according to what is allowed for in the legal authority (Wroblewski, 1989). In the US, this principle is based on the Supreme Court case, Chevron U.S.A., Inc. v. Natural Resources Defense Council (467 U.S. 837, 1984); the prevailing view, favoring the US Environmental Protection Agency, was that

> An agency, to engage in informed rulemaking, must consider varying interpretations and the wisdom of its policy on a continuing basis. Policy arguments ... should be addressed to legislators or administrators, not to judges. The EPA's interpretation of the statute here represents a reasonable accommodation of manifestly competing interests, and is entitled to deference.

However, even where an agency's discretion is specifically allowed for by law, the public may be disillusioned with what it perceives as bureaucratic overreach, and may find administrators to be both unelected and unaccountable to the public will. The popular perception of the agency working within bounds may become the reality. Choices made in the public interest only work as a compelling story for actionable public policy if the story is believed, or perceived as trustworthy.

There is an enforcement mechanism of considerable potency at work at the FDA; that an enforcement arm should be keen to show its productivity as a matter of accountability is understandable. Providing account is an important aspect of administration; it shows that responsibilities have been executed, ideally. At scheduled times throughout a year, reports of measured performance may be made, aligning with performance reporting expectations, using prescribed formats, with explanations as needed to further detail any apparent inconsistencies or provide additional information on specific cases. The careful tracking of performance, and its consistent, timely, accurate reporting, are required for the continuation of the relationship between principal and agent – the officials responsible directly to the public, and the administrators carrying out implementation and enforcement of rules (Farrell, Morris, & Ranson, 2017).

As long as this carefully choreographed dance plays itself out regularly and without fail, one might worry little, as government is operating as expected. This may be how the public sees government's operation, but the dance of accountability itself means little if the system fails to achieve the goals assigned to it. The interaction itself is no measure of quality of its own; no ascription of good government should be made to a process that exists of its own accord, running senselessly, unobserved, and largely unused by the public. The proof of the worth of a system lies in its usefulness, and the reality of any affectation to accountability. Otherwise, the supposed display of accountability is merely performance in an empty theatre; the audience itself may be removed, existing only to the extent that not reporting at all would raise a red flag, inviting review. The mechanism might not be taken at all to be a genuine invitation for review and discourse, important to legitimate accountability, particularly if the means of understanding are obscured, or the form of announcement befogged (Farrell, Morris, & Ranson, 2017).

Government regularly makes decisions of a technical nature. As a result, it relies upon forms of inquiry and reporting that tend toward the voluminous, with mounds of data that are likely not well understood by a lay public, elaborate or intricate analysis, and assumptions being made that might be of a political nature or that favor interest groups. The purpose of the great detail in such reporting and analysis has less to do with the outcome of the analysis, which might well have been presupposed given the government's desire to effect policy in one way or another, and more to do with conferring legitimacy upon a process of inquiry (Loughlin, 1990). Government has a need to be, or at least to appear, fair and transparent to all concerned; it should demonstrate that it has reviewed in due diligence the matter before it, and *showed its work*, so to speak. What government misses in achieving fairness, it perhaps hopes to make up in consideration of all views in open forums, even though this approach may lack authenticity. Analysis with attention to signs and underlying meaning is essential to uncover such matters.

Food Regulations and Enforcement

The criticisms leveled against food regulation and enforcement schemes are not much different than they were a century ago, and so one might question how consequential efforts have been in the long run. Also, there is a lack of alignment in the efforts of various agencies, so if a consumer were to take the sum total of all government advice, they might be confused by conflicting information. Consumers essentially want to be told that a food or product is safe. What instead occurs is that government agencies act as proxies in a battle between corporate competitors, taking out this or that rival product in the name of the public good, when it is questionable whether public interest has anything to do with the matter. Instead, we are left with a view of competing interests, and winners and losers, with the consumer good being largely an incidental matter (Coppin & High, 1999).

Given the need for quick resolution to a variety of complaints, the public has historically had a role in supporting unproven, potentially dangerous consumer goods, from patent medicines to today's supplements. In the US' example, the regulatory system for public health and purity of food and drugs has had before it a rather expansive mandate, to protect the public, though it clearly has failed on a regular basis. Even government efforts to require labeling of products, and truth in advertisement that products be safe and effective, have not entirely addressed the problem of gullibility. It is a mark of human nature that people are overconfident in their ability to address their own problems, through a variety of home-cure and pharmacy solutions, and to expect that manufacturers and other businesses would not create a product that would harm. This potential source of concern is compounded by the desire for government to get out of the way of business, and to allow the market to bring products to meet consumer demands, even as government is called upon to contain excesses and damage after the fact. As a historical consideration, there are plenty of examples of products that failed to meet the standard of due care for human life, but this market demand has always been spurred along by consumers (E1 Entertainment, 2010). Even in a litigious society, with offers of legal representation against pharmaceutical companies becoming a hallmark of television advertising, there is still some level of surprise when the promised benefits do not materialize, or the palliative aggravates an illness or causes some other harm through unspeakable side effects. The belief in product potential is ingrained in the collective – science and advancement will fix our ills.

Instead of public interest, it is perhaps more probable that regulation is operated in the interest of industrial players, and particularly those players who can afford to make their preferences known. This thinking, put forward by Gabriel Kolko and George Stigler, gave rise to capture theory. The prominence and ability of certain preferences to cut through the noise of the interest marketplace and essentially direct the forming and enforcing of a regulatory framework shows the importance of competitive advantage, in that inefficient businesses, are forced out of the market, potentially, by the imposition of regulatory efforts that may on their surface simply support 'fairness' in an industry. In other words, a firm that produces cheaply and quickly will potentially benefit more from a regulatory framework than a slow, inefficient product production approach (Coppin & High, 1999).

Industrialization, in some respect, has been taken as a representation for quality. In the interest of reducing potential for illness, the cause of purity necessitated a heavy toll on food production, namely that foods produced in traditional methods were made suspect. People may have wanted to maintain traditional diets, but found it difficult in light of regulatory enhancements. In those instances, it is easier to overlook scattered, disorganized individuals in favor of organized constituencies, even if the resulting regulatory structure fails to take a position in matters of substantive importance. To get a law passed, sometimes deals are made with national interests, so that their support can be gained. Certain products can be named wholesome, and others deleterious; government gains a role and importance for itself in becoming the arbiter of purity, whether the product is healthful, or whether it is simply asserting that the whiskey in one's bottle is rye or rotgut (Coppin & High, 1999). This serves primarily as a benefit to bureaucratic interests (the people writing the rules, and implementing the regulations, as a matter of entrepreneurial gain) and to corporate interests, in crowding out competing product (Coppin & High, 1999), which while of greater inefficiency in production and more trouble to review from an enforcement standpoint, could prove to be of vastly superior quality.

Because regulators have limited resources with which to work, it might be expected that addressing shortcomings in approaches to protecting the public health against unhealthy food could be prioritized; the approach historically to handling these issues has, however, been largely reactionary, shifting from one crisis to the next. The FDA has far-reaching enforcement authority, though the agency does tend to focus on areas of greatest risk (among those areas, imported food has been emphasized). The relationship between the FDA and the industries it regulates is, at root and by design, adversarial. It is incumbent upon industry to provide for safe product, and to document safety and argue the point when challenged (Hardy, 1990). However, the nature of this relationship has encouraged bad actors to avoid compliance in creative ways, even as the FDA has sought to bring serious and significant enforcement in situations where some reticence might be in order. The FDA must learn more about the products it polices and apply rules fairly across the board, but there is also understanding that the agency could become more emboldened in process on a selective basis, potentially leading to an allegation that its activities could approach the arbitrary or even favor certain interests over others.

In FDA use, words like 'harmlessness' and 'safety' have been subject to interpretation – distinctions were made, and lines between harmless and not harmless drawn based on practical considerations, even if other forms of evidence, like laboratory trials, suggested some risk (Hisano, 2016). There are timescales and consumption rates for what might be considered harmless. Elsewhere, it was thought that having created standards for purity, and that meeting these standards rendered something 'pure,' even given evidence to the contrary. Water, for example, might meet purity standards and yet still be contaminated in a way that is unacceptable; what exists in the water may adversely impact certain individuals (with illnesses, for illustration's sake), and not others. Community and cultural standards may play a role (Schell,

Gallo, & Cook, 2012). There is a lack of clarity in defining the line between clean and impure – safe and unsafe (Nash, 2008). The idea of 'natural' food colors is not universally agreed upon, and the FDA does not certify them; additives used to make food more attractive nevertheless could present major risks to consumers. There is no 'generally recognized as safe' (GRAS) standard for food colors; this represents a whole segment of oversight that does not, for practical purposes, exist in the regulatory framework, except in the event the additive is not listed and then identified. The sources of coloring, even if natural, may be adulterated themselves, and could be harmful (Simon et al., 2017). Quality as a term of art in food regulation is practically meaningless and has a tendency to devolve to something that is measurable (like strength of an extract as a proxy); this says little about quality, and we may not even be getting the product we think we are buying (Berenstein, 2016). As consumers, we are very trusting, of the regulations that exist and enforcement that takes place, but possibly a bit credulous as well.

Science can help us understand more about the line and the nature of the difference, but that does not release one from the need to be cautious in action and approach to regulation (Nash, 2008); better science can help, too, but rejecting knowledge of risk on the lack of absolute certainty is childish. There is wisdom in knowing the difference. The language of 'filth' and 'adulteration' itself is a regression to earlier times, before ice cream poisoning and so-called ptomaine were seen for what they were – bacterial poisoning (Geist, 2012). It is a useful shorthand, in that the label may resist questioning.

Offering a counter-narrative of purity, through shrewd marketing, with American products reaching global consumers in a manner corresponding to the range of Western civilization, helped differentiate some industry-led products from others (Domosh, 2003). The demonstration of the claims as valid was (and still arguably is) significantly less important than the acceptance of such claims by the public. After all, a certain segment of the public enjoys television programs and internet content about gourmet, fresh, healthy cooking, and then still eats the same food, of the same negligible quality and healthfulness, as it would have anyway. The audience is both tired and lacking money to engage in the food discourse otherwise – the public is not ignorant of the point, generally speaking, as it understands the ideals and risks, and yet makes the choices it makes and does so knowingly (Peterson & Turner, 2014). The regulatory system, it would seem, cannot be bothered to change with the times or be cognizant of the public's viewpoint; even if a public benefit is not entirely clear, the public's viewpoint is largely irrelevant to the governmental activity, as long as the system continues to operate steadily, and to appear to be of benefit. Consumer choices are emotional choices, at least initially, before brand loyalty and taste have a chance to set in. Industry not only understands this – it depends upon the inability for consumers to recognize the limitations of their decision-making faculties.

Mimolette

Mimolette is a hard cheese, sometimes called Boule de Lille, related to the Dutch Edam, and most likely having origins in the reign of King Louis XIV. It is made by master French cheesemakers "around the town of Lille, in the Flanders area of Pas-de-Calais, northern France" (*Culture*, 2018), like those of Isigny-sur-Mer, in mild, moist Calvados, for example. The flavor of mimolette, called fruity, nutty, and intense, with a distinct aftertaste, comes from the diet of the cows – herbs and grasses – so it is 'of the place' that produces it. Others claim a tasting profile of "bacon, caramel, butterscotch and toasted nuts, with an underlying sweetness that is not cloying" (*Culture*, 2018). The vibrant orange color is from annatto. It bears little resemblance in appearance or tasting profile to modern commodified cheese, and this is to its benefit (Figure 3.1).

Flour mites or cheese mites when they are working their magic on cheese, identified as *Acarus siro L* (Melnyk, Smith, Scott-Dupree, Marcone, & Hill, 2010) contribute to mimolette's flavor and distinctive crusty rind, which is like a dusty cannonball or a cantaloupe. The mites, in delving into the rind, stimulate air flow (Johnson & Johnson, 2018). "They nibble relentlessly, burrowing into the crust, aerating the cheese, and dramatically reducing the mimolette's bulk. The result is a dense, salty cheese, with earthy, sweet, almost caramel, undertones" (Meier, 2017). When the cheese is ready to consume, the mites are (mostly) blown off with compressed air (Dennis, 2013). The production of cheese, of course, involves living processes. "The molds, bacteria, yeasts and mites make cheese what it is: delicious" (Thomson, 2014).

Figure 3.1 Mimolette, aged 12 months.
Source: photo credit, Allison Atkinson, September 2018.

Where Is It Written?

The regulatory standard for filthy is disputed. "There's no record of a significant health threat – or any health threat – from mimolette... What's been put in place by the Federal government is not exactly a ban, just a regulation that has the same effect" (Dickey & Guilhamon, 2013). In the Washington Post piece by Brady Dennis, a seeming rule of thumb of six mites per square inch was referenced as "a level of concern for field laboratories" (2013), meaning, one would gather, meeting the standard for achieving filth (as far as cheese is concerned, anyway). Elsewhere, the FDA rule was described by virtue of what had been enforced: "Since 1940, the FDA has enforced a limit of six mites per square inch of cheese" (Barry, 2013); alternatively, "six mites per inch *permitted in cheeses by federal law*" (Toobin, 2013) (emphasis mine). French journalist Cecile Delarue countered the limit with "Why not seven? Or five and a half?" (Barry, 2013). Beyond the precision of the number six, this appears to be a standard without purpose. This does not mean in any way that process was not followed. Process was followed in reviewing mimolette shipments. It is painfully apparently from reviewing the voluminous nature of data in the import refusal reporting system (OASIS) used by the US FDA, that product codes and descriptions, FDA districts, points of entry into the US, FDA analyses, and violations charged were all noted. The point is that following the process did not accomplish anything of value.

When asked why the FDA had shifted in enforcement on mimolette, considering it filthy after many years of allowing its importation, FDA spokeswoman Patricia El-Hinnawy commented: "The only thing we can do is cite our regulations, which show very clearly that our job is to protect the food supply" (Dennis, 2013). Benoit de Vitton, the representative for Isigny Sainte-Mère, opined, "It's completely natural. You have bugs on every single cheese you leave in the open air... You can't have Mimolette without cheese mites. It wouldn't be Mimolette" (Dennis, 2013). During the summer of 2013, "all three thousand two hundred and ninety-seven pounds of Mimolette were tossed into dumpsters and doused in bleach" (Toobin, 2013). Cheesemakers and cheese cognoscentes alike were disconsolate. We might note for a moment the apparent double standard for domestic cheese manufacturers, the presence of mites in domestic cheese production, and how Americans consume products that are potentially injurious (Richmond, 2013). Relative to other parts of the world, the US seems to lack a guiding precautionary principle in many respects for public policy, notably where its concerns consumer products and where industry lobbyists have the ear of lawmakers.

The basis of a ban on mimolette is different than a ban on trans-unsaturated fatty acids, for example; trans fats are thought to be linked to heart disease, and so they are unhealthy. Unhealthy foods lead to diseases that increase public health costs, and those are shared by the general population. The foods containing trans fats might also be delicious, and one may reject government's intercession on one's behalf, forbidding the toxic deliciousness (Reinarman, 2007). But mimolette is not poison. It is not even as bad as trans-unsaturated fatty acids (in moderation of course). It is cheese. Cheese mites do not cause harm (beyond the occasional allergy); the product could not be created without them. As Chimileski noted,

> There are 50,000 or so described mite species and only guesses of how many more exist across the planet. We can pretend that there aren't mites on our cheese, just like we can pretend that there aren't mites on our faces, but we might as well accept that they are there.
>
> (2016)

He is correct, of course: It has been suggested that 100% of human beings are covered with *Demodex* mites (Thoemmes, Fergus, Urban, Trautwein, & Dunn, 2014); then again, those mites are personal, and we probably would rather not think about it.

The importation of mimolette causes no harm appreciably greater than eating any other sort of allowable, legal cheese; consider cheese in its various forms, including some heavily processed forms of 'cheese food.' French cheesemakers do consumers a favor by engaging in their craft and providing better, or even conservatively, other options. This says nothing of the net benefit of the enforcement action in the first place, even if "human nature often favors a quick buck over a pure product" (Avorn, 2008, p. 2430). There is nothing impure or injurious about the product, so the imposition of the enforcement mechanism is suspect – a going-through-the-motions of a process with no discernible benefit. The fact that mimolette can now be enjoyed in the US perhaps indicates that, somewhere along the way, a mistake was made, and someone overreached?

Methods and Materials

It occurred to me that after several semesters of teaching a regulation course and questioning this definition of 'filth,' as applied to cheese, I might want to ask the FDA about it directly. I entered a public records request in February 2018, specifically asking for documentation and procedures on the enforcement rules for six mites per square inch on cheese for filth/adulteration. The FDA responded to my request in part, in July 2018; some documentation was considered exempt from disclosure based upon the Freedom of Information Act (FOIA) law, 5 USC 552,

> Exemption (b)(5) permits the withholding of inter-agency or intra-agency communications records which are part of the deliberative process and pre-decisional. Disclosure of such material could inhibit

the open and candid expression of opinions and diminish the quality of the decision-making process.

Of interest, the FDA provided me with a copy of a letter from August 19, 1940, which, referencing enforcement considerations around that time,

> we...believe that from time to time checks should be made upon stocks of process cheese on dealers' shelves with a view to action against stocks which [sic] are found to be infested. In this program we suggest that the tolerance of 6 mites per square inch of surface of the cheese be used as a basis for recommending action.

The letter was signed by P.B. Dunbar, who had been instrumental in creation of the 1938 FD&C Act, and eventually served as FDA commissioner.[1] The FDA also provided a copy of their compliance manual chapter for foodborne biological hazards, specifically the section for domestic and imported cheese and cheese products (program 7303.037). This document outlines various enforcement actions (recall, detainment, seizure, detention) and when those approaches should be taken. Detention would be most appropriate in instances where imported product is at issue, according to this document.

As expected, the FDA does have a system that tracks instances of import refusal. As of this writing, US FDA Import Refusal Reports reside in an online system.[2] FDA explains the reports as follows:

> The Food, Drug, and Cosmetic Act (the Act) authorizes FDA to detain a regulated product that appears to be out of compliance with the Act. The FDA district office will then issue a "Notice of FDA Action" specifying the nature of the violation to the owner or consignee. The owner or consignee is entitled to an informal hearing in order to provide testimony regarding the admissibility of the product. If the owner fails to submit evidence that the product is in compliance or fails to submit a plan to bring the product into compliance, FDA will issue another "Notice of FDA Action" refusing admission to the product. The product then has to be exported or destroyed within 90 days.
>
> The IRR reports on those products for which a determination was to refuse admission to part or all of the product offered for importation...FDA has prepared this information in an effort to provide the public with information on products that have been found to appear in violation of the Act.

Analysis

With regard to the first question – about the six mites per square inch: Despite the FDA's valiant effort to find and send to me what appears to be the original source of this internal direction for counting mites on cheese, and aside from the great interest I took in seeing this historical administrative document, I must point out that the counting of six mites on cheese seems even more arbitrary now given this original founding interpretation and direction. While the six mites amount is present in the administrative letter, it refers to cheese on dealer's shelves; there is no distinction of domestic or international product. There is no reference to documenting the guideline as an absolute; it is a rule of thumb, at best.

Further, the enforcement documentation, with its allowance for detention in the case of affected product from foreign locations, seems limited in its ability to consider genuine risk. This appears to be a regulation and basis for enforcement built on a historic rule of thumb but implemented as if there is a level of precision necessary, without which there may be dread damage to the public interest. We are left with a simple concept – mites are necessary to make certain kinds of cheese, including mimolette, and their presence does not necessarily imply anything other than delicious cheese. It is frustrating to wait months for an answer from a Federal agency, but I am cheered by their transparency (Figure 3.2).

The second question, about the import refusal system, provides for a richer analysis. In 1977, Tukey wrote that "There is no excuse for failing to plot and look" (p. 43). Exploratory analysis is about "finding and revealing the clues" (p. 21). We might see how the data separate themselves into groups, how the data points trail off more in one direction than another, how certain points are more popular or unpopular than others, where the points center themselves, and how much the points spread out. Most probably, our data will not tell us how they would prefer to be analyzed. Instead, we look for examples in similar work, or we have had experiences that we can call upon to help us with the analysis (Tukey, 1977). Taking Tukey's sage advice, the first thing to do with the import refusal data is, reasonably enough, to 'plot and look.'

First, we examine the reasons given for import refusal. Table 3.1 includes reasons for refusal, and their cumulative presence as a given rationale over the dataset. The reasons are given as first, second, third, etc., in order of priority for the rationale. While other codes are also included in the dataset, the codes in this table are most common.

The list of Act section charges includes 281 codes for import refusal; some of the codes do not have any listed description, but instead refer to sections of the Act (example: 2760 means '402(a)(3)'). The FDA does no one any favors (except maybe themselves) by putting all the reasons for import refusal for each case in one column on the report, separating each reason with commas. The period from January 1, 2002 to February 28, 2018 included 367,844 cases (rows) of import refusal. Considering up to six refusal codes assigned to each case, there are 523,152 codes assigned to the database. All 367,844 have at least one code assigned; this number drops substantially as additional codes are

CHIEF, EASTERN DISTRICT:

We have your letter of August 8 in regard to process cheese infested with mites.

We have discussed with Doctor Hodges of Microanalytical Division his report of August 2, 1940, and we have seen two of the specimen packages of the infested process cheese which he has left from his experiments. As we understand it, while the cause of the infestation may lie in insanitary conditions in the plant, the condition apparently does not manifest itself so far as being objectively determinable until the product is out on the market and subjected perhaps to too long or adverse storage conditions. We should judge, therefore, that it is a situation somewhat comparable to the development of active infestation in confectionery held too long in dealers' establishments. We believe that it is a condition which would therefore be encountered only sporadically, and when process cheese does begin to exhibit signs of the activities of mites, probably it rapidly becomes unmerchantable. As a matter of fact, we understand that the process cheese industry is rapidly turning to the use of transparent "Parafilm" wraps which, as you indicated in your letter of February 26, 1940, are said to be practically impervious to mite invasion.

We therefore feel that this will not be found to constitute a major regulatory problem but believe that from time to time checks should be made upon stocks of process cheese on dealers' shelves with a view to action against stocks which are found to be infested. In this program we suggest that the tolerance of 6 mites per square inch of surface of the cheese be used as a basis for recommending action. In the case of any of the initial actions recommended we would like to have submitted to us one or two subdivisions illustrating the type and extent of infestation upon which action is recommended.

Very truly yours,

Enclosure
   Copy of this ltr

cc CD WD

cc Micro Div

LDE:chj
8/9/40

P. B. DUNBAR

Figure 3.2 US FDA Dunbar letter, 1940.

Source: internal memorandum, U.S. Food and Drug Administration, obtained via a Freedom of Information Act request.

Table 3.1 Rationale for import refusal, by cumulative use in import refusal system

Refusal description	Refusal code	First	Second	Third	Fourth	Fifth	Sixth	Total	Codes used (%)
Cases with code listed		367,844	105,964	40,401	5,753	2,320	870	523,152	100.00
It appears the drug or device is not included in a list required by Section 510(j), or a notice or other information respecting it was not provided as required by Section 510(j) or 510(k).	118	91,294	14,980	4,392	188	118	25	110,997	21.22
The article appears to be a new drug without an approved new drug application.	75	38,798	7,896	1,680	104	28	11	48,517	9.27
The article appears to consist in whole or in part of a filthy, putrid, or decomposed substance or be otherwise unfit for food.	249	26,574	2,529	426	80	26	10	29,645	5.67
The article appears to be misbranded in that the label or labeling fails to bear the required nutrition information.	482	11,477	8,194	4,193	681	265	89	24,899	4.76
The article appears to be, or to bear or contain a color additive which is unsafe within the meaning of Section 721(a).	11	13,435	3,423	1,299	246	92	18	18,513	3.54
…the manufacturer's failure to file a scheduled process demonstrates that the product is not being manufactured under the mandatory provisions of 21 CFR Part 108 and therefore appears to have been manufactured, processed, or packed, under insanitary conditions whereby it may have been rendered injurious to health.	83	11,843	5,492	950	130	58	22	18,495	3.54
The article is subject to refusal of admission pursuant Section 801(a)(3) in that it appears to contain Salmonella, a poisonous and deleterious substance which may render it injurious to health. [Adulteration, Section 402(a)(1)]	9	16,594	1,322	169	11	3	4	18,103	3.46

(Continued)

Refusal description	Refusal code	First	Second	Third	Fourth	Fifth	Sixth	Total	Codes used (%)
It appears the device is subject to listing under 510(j) and the initial distributor has not registered as required by 21 CFR 807.20 (a)(5).	341	9,340	4,603	1,701	61	17	5	15,727	3.01
…fabricated from two or more ingredients and the label fails to bear the common or usual name of each such ingredient and/or the article purports to be a beverage containing vegetable or fruit juice, but does not bear a statement with appropriate prominence on the information panel of the total percentage of such fruit or vegetable juice contained in the food.	218	6,680	4,296.0	2,534	583	256	90	14,439	2.76
The article is subject to refusal of admission pursuant to Section 801(a)(3) in that it appears to be a post-1976 device for which a Section 510(k) application has not been determined substantially equivalent or a 510(k) has not been filed.	508	6,913	4,396	1,875	65	21	3	13,273	2.54
It appears the manufacturer is not registered as a low-acid canned food or acidified food manufacturer pursuant to 21 CFR 108.25(c)(1) or 108.35(c)(1).	62	6,575	4,653.0	723	121	43	10	12,125	2.32
The article is subject to refusal of admission pursuant to Section 801(a)(3) in that it appears to bear or contain a pesticide chemical residue, which causes the article to be adulterated within the meaning of Section 402(a)(2)(B) of the FD&C Act.	241	11,565	178	21	1	0	0	11,765	2.25
…appears to be misbranded within the meaning of Section 403(f) of the FD&C Act in that any word, statement, or other information required by or under the authority of the FD&C Act to appear on the label or labeling is not prominently placed thereon with such conspicuousness (as compared with other words, statements, designs, or devices, in the labeling) and in such terms as to render it likely to be	324	7,987	2,877	25	268	134	73	11,364	2.17

Description									
read and understood by the ordinary individual under customary terms of purchase and use (for example, label contains information in two or more languages but fails to repeat all required information in both languages in accordance with 21 CFR 101.15(c)(2), or label fails to include all required information in English in accordance with 21 CFR 101.15(c)(1)...									
...the food is in package form and the label fails to bear an accurate statement of the quantity of the contents in terms of weight, measure, or numerical count in accordance with Section 403(e)(2) of the FD&C Act.	321	4,094	3,718.0	2,438	526	220	75	11,071	2.12
The article appears to bear or contain a substance which is unsafe within the meaning of Section 406.	3,280	4,379	3,879.0	2,140	116	27	6	10,547	2.02
The article appears in violation of FPLA because of its placement, form and/or contents statement.	473	5,280	2,918.0	1,429	241	81	38	9,987	1.91
The article appears to lack adequate directions for use.	16	5,587	2,676.0	1,243	183	48	21	9,758	1.87
The labeling appears to fail to comply with cosmetic labeling requirements of Section 602(a), and/or (b), and/or (c), and as identified by 21 C.F.R. Part 701.	471	4,893	1,028.0	256	6	3	1	6,187	1.18
The article is subject to refusal of admission pursuant to section 801(a)(3) in that it appears to be adulterated because it contains a pesticide chemical, which is in violation of Section 402(a)(2)(B).	3,721	4,415	128.0	17	0	0	0	4,560	0.87
The article is subject to refusal of admission pursuant to Section 801(a)(3) in that it appears to contain a color additive which is unsafe within the meaning of Section 721(a) which renders it adulterated under Section 601(e).	197	3,713	635.0	196	2	2	1	4,549	0.87
It appears that the article fails to comply with applicable standards prescribed under Section 534.	47	3,550	337.0	79	5	1	0	3,972	0.76
	29,4986	80,158		27,786	3,618	1,443	502	408,493	78.08

Source: Created by C.A., using Import Refusal Data Files, U.S. Food and Drug Administration Import Refusal Reports for OASIS.

added. Only 28.8% of all cases have a second code, and so on (see Table 3.2). Twenty-one refusal codes (about 7.5% of all codes) account for just over 78% of all codes applied. While the system appears complex, with its 281 codes, in practice, these 21 codes account for the vast majority of import refusal code assignments. The first item on the list, with its reference to Section 510(j), is a requirement that the manufacturer has on file a list

> of all drugs and a list of all devices and a brief statement of the basis
> for *believing* that each device included in the list is a device rather
> than a drug...which are being manufactured, prepared, propagated,
> compounded, or processed by him for commercial distribution and
> which he has not included in any list of drugs or devices filed by
> him with the Secretary under this paragraph...before such time of
> registration.

Other requirements, including biannual reporting, are also included. The Secretary can apparently forego reporting for certain products (Class 1 devices) given "reasonable assurance of safety and effectiveness" (Sec. 510(l)(2)). We take some time with this 501(j) requirement because it accounts for 21.22% of refusal codes. One hopes that this bureaucratic work leads to outcomes of safety and product effectiveness, but with words like 'believing' in the statement requirement, the scientific basis is perhaps reduced from the outset. Code 249, for "filthy, putrid, or decomposed substance," at least makes the top three, accounting for 5.67% of all codes used.

Immediately upon reviewing the data, though, I noticed a spike in import refusals from 2011 (see Figure 3.3).

This spike was most associated with import refusal for products from Mexico, and accounted for a large portion of Mexican goods refused during the period. This is notable given the volume of trade – refusals for Mexican product are higher than China, India, Canada, or Great Britain, the other leaders on the import refusal board (see Table 3.2). My initial attempt to chart the incidence of import refusals by country over the period from 2002 to 2018 was thrown out of proportion by the spike.

The problem was not a war on cheese, as I might have anticipated, but bad papaya. Mexican papaya represents 11% of the world's market, and 65% of the papaya imported into the US. In 2010, Mexican papaya represented 75% of all papaya imported (Flynn, 2011). A 2011 outbreak of *Salmonella Agona*, stemming from Mexican papaya, affected people in 23 US states (Entis, 2011).

The US FDA wrote of the 2011 outbreak, "More than 100 people were infected with the outbreak organism in multiple states...the outbreak has been associated with papaya from at least one grower and its shipper in

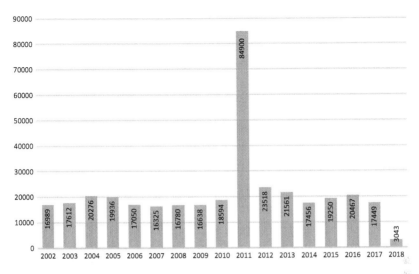

Figure 3.3 Volume of instances of import refusal, by year.
Source: Created by C.A., using Import Refusal Data Files, U.S. Food and Drug Administration Import Refusal Reports for OASIS.

Table 3.2 Frequency of import refusal, by country

	Frequency	*Percent (%)*
Mexico	91,311	24.8
China	32,946	9.0
India	31,474	8.6
Canada	17,359	4.7
Great Britain	13,252	3.6

Source: Created by C.A., using Import Refusal Data Files, U.S. Food and Drug Administration Import Refusal Reports for OASIS.

Mexico" (2018). Rothschild (2011) is more specific, attributing the salmonella to a single importer in Texas. The Centers for Disease Control indicated that illnesses related to salmonella from papaya had also occurred the previous year (Rothschild, 2011). The source of the salmonella contamination in Mexico was said to be water at the exporting operation – something that could be resolved with filters and water treatment (The Packer, 2012). Health concerns associated with food imports were hardly a new concern (Marks, 2015). A major fear was that America had many trading partners with different standards of product quality. The disconnect may lie with the system that the US employs to ensure safety and quality of imported goods.[3]

In its tests in 2011, the US FDA found that Mexican papaya had a 15.6% adulteration rate, due to contamination from salmonella. At that time, it was determined that "Districts may detain, without physical examination, all raw, fresh and raw, fresh refrigerated papaya offered for entry from the country of Mexico, unless exempted (on the Green List)" (2018). Refusal was more or less automatic at that point. In the instance of a detained shipment, "the importer should provide results of a third-party laboratory analysis, which verifies the product does not contain Salmonella" (2018). To be removed from the list, a papaya exporter in Mexico

> should provide documentation with sufficient evidence that future shipments of their papaya will not be adulterated. FDA may consider five consecutive commercial shipments over a period of time, analyzed as described in the preceding paragraph, as being adequate for removal from DWPE [detained without physical examination].
>
> (2018)

This goes against the typical FDA approach, which is to assume that a product is safe unless shown otherwise, and is different from proactive measures that might be employed, such as active testing of potentially unsafe products, on an ongoing basis, at a level relative to the demonstrated threat of the product. Importers, for example, could be required to submit test results for a product to show that the products are safe, as a matter of course (Entis, 2011). There were allegations made that the "U.S. was targeting Mexico's fruit out of protectionist motives by going after Agromod Products Inc., the world's largest grower of Maradol papayas" (Flynn, 2011). Around the time the ban was implemented, the US began allowing Malaysian papayas into the country, with the caveat that they be irradiated (Flynn, 2011).

Discussion

If a law, its accompanying rules, and program implementation are not accomplishing what is desired of them, what, if anything, are they accomplishing? The purpose of import refusal under the Food, Drug, and Cosmetic Act (FD&C) Act is to "detain a regulated product that appears to be out of compliance with the Act." The FD&C Act outlines how the FDA conducts business. The FDA is "responsible for protecting the public health by ensuring the safety, efficacy, and security of human and veterinary drugs, biological products, and medical devices; and by *ensuring the safety of our nation's food supply*, cosmetics, and products that emit radiation." What is meant by ensure, beyond making certain of this outcome? This would not seem to mean the same thing as sounding an alarm when a food problem is already widely known, nor does it appear to mean the detention of otherwise sound/healthy food.

FDA creates a large volume of data through its import refusal program, and this information is dutifully recorded to, stored in, and retrieved from this system. The database itself is impressive in its volume, but less so in its value. This is a bulk of material that simulates a stability in how data are being handled over time, and thus the assumption is that the program itself, represented by these data, is also stable and, one would think, working effectively. The entering, storage, and retrieval of information is akin to bureaucratic ritual; this activity enters the ambit of semiotics, with records of administrative actions existing outside of space and time, removed from their active instance (Hull, 2012). Together, the records form a veritable fortress, indicating unquestionable, rigid implementation of a rule. There is little to speak of in engagement or questioning of a process, because processes are not questioned and do not exist in this system; this is one side of the story, and the lack of discourse helps to cement the likely mistaken notion that the efforts documented within the arrangement are themselves unchanging, consistent, and fair.

The information retrieval system is not easily used or interpreted, and it is not clear that its use is intended for the public generally. Rather, the system assumes a level of technical competency to find in the FDA website (the term "import refusal" itself is technocratic and off-putting), or via search engines; the system requires competency to use the search features, retrieve the data, and interpret the findings. The coding system even exists as a separate file, which must be matched against the data output to interpret the material. Even then, the interpretations themselves are often vague; it can be difficult to understand what specifically was intended. The system behaves as if it is a "stable reference" (Hull, 2012, p. 133), and artifactually fixed although new records are being added to it, professing administration in a solid/completed form. The records within the system do not directly relate to administrative process, enforcement quality, or the activity within the system; it is not necessary for the system to function in a way to encourage transparency or accountability. That is not why it exists at all.

One might respond with the idea that, even if the system is one side of the enforcement story, there is still an opportunity for businesses to respond within this regulatory framework, in a way that is fair. "FDA, like everyone, occasionally makes mistakes and wrongly refuses some entries. Thankfully, when confronted by the right arguments, FDA will rescind a refusal upon demonstrating that it made a clear and unmistakable error" (FDAimports.com, 2011). Given the potential to make error, there is a high level of specificity signified in "clear and unmistakable," indicating a high burden on the party bringing the request for withdrawing an order against an intended import.

The response during the papaya incident was especially concerning. The tendency seems to be reactive work on the part of import refusal, when it is found that a public health emergency exists. The system is not able to root out such widespread threats proactively. Inasmuch as the system documents efforts on import refusal, the US is not necessarily effective at protecting public health on food quality enforcement on a domestic basis, as evidenced by domestic romaine lettuce contamination with *Escherichia coli (E. coli)* in 2018 (Lempert, 2018). Even if food production is safe, distribution may sully product with dangerous results.

We want to believe that our modern food system is safe, but it just is not in many respects, and government is mostly not willing to admit the extent of the problem, from policy design through implementation and evaluation. The system is broken. The US is not the only example, and certainly not the worst among nations, but this does represent a larger issue about the breakdown between policy intent and outcomes; given the public health impact, the outcome of failure is all the more notable and unacceptable.

For a long time, the US and Mexico have had more than a few issues to resolve with trade of injurious materials across the border. It could be suggested that the porosity of a border wall is acceptable insofar as it serves the purposes of the more powerful partner. A good example of this is the US allowing companies to send dangerous old batteries across the border to Mexico for recycling – an example of a system with apparently two standards. The proximity alone of Mexico to the US should give both countries worry about how they manage handling of potential toxics. There have been documented results of negative impacts to Mexican children because of unsafe recycling practices; those companies are only partially to blame, because those batteries are a problem exported from the US, without benefit of regulations necessary to protect the environment and public health from that threat. American companies regularly tout the success of their recycling programs for batteries, but the traceability of the recycled materials gets lost amid third-parties and deals, and may have far-reaching impacts for affected parties in developing areas (Rosenthal, 2011).

Simply sending materials south across the border, as if any problem that they represent has been addressed, is on its merits relatively more irresponsible than the recklessness of one importer, against a shutdown of an entire line of produce that had not, apparently, been an issue beyond one firm. If anything, FDA might have increased its enforcement efforts to ensure that papayas from Mexico were safe on an ongoing basis. As it is, FDA did not proactively catch the problem in a manner that would have allowed it to be stopped before it made people sick. A total ban after-the-fact does not make up for the point that the system, in its processes and for its intended purpose, failed.

Concluding Thoughts

The regulatory process, at least possibly intended to protect the public, is seen as something that stands in the way of businesses getting what they want – something to be overcome, rather than understood as a basis of rules within which to work for the benefit of the entire public, not to mention the health of a business's own customers. The focus becomes too much on paperwork and process. Instead of protection, the result is instrumentation, process, and 'officialness' of documents and whether all forms are completed and boxes checked; there is an ecology of the movement of paper and whims of process. Taken with creation and maintenance of official artifacts, organizations begin to exist for their own ends, and their work products as autonomous objects removed from context (Hull, 2012). This activity can act as a substitute for the primary intended activity, because the bureaucratic object has been interpreted as having the same effect as what was originally intended.

In the context of discussing the visual illustration of quantitative data, Tufte (2001) included a section in his book that spoke to the conjecture that, in so many words, the audience is unsophisticated. He warned that this thinking leads to convoluted presentation and a lack of erudition in the means used to present complicated numerical data and analyses to the public; this was especially true in the US, with Asian and European countries showing more sophistication in reporting and illustrating this information. He quoted two sources that guide thinking in this area: The first, a national television news director, said "If you have to explain it, don't use it" (p. 81). The second quotation, from E. B. White, was that "No one can write decently who is distrustful of the reader's intelligence, or whose attitude is patronizing" (quoted in Tufte, 2001, p. 81). There is plenty of patronization to be had in government language.

Perhaps, a sure proof of the playing of a bureaucratic game is that there is plenty of activity, but documentation is neither approachable nor readily understood. The public is essentially waived off from a close look at what is going on; the online system is a wall rather than a bridge. The problem, of course, is that the FDA's work and mission are extremely important – and failure in this regard is a matter of grave consequence, even if not being able to access import cheese is largely just an inconvenience. Sometimes, foundational elements of administrative work are shaky or even absent, and it is worthwhile to identify those instances and correct them, if possible.

Notes

1 https://www.fda.gov/AboutFDA/History/FOrgsHistory/Leaders/ucm093758. htm.
2 US Food and Drug Administration Import Refusal Reports https://www. accessdata.fda.gov/scripts/ImportRefusals/index.cfm).
3 The article on food import safety and the impact of regulatory modernization and reform by Alexia Brunet Marks (2015) provides an overview of related concerns.

References

Avorn, J. (2008). Coagulation and adulteration – Building on science and policy lessons from 1905. *The New England Journal of Medicine, 358*(23), 2429–2431.

Barry, F. (2013, August 5). Mimolette 'mite' be blocked if levels are too high says FDA. *Food Quality News.* Retrieved from https://www.foodqualitynews.com/Article/2013/08/06/Mimolette-cheese-mite-be-restricted-by-FDA.

Béland, D. (2010). The idea of power and the role of ideas. *Political Studies Review, 8*(2), 145–154.

Berenstein, N. (2016). Making a global sensation: Vanilla flavor, synthetic chemistry, and the meanings of purity. *History of Science, 54*(4), 399–424.

Callahan, K. (2007). *Elements of effective governance: Measurement, accountability, and participation.* Boca Raton, FL: CRC Press.

Chimileski, S. (2016). The natural history of cheese mites. *American Society for Microbiology General Science Blog.* Retrieved from https://www.asm.org/index.php/general-science-blog/item/4433-the-natural-history-of-cheese-mites.

Coppin, C. A., & High, J. (1999). *The politics of purity: Harvey Washington Wiley and the origins of federal food policy.* Ann Arbor: University of Michigan Press.

Culture. (2018). Mimolette – Extra vielle. Retrieved from https://culturecheesemag.com/cheese-library/Mimolette—Extra-Vielle.

Dennis, B. (2013, June 28). Mimolette cheese shipments blocked by FDA, fans fume. *The Washington Post.* Retrieved from https://www.washingtonpost.com/national/health-science/au-revoir-mimolette-fans-unhappy-as-fda-blocks-french-cheese-shipments-over-mites/2013/06/28/08ed8c56-dda6-11e2-948c-d644453cf169_story.html?utm_term=.047420764db1.

Dickey, C., & Guilhamon, A. (2013, July 20). U. S. wants freedom from 'filthy' French cheese. *The Daily Beast.* Retrieved from https://www.thedailybeast.com/us-wants-freedom-from-filthy-french-cheese.

Domosh, M. (2003). Pickles and purity: Discourses of food, empire and work in turn-of-the-century USA. *Social & Cultural Geography, 4*(1), 7–26.

El Entertainment. (2010, orig. 1999). *In search of history: Potions or poisons?* (DVD). Retrieved from https://www.youtube.com/watch?v=TZdwM4sAfCk.

Entis, P. (2011). FDA import alert on Mexican papayas, effective immediately. *eFoodAlert.* Retrieved from https://efoodalert.wordpress.com/2011/08/25/fda-import-alert-on-mexican-papayas-effective-immediately/.

Farrell, C., Morris, J., & Ranson, S. (2017). The theatricality of accountability: The operation of governing bodies in schools. *Public Policy and Administration, 32*(3), 214–231.

Fdaimports.com. (2011). The FDA import refusal report: Many ways in, no way out? *FDAimports.com.* Retrieved from https://www.fdaimports.com/blog/the-fda-import-refusal-report-many-ways-in-no-way-out/.

Flynn, D. (2011, August 26). Mexican papayas detained at the border. *Food Safety News.* Retrieved from http://www.foodsafetynews.com/2011/08/mexican-papayas-will-now-be-detained-at-border/.

Geist, E. (2012). When ice cream was poisonous: Adulteration, ptomaines, and bacteriology in the United States, 1850–1910. *Bulletin of the History of Medicine, 86*(3), 333–360.

Hardy, S. B. (1990). Assuring a healthy food supply: A case for fundamental reform of regulatory programs. *American Review of Public Administration, 20*(4), 227–243.

Hisano, A. (2016). The rise of synthetic colors in the American food industry, 1870–1940. *Business History Review, 90*(Autumn), 483–504.

Hookway, C. (1988). *Quine: Language, experience and reality.* Stanford, CA: Stanford University Press.

Hull, M. S. (2012). Documents and bureaucracy. *Annual Review of Anthropology, 41,* 251–267.

Johnson, D., & Johnson, E. (2018). Mimolette cheese. Retrieved from https:// eatingrichly.com/mimolette-cheese/.

Kerwin, C. M., & Furlong, S. R. (2011). *Rulemaking: How government agencies write law and make policy.* Washington, DC: CQ Press.

Kingdon, J. W. (2003). *Agendas, alternatives, and public policies,* 2nd edition. New York: Longman.

Lempert, P. (2018, April 29). E. coli outbreak in romaine lettuce underscores need for change and technology. *Forbes.* Retrieved from https://www.forbes. com/sites/phillempert/2018/04/29/latest-e-coli-outbreak-in-romaine-lettuce-underscores-the-need-for-change-and-technology/#792dbe1e50c8.

Loughlin, M. (1990). The public local inquiry, the political system, and the public sphere. *International Journal for the Semiotics of Law, 3*(9), 319–328.

Maasik, S., & Solomon, J. (2012). *Signs of life in the U.S.A.: Readings on popular culture for writers,* 7th edition. Boston, MA: Bedford/St. Martin's.

Marks, A. B. (2015). The risks we are willing to eat: Food imports and safety. *Harvard Journal on Legislation, 52,* 125–172.

Meier, J. (2017, February 17). What are cheese mites? *The Spruce.* Retrieved from https://www.thespruce.com/what-are-cheese-mites-591196.

Melnyk, J. P., Smith, A., Scott-Dupree, C., Marcone, M. F., & Hill, A. (2010). Identification of cheese mite species inoculated on Mimolette and Milbenkase cheese through cryogenic scanning electron microscopy. *Journal of Dairy Science, 93*(8), 3461–3468.

Nash, L. (2008). Purity and danger: Historical reflections on the regulation of environmental pollutants. *Environmental History, 13*(4), 651–658.

Peterson, T. L., & Turner, K. L. (2014). "Extravagance and folly" versus "proper food": Domestic scientists, celebrity chefs, and the ongoing food reform movement. *The Journal of Popular Culture, 47*(4), 817–837.

Reinarman, C. (2007). Policing pleasure: Food, drugs, and the politics of ingestion. *Gastronomica, 7*(3), 53–61.

Richmond, H. (2013, July 9). French are pissed we banned their 'filthy, putrid' cheese. *Grist.* Retrieved from https://grist.org/food/french-are-pissed-we-banned-their-filthy-putrid-cheese/.

Rosenthal, E. (2011, December 8). Lead from old U.S. batteries sent to Mexico raises risks. *The New York Times.* Retrieved from https://www.nytimes. com/2011/12/09/science/earth/recycled-battery-lead-puts-mexicans-in-danger. html.

Rothschild, M. (2011, July 27). Papaya outbreak strain also seen in 2010. *Food Safety News.* Retrieved from http://www.foodsafetynews.com/2011/07/ papaya-outbreak-strain-was-also-seen-in-2010/.

Schell, L. M., Gallo, M. V., & Cook, K. (2012). What's not to eat – Food adulteration in the context of human biology. *American Journal of Human Biology, 24,* 139–148.

Sennett, R. (2017, orig. 1974). *The fall of public man.* New York: W.W. Norton.

Shanahan, E. A., Jones, M. D., McBeth, M. K., & Lane, R. R. (2013). An angel on the wind: How heroic policy narratives shape policy realities. *Policy Studies Journal, 41*(3), 453–483.

Siffin, W. J. (2001). Problem of development administration. In A. Farazmand (Ed.), *Handbook of comparative and development public administration, 2nd edition, revised and expanded, 1–8*. New York: Marcel Dekker.

Simon, J. E. et al. (2017). Establishing standards on colors from natural sources. *Journal of Food Science, 82*(11), 2539–2553.

The Packer. (2012). Updated: Mexican papaya alert continues, as do recalls. *The Packer.* Retrieved from https://www.thepacker.com/article/updated-mexican-papaya-alert-continues-do-recalls.

Thoemmes, M. S., Fergus, D. J., Urban, J., Trautwein, M., & Dunn, R. R. (2014). Ubiquity and diversity of human-associated demodex mites. *PLOS One,* doi:10.1371/journal.pone.0106265.

Thomson, J. R. (2014, April 4). Your cheese might be covered in mites, and that's a good thing. *Huffington Post.* Retrieved from https://www.huffingtonpost.com/2014/04/04/cheese-mites_n_5083137.html.

Toobin, J. (2013, December 9). The cheese stands alone. *The New Yorker.* Retrieved from https://www.newyorker.com/magazine/2013/12/09/the-cheese-stands-alone-2.

Tufte, E. R. (2001). *The visual display of quantitative information,* 2nd edition. Cheshire, CT: Graphics Press.

Tukey, J. W. (1977). *Exploratory data analysis.* Reading, MA: Addison-Wesley.

U. S. Food & Drug Administration (USFDA). (2018). Import Alert 21-17: Countrywide detention without physical examination of papaya from Mexico. Retrieved from https://www.accessdata.fda.gov/cms_ia/importalert_721.html.

Wroblewski, J. (1989). Proof in law: Legal language and legal institutions. *International Journal for the Semiotics of Law, 2*(4), 3–16.

4   A Semiotic Analysis of Green Public Procurement

Government procurement is a big business. "Government is often the single biggest customer within a country, and governments can potentially use this purchasing power to influence the behaviour of private sector organisations," and by giving attention to "broader government objectives" (Walker & Brammer, 2009, p. 128). As an example, since at least the 1970s the US government has concerned itself with the environmental implications of the goods it uses in the conduct of the public's business. Inherent in the greening – or growing environmental consciousness – of public procurement is a shift in buying decisions with an intent toward positive environmental impact beyond the walls of city hall. This change typically involves purchasing products that are relatively more *green* (that use more recycled materials, can be re-used more, have a longer operating or useful life) instead of *brown* products (that use new paper with no recycled content, that are intended to be thrown away after use, or that involve planned obsolescence). The notion is that substituting green products for brown ones will ultimately help the environment, by reducing use, production, or further waste.

Green practices have been termed environmentally preferable purchasing (EPP), meaning that, as a result of the large aggregate purchases of goods and services made by governments, environmentally friendly choices can yield a clean environment (Coggburn & Rahm, 2005), or at least one where the adverse impact of government's buying habits and product/service use is lessened. Government has sought to balance environmental preferences, price, and performance; the US Environmental Protection Agency's efforts are indicative of the lengths to which governments have gone to translate environmental values into policy actions (EPA, 2016). In considering these issues, some efforts, like the Framework for Responsible Environmental Decision-making (FRED), have not considered other issues of policy importance, like worker safety or socioeconomic priorities (Curran, 2001). Also, decision-making tools for public procurement (choosing between the greener of two products, for example) may not create an environment that is, strictly speaking, sustainable.

The chapter explores an example of semiotic analysis of a policy debate – where normative values and rhetoric are considered in their sign function together with competing values and program outcomes. The conceptual effort employs a Greimas square to discern underlying issues in the debate and discourse surrounding green public procurement. Understanding is furthered through an analysis for sign and symbol of green public procurement language in the EU case.

Abstractions and the Birth of Public Texts

The written word is not complete unto itself, bearing totality in its abstraction. Writing gains meaning from various practices and culture-based settings, and this meaning can be discerned through analysis. Given the context of the public sphere, the rhetorical instance provides an opportunity to persuade through the written statement. There is an establishment not only of argument of but also credibility of the person or group making the statement (ethos). This rhetorical purpose may influence both deed and conviction of the public. In analyzing public-facing texts, we may become very interested in how these texts accomplish intended results, or even result in inadvertent activity depending on how statements are made (Bazerman & Prior, 2009).

Bazerman wrote that "we create our texts out of the sea of former texts that surround us, the sea of language we live in" (2009, p. 84). The origins of texts might be acknowledged or ignored, and when we are acting as readers, we may recognize the origins of texts or sense something about them that is familiar. The concept of intertextuality – or how texts relate to other texts that provide context – is relevant because it shows us how understanding and knowledge are created, and how terms alien to a context can nevertheless be used to make persuasive arguments in the public sphere. One may choose to take terms at face value, or look for the underlying elements that may inform a more thorough understanding, whether those references to other texts occur within a document or communication, or to other texts or bodies of knowledge (Bazerman, 2009).

We may seek to understand the motivations behind the creation of a public text, particularly when the text outlines a formal process or legal requirement. When texts situate themselves within a larger tradition, the tendency is to quote other works, and tie the material presently under scrutiny to previous accepted work (Prior, 2009). This occurs in academic writing, such as the present text, as a primary activity. An absence of reference to other work would be frowned upon, because there is already an understanding that much has come before the present work, and this knowledge should be understood and cited. Without a firm basis in the tradition of knowledge-building, an academic work is suspect. The enterprise of public policy provides expectations that are similar in a variety of respects – attention to previous legal tradition, awareness of context and public attitude, and the symbolic value of various actions vis-à-vis the potential for follow-up on performance and productivity in achievement of gains for given policy pursuits. The reader also needs to know who wrote the work, or participated in its drafting (Prior, 2009), if full information is to be shared about the process and intent. Otherwise, policy appears unapproachable and opaque, or the policy appears multi-voiced, to the point of denying authorship.

The rhetoric of policy may form the motivation for creation of a text, in this case, a bill or proposed ordinance, for example, which may eventually be made law. The initiating text (Prior, 2009) may be an angry letter from a constituent, demanding change, or as another form of 'text,' media coverage of an event leads to disagreeable sentiment in the public mindset. The resulting official text need not be purposeful; it may be ceremonial, serving as acknowledgment of public anger. This may prove enough to allow public discourse to move to another topic; refusal to provide for substantive official response may make the public even more livid. The success of the policy approach as an official statement, able to persuade (ethos) may depend on alignment with zealous public reaction and expression of passions (pathos), and/or appeals to reason (logos). The value of appealing to emotion should not be under-estimated (Selzer, 2009).

Gaines (2001) called for "developing a method that recalls the structural origins of the discipline and builds a formula to support interpretive analysis" (para. 6), to bring semiotics to a more impactful place. The assumptions made in creation of myth and symbol be open to analysis. Symbol and myth-making get in the way of connecting communication with content; assumptions are being made when a sign or symbol connotes something beyond a direct referent. Those assumptions deserve to be brought out and challenged, if necessary, to the extent that they differ strongly from matters of fact or in ways that serve privileged groups over others, contrary to serving the larger public interest. Such a statement itself may be construed as problematic, because it implies that the whole of society has a right to have some role in public discourse and the larger discussion of societal priorities. These discussions about challenges facing humanity affect all of us. Otherwise, we cannot change our focus to context as a driving force in the shaping of meaning (Gaines, 2001), and become aware of the fuller impact of symbols and myths, and how they play upon our thinking and decision-making.

When analyzing texts, there are a variety of perspectives worth considering: What does the text mean to the analyst, to its intended recipient (primary addressee), to the person or people sending it? Some of this is conjecture and the quality of the analysis is informed by how well we understand the client populations, communities served by programs, or government structures that implement programs. From the viewpoint of public policy and regulation, that the original program-matic intent cannot be entirely and completely reconstructed is less ob-jectionable, perhaps, because we must at some point come to terms that programs outlive their creators. Constitutions may exist in force for hundreds of years, and their underlying thematic elements even longer. Yet, from a legal perspective, the interpretations of those outside the policymaking, regulatory, and legal communities matter less, because their position does not ultimately allow them to determine the meaning of policy or legal documents. They must simply live with the conse-quences of such determinations. This also reflects one of the problems of public administration, on the cusp of legal policymaking and client advocacy, and being able to see both sides of a program – its intent and consequences.

Authors of certain texts (such as those of law) have in mind very spe-cific contexts and meanings; "unforeseeable interpretations" may result, because "a text so immoderately 'open' to every possible interpretation will be called a closed one" (Eco, 1979, p. 8). Open texts are more "defined by the lexical and the syntactical organization of the text...the semantic-pragmatic production of its own Model Reader" (Eco, 1979, p. 10). Law, then, is a closed text because it is not planned that readers may exert free interpretation upon the text, even though that is often what ends up oc-curring in practice (and in the courts). Law as a closed text is, however, incomplete, and while it rejects consistent interpretation and clarity as a matter of course, it nevertheless demands interpretation and an open-text like readerly role, from those in the legal profession, administrators, and any public willing to approach and seek to understand law. One may find repeated appearance of "figurative and/or referential words or phrases" – and this can be indicative of values and interests of outside collectives (Arrigo, 1999, p. 96). Taking these words and phrases back to their origin(s) may provide a greater understanding of the nature not only of policy, but decision-making in the public sphere as well.

It is important not to consider only the text on its own. The text exists in context – it is of a time and place, created by people with viewpoints and various considerations and rationales for action. This larger 'com-munication chain' approach gives additional meaning to any signs that are placed in policy, through rhetorical statements or eventually in law. One should also consider the audience of these attempts at communica-tion. One may ask a variety of questions related to policy, patterned after considerations raised by Selzer (2009): Were the efforts to communicate successful? Did the audience respond favorably or not? Did the policy work define future community realities in positive or negative ways, or otherwise impact societal discourse? Were arguments compelling on their own in ways that had symbolic value in their own right? Finally, did resultant programs lead to outcomes that were quantifiable and consis-tent with original legal intent?

The Aims and Needs of Government

Public administration sets in motion systems because collectively it wants to help and it believes it can solve problems with technical knowledge, systems, and processes. However, "there is a paradox between public administration as promoter of technological system and...facilitator of individuality...in the incongruence of system and system environment" (Farmer, 1995, p. 102). For the same reason that agencies rarely fall out of existence, we may expect that agencies once born find activities to fill their time; they continue to devour resources even when obvious tears with social fabric and individual needs of clients become evident.

Considering the underlying meaning in political rhetoric and text, critical in what is being said or written is what is absent. There are elements of deconstruction in separating surface terminology from assumptions and contexts that allow such terms to obtain meaning. In politics, and subsequently finding expression in the public policies of administrations, there is often a need to show how change has been effected – that there has been a clear break somehow with what has come before.

Governments have to figure out relationships with the public; the public might be citizens, customers, voters, subjects, or any number of other frames of the day, and administrators might be rulers, experts, employees, or servants, among other options (Callahan, 2007). Governments associate with truth and justice and position as arbiters and bringers of both. Truth in an objectivist sense means something absolute and unconditional and unrelated to context or individual perspective; it could be argued that there is a strong sense in politics that truth might actually exist in an objectivist sense (Lakoff & Johnson, 1980). This affects policy because from a perspective of implementation, and evaluation of programs informed by the scientific method, what individuals consider to be true is absolutely true from where they might sit, but it might have nothing at all to do with an evaluator's view of how a program has or has not achieved program outcomes, or how clients see the program. Belief aside, facts do not, in any event, speak for themselves. There are different 'truths' and few of them are universal. Objectivism is perhaps most dangerous because it imbues decisions with a false sense of security.

Administration has held close for much of its self-aware existence to the idea that it had the knowledge and technique to implement programs and fix problems. Public administration has been quick to point a finger at politics for causing many of its problems with vague, value-laden laws that translate poorly into implementable programs that yield measurable outputs and outcomes. Administration, for its part, has done itself no favors in creating a convoluted, unnecessarily difficult miasma of bureaucratese, which is as breathtakingly obtuse as it is unapproachable. Careers have been built on a lack of success in program implementation and breakdowns in communication between the political and administrative spheres. One could say that this is completely unaccept-able and stamp our feet about it; however, it is perhaps totally acceptable and worse, it is probably the preferred approach for lengthening one's career in public service. Administration is not built upon failure – upon innovation and trying new ways forward – it is built on stability. The public criticizes the government but at least it is there to criticize or rail against when the mood suits.

The public is somewhat complicit in the arrangement, because of its willingness to go along with intellectually lazy patter that poses as broad pronouncements of a better future for us all. We might feel it innocuous or even efficient to "willfully shut...eyes to the fact" (Heffernan, 2011, p. 2) and employ various filters that help us retain what makes us feel better about ourselves and our contexts, and dis-pense with that which may make us uncomfortable. For the most part this is advantageous because without filtering we may not be able to proceed with our day's activities. But this process may create habits that make us more obedient; the occasion may rise when people have a more obligation to be disobedient, but at that point, it may be im-possible to resist the imposition of further demands. There is a need in society for "heroic dissent [that] sets a standard for critical thinking" (Heffernan, 2011, p. 245). When one fails to make noise against what one knows to be wrong, then one may be complicit in the failure or transgression against the public good.

Performance of Green Public Procurement as Policy Symbol

Green buying is spurred by various factors, among them a need to satisfy customers, reduce pollution, and remain within regulatory requirements. Rao (2008) pointed out that Asian businesses have an increasing expec-tation to consider environmental performance in their business and pro-ductive capacity, to stay in advance of rival companies, and be acceptable to the global market. There is a need to not only reduce waste and dam-age to the environment from a corporate social responsibility standpoint, but also to stay in step with regulatory expectations and the threat (if not reality) of hefty fines for pollution leading to environment degradation and damage to public health. Other considerations include the health and safety of employees. Large businesses with significant resources to make positive changes in sustainability may lead efforts. Sustainability vies with other priorities, among them a need to provide enhanced prod-ucts for lower costs, for business and government attention, even though there has been additional consideration given of the value of long-term relationships in business, and treating others and the environment as a resource-base with respect. Strategic planning has occurred in support of sustainability and sustainable development, as awareness of pollution, its impacts, and the need for mitigation has increased. Planning must, however, shift to action in implementation, and be driven by employees and officials directly involved in supply chains, and who design and implement procedures for procurement (Rao, 2008). Good governance is essential to achievement of sustainability (Alibašić, 2018).

In procurement, the problem of greening and sustainability can be hampered by the supply chain's emphasis on suppliers, what they are doing to support such efforts, and the products being offered. Statements in support of green procurement are fine, but do not amount to much without the ability to buy green products. If it is not possible to source green products, it might be feasible to reduce the amount of product being purchased, or the utilization of polluting materials or supplies that encourage waste production. Many procurement organizations focus on the purchase and use of recycled materials, such as recycled paper. The success of the effort is dictated by matters that typically affect advocacy: whether top management support the effort, whether the effort has been made an organization-wide initiative with appropriate buy-in, whether there is personal responsibility on the part of staff for various aspects of the program, and whether knowledge-sharing networks have been created to support the longevity of the effort. The form of the program may draw from a number of perspectives: placing the emphasis on suppliers to document the 'greenness' of products, requiring the purchase of 'green' products of specific content, or even educating suppliers and working with them to developer greener products (Rao, 2008). There is no guarantee that a pronouncement of the government that it supports green procurement will accomplish a green supply chain – the connection with suppliers must be made and remade on an active basis to accomplish such a far-reaching goal.

Many in procurement have been involved in green buying initiatives, but it is worth asking – what is the benefit of these programs in substantive terms? Awareness alone does not yield a desired outcome. True stewardship does not rest on pronouncements, but in working with partners to achieve the intended goals of a program.

In reviewing the evolving study of organizational purchasing, Green, Morton, and New (2000) offered that contractual engagement takes place in an environment of relationships, sometimes with great longevity, where there is an advantage in trust between sellers and buyers; the operating environment itself, with its values and expectations, can impact procurement processes, and what is considered acceptable and appropriate in a given context. Consumers (both end users and as organizations) can demand greater attention to environmental priorities, including the purchasing of green products. This can impact organizational decisions and decisions around the organization (within the supply chain, in communities, and at other levels of government, through spread of what are felt to be best practices).

Walker and Brammer (2009) indicated that local small business contracting activity had positive implications for sustainability, but that in the UK context environmental measures lagged behind. Nijaki and Worrel (2012) suggested that attentions to buying local and green could be joined as an approach to economic development, in view of encouraging attention to equity, environmental values, and economic goals as factors in strategic procurement, within a larger sustainable development plan. Still, as a policy intervention, focus on replacing brown products with greener products ignores consumptive practices, consumer behaviors, and potentially cost more, so "green procurement can produce significant benefits only under certain circumstances" (Marron, 1997, p. 299). Even though Coggburn and Rahm noted that efforts have been made to address unfair myths associated with green products – that such products are more expensive, inferior in quality, and harder to acquire – governments preside over large environmental footprints. Efforts to balance procurement priorities against long-term priorities like environmental protection are occurring, but consumption and waste continue, and expectations of public procurement for fairness, efficiency, and best product for the price remain constant urgencies (2005).

Greimas, the Nature of Meaning, and the Semiotic Square

In his work, A. J. Greimas explored the nature of communication processes, and the creation of meaning and reality as a reception of language, rather than its expression. Uncovering ideology, its discernment and transmission, plays a role in this work. Greimas followed Saussure in suggesting linguistics as a study in opposition – defining the value of a term by what it is not. In communication, what something is, and how it is expressed, is versed in terms of a countering object or concept. Within a system of relations and oppositions, in an inherent duality between terms, there is no absolute meaning, but rather understanding being created in the moment, between terms that support or differ with one another. The intelligibility of the world in this view tends to rest on a system where terms presuppose one another. Language is unclean in that it is equivocal, and focusing in on terms and their relationships with one another allows a more coherent view of communication efforts as they are put forward. There is not a meaning and an absence of meaning, but rather a meaning that is allowed by the presence of its contrary. The system is not logical, with terms purely set against one another, but semantic, with terms possibly confounding one another, as each seeks to impact meaning. While rhetoric is one form of communication, discourse, and the push-and-pull between competing factors in meaning, is informed by oppositions and misalignment (Schleifer, 2017, orig. 1987).

Policy has an odd placement in this system-thinking. It is an expression of collective will, seeks a manifestation of desired phenomena (program outcomes), at least as stated in laws, rules, and program materials, and acts as if it is anonymous when cited. Rules, for example, are referenced in often complex strings of acronyms, letters, and numbers, derived from a particular system that may defy popular understanding. The message is that policies and laws could be disengaged, and in their formalization above the fray, but this message is false. Rules and public program documents have authors, of course, despite the anonymization of the formalized legal construction.

It is worth considering the number of dichotomous relationships in the discourse on green purchasing. First, there is the relationship of green (environmentally conscious, clean, responsible) to brown (environmental degrading, dirty, irresponsible) products. One may set aside for a moment that there is disagreement on the definition of a green product compared with a brown product, and consider all products along a semantic spectrum of relatively more or less green (with brown products effectively being 'non-green'). At the same time, there is a competing relationship addressing financial responsibility and accountability; public purchasing often requires an award for the lowest price that meets technical specifications, and decisions that are seen to not give adequate attention to this aspect may be deemed wasteful. As another element of detail, other socio-economic considerations, such as worker's rights and equity, may affect how placements along semantic axes are perceived. Under certain circumstances when workers' issues or equity considerations are not primary points in the policy context, making a case for green purchasing may be relatively more straightforward, even if cost is a consideration. When those other contexts compete for policy attention, green considerations may be seen as relatively more wasteful or less important than those other socio-economic considerations.

The above complementary semantic relationships, and their essential sign-bearing elements, may be depicted with the help of a semiotic square, also known as a Greimas square. "By semiotic square is meant the visual representation of the logical articulation of any semantic category" (Greimas & Courtâes, 1982, p. 308). In Figure 4.1, *green* and *fiscally responsible* may exist concurrently and be true and/or false at the same time, at varying levels. They may be cooperative with or contrary to one another. As green asserts one set of values, 'fiscally responsible' may be taken, depending on how portrayed, to negate such values. S_1 and S_2 have a relationship of contrariety; they may at times be assumed as opposed to one another.

The first generation of terms may lead to a second level of understanding with consequential categorical terms, which lie outside the semiotic square. In a hierarchical sense, *truth* and *falseness*, or "contradictory metaterms" (p. 310) may be equated with 'sustainability' and 'impermanence' (above and below the semiotic square). Sustainability itself is a disputed term, even more than green procurement, because it involves

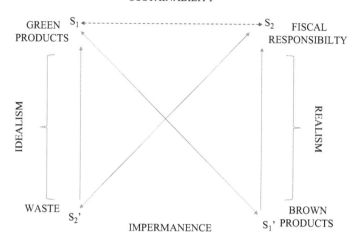

Figure 4.1 Semiotic square, green products and fiscal responsibility.
Source: Created by C.A., original work. Based on theory of Greimas and Courtâes (1982, pp. 309–310).

a variety of aspects contributing to societal longevity that might be disputed depending on one's viewpoint. As an example, sustainability can be defined as "the persistence over an apparently indefinite future of certain *necessary* and *desired* [emphasis mine] characteristics of the socio-political system and its natural environment" (Robinson, Francis, Lerner, & Legge, 1996, p. 31). Within this definition is the idea that people will come to some agreement as part of a civil society about its values to the extent necessary to accomplish long-term stewardship of not only the natural environment, but societal constructs. Impermanence is, like brown products as an opposite of green products, an absence – in this case, the absence of sustainability.

Interestingly, within the square itself, the assertion of green products would seem to negate waste in fiscal terms, and the assertion of fiscal responsibility would negate the use of brown products. Both of these evocations may seem contrary to forms of thinking that focus on short-run gains (i.e. impermanence), but are consistent with ideas of sustainability. Another way of exploring the square is that green approaches themselves are wasteful, and that fiscal responsibility implies limited focus on short-run gains only.

To the right and left of the square, replacing the *secret* and *lie* of the Greimas and Courtâes example, are "contrary metaterms" (1982, p. 310) adjustable to the subject matter under review: in this case 'idealism' and 're-alism' – where the green of idealism is confronted with budget realities and resource considerations in policy debates. The third level of understanding may be mythic, or at least myth-making: In policy circles, the value of the symbolic cannot be overlooked, and to the extent that the push-and-pull of these dyads and contrary relationships exists, the larger issue and rationale may be symbolic in nature, more than serving quantifiable ends, with consistently measurable value. As sustainability is assumed a positive pursuit, even when poorly defined, there is allowance for exploratory approaches and some lack of clarity in measurement of outcomes. Intent and belief are undeniably important in the making of public meaning.

The terms within the semiotic square, in their effort toward the construction of meaning, are allowed to play with and against one another, in a fashion relatively independent of outcome. As with other language games, the language of green policy and fiscal responsibility can tend toward clever and technical wordplay. As Tinsley (2015) suggested in his review of language games in economic development, building upon Wittgenstein and Baudrillard, refinement of terms continues "through a series of repetitive interactions that reinforce not only the intended meaning of certain language, but that also help the game participants to share perspectives" (p. 34); outsiders to the game may have little concept of the intended meaning of term use, but those playing within the game are aware of what the terms mean. The result of the wordplay in policy circles may mean very little, ultimately; policy assumptions are seldom challenged, and no outcomes need necessarily result for a program to be extended. The benefit may exist primarily in the rhetorical weight of seeming to affect a policy area of acute importance, like the environment, in a profound way.

With green purchasing, what results is a series of trade-offs in consumer/organizational behavior, leading to decisions that are reflective of the proclivities of the decision-makers and the values of organizations as much as the broader societal decision-making environment. Further, because consumer beliefs and actions are sometimes different, it is possible that consumers and organizations might indicate a preference for green purchasing, even with an increased cost or potential impact for other considerations, and then behave quite differently when the matter of procurement actually arises. An increased cost may be acceptable as a conceptual matter but when confronted with the choice to pay a certain amount substantially higher than a 'brown' choice, the decision becomes more difficult and the choice more conflicted. Convenient or easy options are often preferred, even with societal values in play (Earl & Clift, 1999). When additional considerations, such as equity in sourcing or budgeting priorities for various programs are taken into considerations, inclinations to support environmental initiatives may still remain a priority, but must effectively compete with other policy priorities. Short-run needs may win out over long-term considerations, even when those long-term goals speak to society's better nature. For green procurement, what we may be left with is mostly symbolic, and with little substance.

The semiotic square is one means of realizing a greater understanding of policy in practice as a function of sign and competing priorities. Other alternatives for semiotic analysis, including the connection of political rhetoric and program language, and assessment of the alignment of law and implementing procedures, can provide additional awareness. We now turn to an example of green public procurement language in practice – websites of the European Commission on green procurement from a general and legal/policy framework, using Infranodus for a topic modeling/bag-of-words view. A specific example – recycled paper – is reviewed to test the content analysis.

Analysis

A straightforward way of approaching analyses of legal documents is content analysis, using legal materials of various sorts as texts in qualitative sense of that term. Content analysis may be defined as "identifying, quantifying, and analyzing of specific words, phrases, concepts, or other observable semantic data in a text or body of texts with the aim of uncovering some underlying thematic or rhetorical pattern running through these texts" (Huckin, 2009, p. 14). Content analysis may be either inductive or deductive. Content analysis considers the meaning of a text through direct examination, "uncovering some underlying thematic or rhetorical pattern running through…texts" (Huckin, 2009, p. 14). The approach may be conceptual (looking for an idea in a text) or relational (seeing how that idea correlates to other concepts throughout a text). The analytical method centers on a practicable research question that considers a conceptual or relatable matter within a text/corpus, counts and otherwise considers the concept or relationship of that concept to others in the text(s), and provides for interpretation (Huckin, 2009).

As semiotic (sign-based, to uncover underlying meaning-making) analysis is often exploratory, one's approaches may seek to confirm or disconfirm a given proposition about relationships between official actors, or between actors and citizens, or the approach may simply seek to understand more about the meaning behind given policy choices, at whatever level of policymaking (Huckin, 2009).

As an example, content analysis relies upon inquiry of texts, implying that appropriate texts should be selected. For public policy, various forms of legal authority may act as texts for analysis. Examples include, but by no means are limited to constitutions, treaties, statutes, common law, contracts, criminal law, and various forms of regulations/administrative law (Mayer, Warner, Siedel, Lieberman, & Martina, 2012). Further, minutes of public meetings, official guidance documents, brochures and pamphlets, and other materials offered to clients/regulated parties/the public may be considered as texts. As semiotics generally has little limit on what may constitute a text, one may conclude that matter related

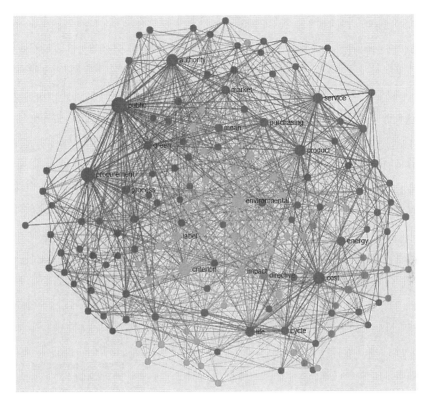

Figure 4.2 Network, general, public-centered websites, EU, green public procurement.
Source: Created by C. A. using InfraNodus from Nodus Labs. The websites included in the analysis are referred to in the text.

in some way to public policy may also be considered a text with potential for analysis.

The choice of which texts to study in any given case should be well determined – the selection should fit the intent. Validity in analysis of texts can be improved when researchers take into consideration the social context of the study. Care must be taken in interpretation to assure reliability; the researcher can assure reliability not only through alignment of opinions of various interpreters (that alone would actually not assure reliability; it might only assure that all interpreters share the same bias), but through assessments of sources themselves as credible, intra-subjectivity (consistency in analysis of a researcher over time), analytical transparency, careful argument, and thought in how questions are posed (Bergström & Boréus, 2017).

In order to visualize the message of green public procurement in the EU case, I used Infranodus[1] – an online tool for text analysis and network visualization – to visit and envisage a series of EU websites on the green public procurement topic. Infranodus generated a visual image of the network of related concepts within the websites visited. I ran two contexts for network analysis – one based on general 'green public procurement' language from the EU website, intended one might suggest for the general public; the other network was based on legal and policy framework portions of the website, which are more complex and possibly difficult to grasp, absent familiarity with legal language and policy discussions (Figure 4.2).[2] I created two text files – copying and pasting the text from the websites by the groups mentioned above into one file per group – and uploaded the text files to Infranodus for analysis (Figure 4.3).

A clear difference is the focus on the energy present in the legal and policy framework websites. Energy impacts play a significant role in determining whether an approach is sufficiently green within this framework. Energy efficiency, renewable energy sources, and consideration of same in the procurement context figure in this. Energy is woven into the framework through connections with the criteria to be employed for discerning whether public procurement is green, and in designating contract

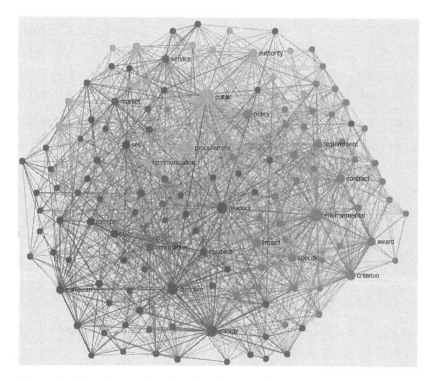

Figure 4.3 Network legal and policy framework websites, EU, green public procurement.

Source: Created by C. A. using InfraNodus from Nodus Labs. The websites included in the analysis are referred to in the text.

requirements and awarding standards; the emphasis in the public-oriented general descriptions of the program is not present at the level it is in the legal and policy framework sites. As a related matter, communication of public procurement policy is third on the list of main topics in the legal/ policy framework, even though communication of the program and its outcomes would seem to be important; it is the top topic on the network for general websites. The final main topic in the legal/policy framework network references European and council, and includes official designation of objectives and regulations as formally agreed to by the EU – this is consistent with the websites being aimed at describing the legal and policy framing for GPP in the EU. Table 4.1 outlines the analysis of the two networks, via the Infranodus platform.

Polysingularity means "the multiple clusters of meaning circulation contained within a text" (Paranyushkin, 2012). Both the public-centered and legal/policy framework websites have a focused discourse. Influence dispersal in the legal/policy framework network is much higher (50% compared with 80%). Whereas the main topics for the public-centered sites were related to public procurement authority; service product cost (some of the hallmarks of procurement language generally); and environmental criterion impact (specific identification of indicators for the green

Table 4.1 Topic and influential word analysis, EU green procurement websites

General public-centered websites	*Legal and policy framework websites*
Main topics (communities detected): 1 public procurement authority 2 service product cost 3 environmental criterion impact 4 directive save vehicle	Main topics (communities detected): 1 energy product information 5 environmental criterion award 6 public procurement authority 7 directive European councils

Most influential words (highest
  betweenness centrality):
  public procurement criterion
  environmental
	Most influential words (highest
	  betweenness centrality): public
	  environmental energy procurement

Question to ask:
What is the relation between 'public –
  procurement – authority' and
  'service – product – cost'?
	Question to ask:
	What is the relation between 'energy –
	  product – information' and
	  'environmental – criterion – award'?

Stats: total 150 words, graph density
  0.090, average degree: 13.37
Discourse polysingularity: focused
  0.23 modularity, 37% of words in
  the top topic (total 4 topics), 100%
  in the main connected component
  (1 in total), influence dispersal 50%
	Stats: total 150 words, graph density
	  0.129, average degree: 19.17
	Discourse polysingularity: focused
	  0.23 modularity, 35% of words in
	  the top topic (total 4 topics), 100%
	  in the main connected component
	  (1 in total), influence dispersal 80%

Source: Created by C.A., using output from InfraNodus from Nodus Labs. (Source websites included in text.)

procurement program, which ostensibly maximizes the environmental benefit of engaging in the effort), the legal and policy framework sites have a different focus.

For sources used, efforts have been made to assure that the sources are authentic, including, for example, downloading official documents from government websites. The corpus for each chapter has been developed accordingly, or via searching criteria and steps that may be replicated by other researchers. Records of original texts have been retained in addition to the analytical files, for additional documentation (Bergström & Boréus, 2017). For purposes of the work in this book, the corpus used for each chapter can be made available to other researchers upon request, so that the results and methods are transparent, and other researcher may attempt the same methods (on this material or other types of material) and reach similar results, given the same assumptions.

Discussion

While this analysis allows us to see major topics and often-used terms, as would be expected from content analyses, we do not have a clear view of what 'green procurement' is, as a defined and implementable concept. Instead, we see the trappings of administrative rules and procedure, addressing concerns on a piecemeal basis, and it is not clear to what end. Looking more closely at the individual websites helps with defining terms from the EU perspective. Green public procurement, for example, is "a process whereby public authorities seek to procure goods, services and works with a reduced environmental impact throughout their life cycle when compared to goods, services and works with the same primary function that would otherwise be procured" (European Commission, 2016). This statement is mostly clear – it puts green in relative terms (as suggested by the Greimas square).

An Micro-Level Example: Recycled Paper

An application of symbol touching upon green procurement is government's obsession with paper. Even where attempts are made to use recycled paper, it is the nature of the machinery of government to print hard copies of documents, to make documents official, to provide documentation of decisions, and to allow officials (mostly) to read through documentation of policy options in order to make the most fully informed decision possible, in theory anyway. The paper itself is "a material object...a semiotic mediational resource – it generates and transfers meaning when used in a specific action" (Dolata & Schwabe, 2017, p. 775). Paper is pointed to as a significant problem for government, as a hindering factor in officials' efforts to make sense of the difficult decisions that they must make. When solution-makers approach government, they put forward the idea of virtualization of government processes, or of the virtues of the so-called paperless office. The advent of email, for example, was supposed to reduce the glut of paper in government, but it does not seem to have accomplished that outcome. The offering of paper serves as a connection to and reification of decisions being made. The display of a lengthy document (like a thick budget book) implies complex calculations and deliberations, even if officials have not fully read or digested the information contained within the document. Paper in government is multimoded and multipurposed; it exists to serve a variety of ends, not all of them evidenced by surface-level production of meaning, and some approaching theater (Dolata & Schwabe, 2017).

When we begin to look more closely at the criteria to be used for determining whether products and services are green, we are confronted with a complex website of green criteria for various product lines.[3] The website suggests that "The EU GPP criteria are developed to facilitate the inclusion of green requirements in public tender documents. While the adopted EU GPP criteria aim to reach a good balance between environmental performance, cost considerations, market availability and ease of verification, procuring authorities may choose, according to their needs and ambition level, to include all or only certain requirements in their tender documents." Elsewhere, the site notes that the green procurement program is voluntary, "which means that Member States and public authorities can determine the extent to which they implement it."

Clicking on the standard for copying and graphic paper, for example, brings up a 13-page pdf document, differentiating paper to be used for office and 'professional use' (not exactly a clear distinction), and requiring evaluation of samples to determine alignment with the rules. To its credit, the EU does acknowledge a number of barriers common to instituting green procurement, but the simplest barrier is that the program is voluntary, complex enough to require training and active thought/participation, and not exactly clear from an action v. outcome standpoint, even if the definition of the program itself is relatively clear.[4] The EU acknowledges that it is still establishing standards. One might imagine that this discussion can be complex in its own right. The good intentions are notable, but turning those intentions into a reality with measurable outcomes for environmental benefit and communicating that benefit is secondary. As these standards are written for the whole of the EU, it is also fairly apparent that allowances for the various nations and their views are included in the establishment of standards. The discussion on allowable paper brightness level (a level of 60–90, based on preference) might well have been left out, given its vagueness. Some aspects of evaluating the acceptability of paper might be considered challenging from the view of a public servant, simply interested in doing the right thing: An example of this is language for "sustainable and/or legal virgin fibre option," which invokes forest stewardship standards, tracing systems, and chains of custody for materials (European Commission, 2008). Consistency aside, the presence of such language in a training toolkit might be off-putting to the level of encouraging program avoidance.

Contrast this with the common existence on the market in the EU of recycled paper. Much A4 paper available for sale in the EU is FSC and EU Ecolabel branded. It is not clear how much of the market for recycled paper is due to green public procurement programs, but a substantial portion of the demand is consumer-based. A question that can be asked is, what is the driving force? The existence of standards and criteria from government, industry-led corporate responsibility initiatives, or general consumer preferences. It is not whether recycled paper saves resources and energy, though there is some discussion about how much energy is saved, or how much pollution is reduced (EPA, archived 2015 though not updated, compared with BIR, 2007). A better question is: Why such a complex statement of requirement for recycled paper – when a few general points on buying recycled could have the same benefit? Hickman (2009) rightly points to the potential for backlash against recycling efforts. In the need to outline criteria for 'green procurement,' opportunities for improving recycling process and public engagement are being missed. The public, in this view, does respond to positive reinforcement; people do want to know that their efforts have a positive outcome, and that it would not be possible without their involvement.

It is troubling then that so much attention is on establishment of criteria in a voluntary program, with relatively little attention being paid to showing outcomes. Adell (2013) indicated that it is difficult to track how much impact green public procurement has; the ability to observe transformation to the market as a result of government efforts is not strong. Actual environmental benefits are "rarely calculated, but of interest" (p. 24). Reporting results becomes essential, but in order to report results, indicators of program success must be tracked and those results communicated to the public in an effective way. There may be assumptions made about performance, but those assumptions turn out not to be true in context. Top-down approaches do not serve the cause of integrating green procurement ideas into the working environment as regular expectations. Incentives and connections to other existing programs can help turn green procurement intentions into measurable accomplishments.[5] Still, the daily working environment of those directly involved with purchasing decisions must be considered, when pressures from a variety of sources may make the good intentions of green procurement secondary considerations, or largely ignored.

Concluding Thoughts

As observed in this example on green procurement, policy can exist on the basis of its own symbolic worth, with little consistent attention to program outcomes across jurisdictions, even though technical language may be similar between locales. Normative considerations and societal values prevail, but in terms of public policy, language games might carry the day, in a manner that brings governments and society no closer to broader objectives like sustainability. This is not good enough. Rather than standing in fear of law as unapproachable, people should seek it out, attempt to understand what is being done in their name, and determine consonance or dissonance with rhetoric. The goods received should match the bill of sale, and account should be regularly demanded – not just from semiotic analysts, but from government itself, by the public. Taking a critical look at signs and symbols may help the public guard against manipulation and get the most from its public service. Even a basic semiotic step, like assembling a Greimas square, can hint at inconsistencies in problem definition and reveal points where clarification may be needed.

Criteria that are already commonly met are listed as standards in some instances. Other criteria of considerable complexity may not be met, which is understandable given that programs are not fully integrated into their operating environments, and are voluntary regardless. Public procurement as a professional field has an increasing intent to be accountable not only within its operating environment internally, within government agencies for example, but also to the community and the larger global context. There is understanding that government has a role that is like a business, in its volume of purchases and utilization of resources, but that government has a larger mandate toward responsibility.

It is all the more important that government statements and practices are meaningful. Unless one is going out of their way to buy virgin-fiber copy paper, it is relatively easy to buy green in this respect. Government gets to point to a supposed gain, but it is not much of a gain – it is the continual achievement of a standard issued years ago. The standard is not an absolute expression of green-ness; it is not relatively greener. The push to buy recycled material in public procurement, from a top-down criteria view, misses the need for involvement of procurement professionals that actually accomplish the work. A standard issued ten years ago (as posted on the EU website at the time of this work) does not indicate that engagement with industry is active and ongoing – important for moving processes toward increasing responsibility and reduced environmental impact.

This is potentially a point for growth for government. Leadership in defining terms and setting the tone for a positive, sustainable future necessitates involvement from the top of the organization as well as its rank-and-file. Directives and establishment of criteria in voluntary programs has symbolic value, but can only take these efforts so far. Where government is successful in green procurement, a wide variety of actors have been involved, from industry supportive of such larger societal goals, as well as public administrators implementing the programs, and people in communities supportive of government efforts to be responsible. Increasing these connections and relationships, and making monitoring and reporting an ongoing aspect of programs, is important, but involvement and integration of green practices into the regular work of government is essential to program success.

Notes

1 https://infranodus.com/.
2 The websites examined for the general audience were http://ec.europa.eu/ environment/gpp/index_en.htm; http://ec.europa.eu/environment/gpp/gpp_ criteria_en.htm; http://ec.europa.eu/environment/gpp/what_en.htm;http://ec. europa.eu/environment/gpp/benefits_en.htm; http://ec.europa.eu/environment/ gpp/barriers_en.htm; http://ec.europa.eu/environment/gpp/versus_en.htm; http://ec.europa.eu/environment/gpp/circular_procurement_en.htm; http://ec. europa.eu/environment/gpp/lcc.htm; http://ec.europa.eu/environment/gpp/ dialogue_en.htm; http://ec.europa.eu/environment/gpp/eco_labels.htm. For the legal and policy examined, the sites visited included: http://ec.europa.eu/ environment/gpp/eu_related_en.htm; http://ec.europa.eu/environment/gpp/ eu_policy_en.htm; http://ec.europa.eu/environment/gpp/gpp_policy_en.htm; http://ec.europa.eu/environment/gpp/commission_guidance_en.htm; http:// ec.europa.eu/environment/gpp/treaty_en.htm; http://ec.europa.eu/environment/ gpp/eu_public_directives_en.htm; http://ec.europa.eu/environment/gpp/case_ law_en.htm.
3 http://ec.europa.eu/environment/gpp/eu_gpp_criteria_en.htm.
4 http://ec.europa.eu/environment/gpp/barriers_en.htm.
5 There are a variety of resources available on the need to report on green procurement efforts and program accomplishments. A useful webinar conducted by Clean Energy Solutions Center, for example, is located at https:// www.youtube.com/watch?v=DsvYc-5yMp4.

References

Adell, A. (2013). Monitoring and evaluation of green public procurement programs. *Ecoinstitut Barcelona*. Retrieved from https://cleanenergysolutions. org/sites/default/files/documents/Ecoinstitut_CESC2013_GPPMonitoring Aure.pdf.
Alibašić, H. (2018). *Sustainability and resilience planning for local governments: The quadruple bottom line strategy.* Cham: Springer International.
Arrigo, B. A. (1999). How has the law gone mad? Reflections on semiotics and postmodernism. *International Journal for the Semiotics of Law, 12*, 95–101.
Bazerman, C. (2009, orig. 2004). Intertextuality: How texts rely on other texts. In C. Bazerman & P. Prior (Eds.), *What writing does and how it does it: An introduction to analyzing texts and textual practices, 83–96.* New York: Routledge.
Bazerman, C., & Prior, P. (2009, orig. 2004). Introduction. In C. Bazerman & P. Prior (Eds.), *What writing does and how it does it: An introduction to analyzing texts and textual practices, 1–10.* New York: Routledge.
Bergström, G., & Boréus, K. (2017). Analyzing text and discourse in the social sciences. In K. Boreus & G. Bergstrom (Eds.), *Analyzing text and discourse:*

Eight approaches for the social sciences, 1–22. Thousand Oaks, CA: Sage Publications.

Bureau of International Recycling (BIR). (2007). About recycling. Retrieved from https://web.archive.org/web/20070927175746/http://www.bir.org/aboutrecycling/index.asp.

Callahan, K. (2007). *Elements of effective governance: Measurement, accountability, and participation.* Boca Raton, FL: CRC Press.

Coggburn, J. D., & Rahm, D. (2005). Environmentally preferable purchasing: Who is doing what in the United States? *Journal of Public Procurement, 5*(1), 23–53.

Curran, M. A. (2001). Developing a tool for environmentally preferable purchasing. *Environmental Management and Health, 12*(3), 244–253.

Dolata, M., & Schwabe, G. (2017). Paper practices in institutional talk: How financial advisors impress their clients. *Computer Supported Cooperative Work, 26,* 769–805.

Earl, G., & Clift, R. (1999). How businesses factor environmental features. *Measuring Business Excellence, 3*(3), 25–33.

Eco, U. (1979). *The role of the reader: Explorations in the semiotics of texts.* Bloomington: Indiana University.

European Commission. (2008). Copying & graphic paper – GPP product sheet. Retrieved from http://ec.europa.eu/environment/gpp/pdf/toolkit/paper_GPP_product_sheet.pdf.

European Commission. (2016). What is GPP. Retrieved from http://ec.europa.eu/environment/gpp/what_en.htm.

Farmer, D. J. (1995). *The language of public administration: Bureaucracy, modernity, and postmodernity.* Tuscaloosa: University of Alabama Press.

Gaines, E. (2001). The semiotic analysis of media myth: A proposal for an applied methodology. *The American Journal of Semiotics, 17*(2), 311–327.

Green, K., Morton, B., & New, S. (2000). Greening organizations: Purchasing, consumption, and innovation. *Organization & Environment, 13*(2), 206–225.

Greimas, A. J., & Courtâes, J. (1982). *Semiotics and language: An analytical dictionary.* Bloomington: Indiana University Press.

Heffernan, M. (2011). *Willful blindness: Why we ignore the obvious at our peril.* London: Simon & Schuster.

Hickman, L. (2009, February 25). The truth about recycling. *The Guardian.* Retrieved from https://www.theguardian.com/environment/2009/feb/26/recycling-waste-environment.

Huckin, T. (2009, orig. 2004). Content analysis: What texts talk about. In C. Bazerman & P. Prior (Eds.), *What writing does and how it does it: An introduction to analyzing texts and textual practices, 13–32.* New York: Routledge.

Lakoff, G., & Johnson, M. (1980). *Metaphors we live by.* Chicago, IL: University of Chicago Press.

Marron, D. B. (1997). Buying green: Government procurement as an instrument of environmental policy. *Public Finance Review, 25*(3), 285–305.

Mayer, D., Warner, D., Siedel, G., Lieberman, J., & Martina, A. (2012). Advanced business law and the legal environment. Retrieved from http://open.umn.edu/opentextbooks/BookDetail.aspx?bookId=121.

Nijaki, L. K., & Worrel, G. (2012). Procurement for sustainable local economic development. *International Journal of Public Sector Management, 25*(2), 133–153.

Paranyushkin, D. (2012). Visualization of text's polysingularity using network analysis. Retrieved from https://noduslabs.com/research/visualization-text-polysingularity-network-analysis/.

Prior, P. (2009, orig. 2004). Tracing process: How texts come into being. In C. Bazerman & P. Prior (Eds.), *What writing does and how it does it: An introduction to analyzing texts and textual practices, 167–200*. New York: Routledge.

Rao, P. H. (2008). *Greening the supply chain. A guide for Asian managers*. Los Angeles, CA: Response.

Robinson, J. B., Francis, G., Lerner, S., & Legge, R. (1996). Defining a sustainable society. In J. B. Robinson (Ed.), *Life in 2030: Exploring a sustainable future for Canada, 26–52*. Vancouver, BC: UBC Press.

Schleifer, R. (2017, orig. 1987). *A. J. Greimas and the nature of meaning: Linguistics, semiotics and discourse theory*. Abingdon, Oxon: Routledge.

Selzer, J. (2009, orig. 2004). Rhetorical analysis: Understanding how texts persuade readers. In C. Bazerman & P. Prior (Eds.), *What writing does and how it does it: An introduction to analyzing texts and textual practices, 279–308*. New York: Routledge.

Tinsley, S. (2015). *Jobs created? Economic development as language games*. PhD dissertation. Retrieved from http://fau.digital.flvc.org/islandora/object/fau%3A32136/datastream/OBJ/download/Jobs_Created__Economic_Development_as_Language_Games.pdf.

US Environmental Protection Agency (EPA). (2015). Wastes – resource conservation – common wastes & materials – paper recycling. Retrieved from https://web.archive.org/web/20150227163026/http://www.epa.gov:80/osw/conserve/materials/paper/basics/index.htm.

US Environmental Protection Agency (EPA). (2016). Environmentally preferable purchasing program history. Retrieved from https://www.epa.gov/greenerproducts/environmentally-preferable-purchasing-program-history.

Walker, H., & Brammer, S. (2009). Sustainable procurement in the United Kingdom public sector. *Supply Chain Management: An International Journal, 14*(2), 128–137.

5   New York City's Conflicts of Interest Law

Compliance versus Ethical Capacity

Introduction

> I believe it may be laid down as a general rule, that [the people's] confidence in and obedience to a government, will commonly be proportioned to the goodness or badness of its administration.
>
> (Hamilton, 1787, para. 1)

The application of ethics to governmental work has been examined with interest in public management literature. Considerations of the social contract and legitimacy of public institutions reach back to the Enlightenment, in the works of Rousseau, Hobbes, Pufendorf, Grotius, and Kant (Bertram, 2004), and flower in *The Federalist* at the founding of the US of America (Richardson, 1997). The roots of contractarianism extend back even further, to Roman, Greek, and Stoic philosophy, and the *Bible* (Boucher & Kelly, 1994). While deliberation on ethics and the social contract is not new, it is still as relevant today as it ever was – perhaps more so given a rhetorical climate often hostile to public-sector work (Chen & Bozeman, 2014).

In an effort to increase the transparency of public-sector activity, enhance accountability, and avoid corruption or at least the appearance of corrupt acts, the public sector has responded with ethics policies and training, and the creation of offices of audit, inspectors general, positions for staff ethicists, and professional standards agencies. Ethics programs involve "a set of activities, policies and procedures intended to support employees to understand and comply with the ethical standards and policies set by the organization" (Park & Blenkinsopp, 2013, p. 521). However, the existence of an ethics program alone does not ensure compliance with ethics rules, nor does it necessarily pre-empt objectionable behavior. Because there is no consistent foundation in ethics among public service employees, it is unreasonable to assume consistency in evaluation criteria for ethical practice, beyond simply abiding by the letter of the law. A pure standard of ethical behavior does not exist in organizations, public or private, and insistence on an adherence to the factor as a baseline for evaluation of performance or quality of governance is a challenging prospect.

A disconnect often exists between the expectations of senior staff and the behavior of line employees. While senior staff members may be more or less committed to the creation and maintenance of an ethical organizational culture, the inability to control informal structures within organizations may render that ideal unattainable. Not every employee behaves in ways equally moral or ethical, and even employees genuinely engaged in ethics programs may find that they cannot find common ground. There may be a lack of congruence in formal and informal ethical standards, creating dissonance for employees between high-level official dictates and customary, even accepted, practice (Pelletier & Bligh, 2006). Employees may then discern a hypocrisy/sincerity continuum when it comes to ethics, as the incentive for positive action is sometimes outweighed by an organizational allowance for behavior clearly at odds with strictly constructed ethics codes; this can lead to cynicism (Fassin & Buelens, 2011).

The ethos of the public service notwithstanding, people enter the public service for a wide variety of reasons. At some level, there is an assumption that employees participate in the public service because they feel akin to some idea of the public good (Perry, 2011); there is a need to convince the public that this positive, outwardly seeking motivation exists (Bergsten, 1985). Still, this assumption may be misplaced. When we consider the historical roots of the public service in the US, we may raise the matter of serving the public interest, which adds complexity. Is the most appropriate responsibility of the public sector in actively serving some deeply held notion of the public interest, or is the role of public administration most appropriately based in a more neutral agency: carrying out the programs of elected officials?

This chapter presents an inquiry into the literature on public-sector ethics programs, and pursues a critical understanding of the break between compliance-based approaches and theoretically preferred methods of increasing ethical integrity. Using the municipal government example of New York City as a point of reference, we reflect on the role of ethics in the public sector, in substance and symbol, and review approaches to ethics regulation. We seek to understand: What ethical aspects are emphasized by the New York City conflict of interest program, and what does the New York City program suggest about the understanding that exists between government and the public? In exploring these questions in the New York City case, it is possible to gain additional understanding of the nature of compliance-based approaches to ethics and how these methods fail to address the public's need for trust in government. It is proposed that compliance approaches to ethics are a useful distraction – they have less to do with the ethical outcome, and more to do with selecting points of transgression to prohibit – possibly satisfying a public angry at government's seeming dishonesty or the perception of treachery, in identifying wrongdoers, but failing to solve the need for greater ethical capacity in the public sector. It is contended that the myth of promoting ethics is a serviceable enough outcome for public-sector ethics programs, but public-centered notions of a broad and consistent impression of right and wrong amongst public-sector employees are, at best, misplaced.

Administrative Ethics as Substance or Symbol?

Administrative ethics has been defined as "ethical standards and choices made by those in administrative positions as these relate to the design and delivery of public sector policies and programs" (Dubnick & Justice, 2006, p. 238). This necessarily involves foundational morals of individuals, which vary widely and are rooted in personal experience and religious preference. In considering administrative ethics, we are reminded of the public sector's deontological (duty-driven) obligations, a duty to serve the population, in addition to the teleological considerations of means-ends tests. The concept of the *public interest* is far from distinct (Pesch, 2008), and the ambiguity of the term yields its greatest use in political rhetoric, where assertions of action in the public interest may have little base in considered thought, regardless of the fire of the speaker.

Competing views of individual morality and public expectations cloud matter further. Many considerations in the public sector amount to a utilitarian weighing of means and ends. Day-to-day public-sector questions are frequently teleological, and not deontological or in direct and conscious support of shared values (axiology), even though those issues may be indirectly linked to processes beyond the decision-making level (Brady, 2003). Seldom do front-line employees find themselves in dilemmas where they invoke Kant's categorical imperative; they may not even be aware of it (Kant, 1785). Attention to detail and enforcement of rules and procedures are valued in public administration, but somewhere along the way, one must admit the field's humanity and the uncertainty in discretionary application of rules, even to the point where practice may result in government that is unfair. In questioning which policies to support, some notion of public obligation or shared values may play a role.

Ethics in American Government

Ethics in American government is an issue as old as the nation (Locke, 1995). "Public administration is driven by responses to scandals and attempts to deter them" (Anechiarico & Jacobs, 1992, p. 580), and this had led to approaches that stress obedience to detailed standards over self-regulation of behavior at the individual level, and efforts to create or maintain an ethical/moral culture within organizations. For public administrators, virtue remains normatively important within public service as a major consideration, along with consequentialism and duty, for ethical decision-making (Svara, 2007). However, because the eventuality of a self-governing, individually mindful class of administrators educated in and aware of universal virtues has not materialized, public-sector ethics is often thought of in terms of compliance approaches. These approaches find formal adoption in codes, thought to be useful for "sharpening awareness" of "the ethical dimensions of [government leaders'] policies and actions" (Eskridge, French, & McThomas, 2012, p. 141).

A primary triggering concern for ethics regimes in the public sector is the desire to reign in administrative authority. This necessitates the creation of sometimes cumbersome legal and regulatory regimes that seek to define ethical behavior by what it is not, and to vaguely outline acceptable and appropriate practice. The 20th century saw much attention to public service ethical codes (see Beyer, 1922, for an example that illustrates how little these issues and expectations have changed over time). Meine and Dunn drew the lineage of ethics codes back even further, to the Athenian code (2013). They suggested that the prevalence of codes stands as a testimony to a widespread belief that they are important to have, though whether ethics codes are necessary remains unclear. There has been little movement in the discussion of how ethics codes might be implemented differently or respond more effectively to the trials confronting public administration as a field; as Svara wrote, "entering 2014, the status of public service codes of ethics approximated the conditions that had existed since 1984" (2014, p. 566). More generally, there remain questions, for example, of congruence of morality and legality in ethics codes across professions (Tamás, 2012).

Bazerman and Tenbrunsel included "codes of ethics, ombudsmen, and ethics training" among the components of an ethics program, and further stated that such programs "are designed to convey the values of an organization and the ethical standards the organization expects its employees to meet" (2011, p. 102). They suggest that these programs are often very expensive and not particularly effective, going as far as stating that ethical codes may have the opposite of their intended effects because they have too narrow of a focus to actually encourage ethical decision-making. Further, consistent with the neo-institutionalist school of thought, the informal organization and culture may be more impactful upon the ethical realities of behavior than an ethical code or staff ethicist remarks, along the lines noted in the literature on counterproductive work behaviors (Bashir, Nasir, Qayyum, & Bashir, 2012). Kaptein (2010) found that ethical culture held high explanatory value for unethical behavior in organizations. Why then do governments both choose to institute these codes and fund large staff of people supposedly engaged in the protection of institutional ethics?

The work of the public service is made complex by its placement outside the boundary of the business world, and involvement in protecting the public interest or at least ideas of what that might constitute. The peculiarities and machinations of the business of government are sometimes the object of ridicule, even where there are acceptable administrative reasons for bureaucratic action or inaction. The public service is frequently in positions that transcend the bureaucratic role of administrative matters; the success or failure of programs and agencies rests on the reality of the agency's work and its worth, and the perception of value on the part of political forces that control government through budgetary authority. It has been suggested that there is an ongoing political confrontation with regulation and regulators that shows little attention to party lines (Cooper, 2009). In seeking to provide the most business or elite-friendly environment possible, governments may have to some extent renounced their responsibility to protect the public or otherwise address the failures of the marketplace through regulation and front-line service. The work of government remains varied and critical, but the esteem of public-sector work has at times waned.

Koh and Boo (2004) suggested positive connections between management support of organizational ethics programs, job satisfaction, and organization outcomes. On the other hand, Bazerman and Tenbrunsel (2011) proposed that the existence of a code of conduct and a compliance scheme may fail to prevent widespread corruption and catastrophic, far-reaching ethical lapses; they invoke the private sector example of Enron, and suggest that informal culture has more to do with whether ethical considerations are a regular part of doing business. Formal systems might be window dressing, with a considerable symbolic value in assuring the public of quality while hiding real concerns in failures elsewhere in the organization, either in production or behavior; formalized codes might not often be relied upon as a touchstone for quality. "Codes of conduct can be mere attempts to convince outsiders, and particularly investors, that the organization is ethical while disguising its more important goals" (Bazerman & Tenbrunsel, 2011, p. 119). It may be that the more an organization talks about how ethical it is, or how much it aspires to achieving ideals of ethical practice, the more it is actually engaged in behavior hostile to those principles. The protestations of honesty seem insincere, if not indicative of treachery under the surface.

In the practice of public administration, public-sector ethics might be relegated to an annual course or webinar identifying basic parameters of what is acceptable under a law, and nothing more than that. While academic programs raise issues of serving the public good, and evaluate the philosophical traditions from which notions of public-sector ethics grow, the purposes of the public sector seek toward other ends. Instead of highlighting or expanding the vital abilities of public-sector staff, or contemplating the moral compass of the public servant, such approaches are content to forbid the acceptance of gifts of certain value, or provide for similar surface-level responses. However, as Atkinson and Bierling put it, ethics is more than simply following rules; "it also involves exercising one's judgement in the pursuit of...virtue" (2005, p. 1007). Public administration misses an opportunity to grow capacity through the *exercise* of judgment.

Performance of public institutions weighs heavily against efforts to assure integrity (Anechiarico & Jacobs, 1996). Self-regulation has been replaced over time by the imposition of sanctions for violation of rules. Brooke speculates that the reasons for the rise of regulators over the recent past include privatization and a lack of trust in officials and instrumentality (2003). One might speculate that these reasons also form the basis of the shift from ethical self-regulation to compliance approaches, to seek to assure loyalty and adherence to obligations where public service motivation either does not or is not believed to exist. Minimally, public employees seem to "have a duty to behave as if they were complying" (von Kriegstein, 2016, p. 445).

Maletz and Herbel advanced the idea that concern about public-sector ethics, which on the surface is a positive matter, has resulted in "public action to codify, supervise, and enforce standards of ethics on a scale unprecedented in our prior historical experience. Yet the officials on the receiving end of these efforts regard them as trivializing" (2000, p. 21).

A survey of values management, that is, the intersection between ethics and responsiveness, found that some of the greatest gaps in values management involved the best use of employee abilities (Berman & West, 1994, p. 14). These gaps still exist in the public sector. While complying with a code of ethics was also listed as an item with a gap suggesting a need for improvement, this suggests that the public sector can do a decent job of complying with a code of ethics without resolving some considerable issues, suggestive of a continuing lack of accountability to the public.

Glor (2001) offered that the shift toward New Public Management caused codes of ethics to become necessary, as public service moved away from a motivation based upon ideals of the public interest and individual responsibility, equality, and fairness. She proposes the possibility of generational differences in approach to public values, and how values of generations (mature, baby boomer, generation X, for example) may be reflected in the styles of service in the public sector. Baby boomers, for instance, do not like being told what to do; for generation X, it is suggested that "Governments cannot count on the commitment of genXs to its values — rather, government must attract genXs on the basis of meeting their needs... Generation X will give value as employees but not commitment" (Glor, 2001, p. 535). In this view, codes of conduct need to be reflective of this different relationship between employee and institution.

Adams and Balfour (2010) pointed out the danger for ethical practice in market-based government. They advised that "the short-term orientation of the new market-state has tended to undermine character, especially those qualities that bind people to each other and furnish the individual with a stable sense of self" (p. 618). In this environment, government agencies may be seen as ineffective and untrustworthy relative to private sector organizations (Adams & Balfour, 2010). The suggestion that privatization of government services holds answers to the ill-health of the public sphere ignores the lack of accountability that exists in the private sector, while short-changing the true role of government. The result has been a growing malignancy which has negatively impacted the potential for accountability and responsibility in the public sector.

It could be said that the triumph of a market-based mentality paints serving the public interest as an outmoded concept, or an unreachable goal in times of scarce resources and public hostility. Rather than countering the hostility, government plays into it further by establishing standards of ethical conduct that may not themselves assure the public of an ethical public sector. Lost in the shuffle, the spirit of public service becomes harder and harder to discern in public work, no matter how dedicated public servants are to the cause. An opportunity for ethical leadership exists but is traded for a far simpler and less effective option in codes of ethics. It is worth recognizing that "a ready willingness to abandon personal principle is at the root of many ethics violations rather than a lack of fortitude or courage, or ethics as a virtue" (Thoms, 2008, p. 422). People do not abandon their ethics because of frivolous reasons – they abandon ethics because organizational culture requires it, or because they abide by codes that may yield *compliance* with the letter of the law, but not ethical/moral behavior or the spirit of public service. The role and importance of the individual in creating and nurturing an ethical environment is lost in favor of following a set of simple rules. Since public-sector leaders may have a limited span of influence anyway (Thoms, 2008), the idea that we can do without an individual sense of ethical right is ludicrous; yet, the public service spends little time defining that sense of right, or emboldening its increase.

As a final thought in reviewing the literature, the symbolic value of programs cannot be overlooked. Murray Edelman wrote that

> it is characteristic of large numbers of people in our society that they see and think in terms of stereotypes, personalization, and oversimplifications, that they cannot recognize or tolerate ambiguous and complex situations, and that they...respond chiefly to symbols that oversimplify and distort.
>
> (1964, p. 31)

Edelman stated that he did not see administrative agencies as instruments serving the public interest (p. 56), and that the institution of administrative programs instead serves political goals. Government does not work in absolutes that provide the mass of people with comfort and certainty;

government operates in discretion and sees its legitimacy either reified or challenged through the active creation of reality through the use of symbol. The public's desires on administrative issues, and the right or wrong behavior of public officials, for example, are not so easily discerned or agreed upon as may be guessed. To borrow Edelman's terms, the dogma of symbol plays in the political sphere, and the rationale and process of administration does not. In fact, appeals to the rational are likely suspect simply because of their perceived intellectualism; if public work cannot be plain-spoken, it must have something to hide.

This review of the literature considered the changing nature of ethics in public service, from a need to serve the public interest broadly to a compliance approach centering on abidance by codes of conduct. While the environment of the public service has grown more complex, ethics training has been overly simplified and even marginalized; this may serve symbolic or political ends but does not adequately address the needs of either the public interest or public-sector employees. Having considered relevant literature on ethics programs and the place of ethics codes within government, we now turn to a discussion of the methodology for evaluating our case example.

Methods – Legal Frameworks for Public Ethics in New York City

The selection of certain qualitative tools over other potential evaluative options requires explanation. I am the sole coder of the texts in this analysis, but worth in qualitative methods does not require groups of coders or general agreement on code selection for the methodology to be valid – the nature of qualitative methodology makes no claim of universal acceptance of interpretation. Instead, the standard for excellence more commonly involves clear problem articulation; sufficient grounding in literature; processes and tools for data collection and analysis described adequately; consequential discussion of results; and overall clarity (Storberg-Walker, 2012). Following Freeman, deMarrais, Preissle, Roulston, and St. Pierre (2007) and Kuckartz (2014), replicability, data, and evidence of the analysis to support claims, trustworthiness of the analysis, and using software tools to enrich analytical sophistication is also important.

Laws and accompanying guidance provide a directive for ethics programs within the governmental enterprise, and as noted in the literature, there is a great reliance on their use in government. In exploring the language of ethical codes and discerning the worth of such approaches, it is advisable to examine law and how it is translated into counsel for the public-sector employee, evaluating where source authority and interpretive 'plain language' may differ in focus. This chapter relies upon qualitative analysis of legal documents and official guidance (Webley, 2010).

Specifically, the analysis focuses on a textual comparison of the New York City Conflicts of Interest rules (referred to as the *Blue Book*, Chapter 68 of the New York City Charter), and *Ethics: A Plain Language Guide to Chapter 68, New York City's Conflicts of Interest Law*, referred to as the *Orange Book* (as these documents existed in 2014 when the research was originally conducted. There have been subsequent revisions to the Orange Book, but the Blue Book appears to have remained the same). The rationale for the approach is that by exploring and contrasting the law and guidance documents we may find better understand the focus and intent of the rule, discern potential problems or points of success within the system, and develop an understanding of practice in ethical rulemaking that may provide useful information beyond the case evaluated here. Analysis of the Blue Book allows for an understanding of the formal, institutional view of what is deemed important as far as ethical considerations are concerned; the Orange Book shows how these official pronouncements are then translated for the rank-and-file. The differences between the documents may be telling about the considerations and priorities at various organizational levels, from political-principal to administrative-agent.

The purpose of this analysis is to create a qualitative understanding of the value of ethics rules in a particular prominent instance and to discuss any alignment of ethics rules and codes with preferred individually centered approaches to public-sector ethics. In addition, such an analysis also allows us to see why certain matters end up as part of ethics rules, why they are dealt with as they are, and how the participants within the case see the situation as they do (Schutt, 2012).

Here, I sought to shed light on a clear dilemma: What ethical aspects are emphasized by the New York City conflicts of interest program, and what does the New York City program suggest about the understanding that exists between government and the public? I desired a method that could be easily understood and applied to readily available source texts, not only for clarity and replicability of the present review but also for the potential of future research elsewhere. The techniques of grounded theory and coding are straightforwardly applied to other instances of ethical law and interpretative guidance, and further work in this area might follow similar methodological lines.

To create this understanding, I engage in a multistage cycle of coding, first with a hybrid descriptive/evaluative coding process, and then with a second-stage coding approach utilizing axial coding. Descriptive coding "summarizes in a word or short phrase...the basic topic of a passage of qualitative data" (Saldaña, 2013, p. 88), while evaluation coding assigns "judgments about the merit, worth, or significance of programs or policy" (p. 119). Axial coding in the second stage reassembles codes of the initial stage and determines which assert dominance as categories (p. 218). In effect, the method disassembles the source documents and considers the parts on their own merits, before comparing the two corpora. Saldaña (2013) points out that ultimately the criteria for analysis come from the texts/data themselves, and this is the case with the New York City documents. Use of these methods draws strength from reliance on the textual basis and evaluation of the significance of this material at an in-depth level. Regarding the case selection, the state of New York and New York City have been examined in the literature because of their size and the perception, real or not, of widespread corruption. The state has had reform-oriented ethics measures going back to the 19th century that have focused on punitive measures for transgressions of rules. These approaches have not been successful in eradicating ethical lapses, even with the longevity and diversity of such efforts, and yet they persist. Anechiarico and Jacobs have offered that efforts toward ethical ends have been damaged not only by the ethical program of public officials but by state efforts to reign in such activity (1996). In a 1992 article, the authors wrote that "the existence of...sprawling legislation casts a long shadow over the public service...although the ethics legislation is comprehensive, it is only minimally enforceable," and referred to enforcement as "quixotic" (Anechiarico & Jacobs, 1992, p. 598). Still, New York City's program has been mentioned as a model ethics program (Greenball, 2003), so the validity of approaches taken by the city government, in this case, is potentially valuable to other governments and worth discussion.

For future research, potential textual sources for comparative analysis at the legislative, regulative, and interpretive levels, are included in Table 5.1. While not exhaustive, the table shows the opportunity that exists for delineating inconsistencies that may exist between legislative intent and rulemaking or even interpretive guidance, through comparative analysis.

Results

Table 5.2 is a contrast table (Miles, Huberman, & Saldaña, 2014, p. 150) comparing analyses of the Blue Book and the Orange Book. The table focuses mostly on common elements between the two texts, with the exception of highlighting a few outliers; between the two texts, it is possible to gain insight into the primary considerations of the city's conflict of interest code and its rationale. Axial coding of the first round evaluative coding led to the assignment of four major categories: public interest goals, structural considerations, education, and vagueness. MaxQDA, a software program for qualitative data analysis, facilitated this coding and comparison of the texts. The table highlights the majority of codes for the two texts – 94.3% for the Blue Book and 88.5% for the Orange Book.

Both documents draw a direct connection between following the conflict of interest rules and outcomes for the public trust, enhanced integrity, and promotion of public confidence. Only the Blue Book makes the

Table 5.1 Potential textual sources for comparative analysis at the legislative, regulative, and interpretive levels

	Legislation	*Regulation*	*Procedures, guidance, interpretation*
Federal	Public law, US code	Code of federal regulations	Federal register notices; official questions and answers; official guidance; desktop procedures, standard operating procedures; website statements; training materials.
State	State statutes	Administrative code	Public hearing minutes; official notices and guidance, desktop procedures, other officially promulgated interpretive material as may be available; training materials.
Local	City or county ordinances	Administrative code	As above.

Source: Created by C.A., original work.

case that code compliance leads to increased efficiency; this may imply that the notion of efficiency is not the prime consideration of the street-level bureaucrat, but also risks missing the broader implications of the program and the employee's place within it, eliminating a potential incentive for active participation.

That both documents place an emphasis on prohibited behaviors and examples of what not to do, rather than providing a more deeply rooted or an individually focused ethical scheme, is consistent with the critique of Bazerman and Tenbrunsel. The Orange Book has more instances of language addressing the philosophy of the program and the rationale for its operation (13% of all codes in the Orange Book, compared with 2.1% in the Blue Book). There is thus some effort to situate the program's importance for employees but it is ultimately limited. Both documents point out many exceptions to more sweeping statements about conflicts of interest. Given the exceptions, which include matters such as a $50 threshold for a valuable gift, existing close personal friendships preceding business relationships being an acceptable pass for gift-giving, and ownership interests of less than $10,000, one may see the exceptions as not broadly defined, but rather arbitrary and seemingly particular to some specific past incident, special interest, or path dependence in committee decision.

Additionally, the Blue Book makes use of what could be termed "dummy rights," or obvious rights broadly accorded, where articulation of such

Table 5.2 Contrast table comparing document analysis of Blue Book and Orange Book

Theme/Code	Blue Book		Orange Book	
	Number of instances	Codes in document (%)	Number of instances	Codes in document (%)
Public interest goals				
Philosophy	6	2.1	17	13.0
Integrity	2	0.7	4	3.1
Promoting public confidence	1	0.4	1	0.8
Public trust	1	0.4	1	0.8
Efficiency	1	0.4	0	0.0
Structural considerations				
Named prohibitions on behavior	27	9.6	31	23.7
Exceptions to rules	22	7.8	22	16.8
'Dummy' rights	8	2.8	0	0.0
Provision of case-specific review on request	6	2.1	13	9.9
Moonlighting, must give notice	0	0.0	6	4.6
Penalties	5	1.8	1	0.8
Education				
Informing about the code/ increasing understanding	1	0.4	7	5.3
Developing educational materials	1	0.4	3	2.3
Training for new and existing employees	1	0.4	2	1.5
Each new employee received code/signs acknowledgment	1	0.4	0	0.0
Vagueness				
Use of the word 'shall'	183	64.9	0	0.0
Ethical standards may vary agency to agency	0	0.0	5	3.8
Acceptable use	0	0.0	3	2.3
Totals	266	94.3	116	88.5

Source: Created by C.A., original work, based on analysis of NYC Blue and Orange Books (ethics program).

rights for public servants seemed odd or misplaced since those rights are generally understood. Examples of this include: no prohibition for

> a public servant from accepting or receiving any benefit or facility which is provided for or made available to citizens or residents, or classes of citizens or residents, under housing or other general welfare legislation or in the exercise of the police power.

or "a public servant from obtaining a loan from any financial institution upon terms and conditions available to members of the public."

In terms of education, both texts make comment directly relating to the educational goals of the code. However, the Blue Book specifically indicates that new employees will receive a copy of the code and sign an acknowledgment that they agree to abide by it. The same document later notes that the employee failing to sign the acknowledgment does not absolve him or her from abiding by the code. The signing of the document is a symbolic form of compliance then, and potentially dredged if the employee eventually transgresses the line of ethical standards, however subjective they may be.

Strikingly, the Blue Book makes considerable use (183 instances) of the vague legal word 'shall.' The word has a variety of meanings, including "has a duty to; more broadly, is required to... This is the mandatory sense that drafters typically intend and that courts typically uphold" (Garner, 2014, p. 1585). Alternate definitions muddy the waters, though, and allow for a potentially useful lack of clarity: "Should (as often interpreted by the courts)...May...Will...[or] is entitled to" (Garner, 2014, p. 1585). The Orange Book makes no reference to the word shall, and the number of *exceptions*[1] in both texts signals that the operative definition at work here is perhaps not the strict requirement, but rather a weak *should* or *may*; in that respect, the drafting does not indicate a mandatory situation, or align with the strongest sense of the definition.[2] For the Orange Book's part, a curious vagueness exists in the five instances where the document points to circumstances where agencies may have more strict ethical standards than the code. In those instances, little explanation is provided for why the code has a less strict standard, or why certain agencies would want firmer rules.

As an example of the irregular word use, consider City Charter section 2603(b), which requires training of all employees (using 'shall'). The city's Conflicts of Interest Board Training Unit, the small group mandated to train the city's workforce, does hold training classes; in 2016, the unit held 855 classes for 32,000 people, but this was a far cry from the more than 300,000 city employees. The mandate was that all employees be trained every two years (Tcholakian, 2016). The same section requires an employee acknowledgment statement of the applicability of Chapter 68 with the more firm word 'must' and demands the same within ten days of an employee becoming a public servant. Paperwork and documentation win out over training.

Discussion

Public administration ethos suggests that those who would seek to engage in the work of the public serve expansive ideas of the public interest or good – ideas that are resistant to stable definition. The public sector finds itself inviting new blood into an environment where public employees are constantly questioned – where honest, principled work is somehow not good enough to justify the pay. Public administration as an academic pursuit teaches the value of serving the public interest, and there is great value placed on such ideals by many new public employees. Yet, the respect and admiration of public employees for the broader society are not often shared by the public itself. The complexity of public-sector work leads to inefficiency and ineffectiveness, and public employees are scorned for not doing more, even though such a mocking tone is wholly inappropriate coming from an otherwise absentee public. The New York City Blue Book, which draws prohibitions on behavior as proxy for ethical practice while barely speaking to the ideals of public service, places public service in a defensive, compliance mode. In fact, the preamble to Chapter 68 makes clear the intent: "prohibitions on the conduct of public servants are enacted to preserve the trust placed in the public servants of the city, to promote public confidence in government, to protect the integrity of government decision-making and to enhance government efficiency" (New York City Charter Chapter 68 § 2600: Preamble). This does not consider public service ethos or individual employee growth, and the approach is unsuccessful in spanning the obvious gap between the public and its government.

Codes, laws, and case studies are the tools of ethical training. It is perhaps unreasonable to believe that a sufficient grounding in administrative ethics can be had for the review of case studies, or the reading and signing of an agreement with the Blue Book. In the New York City case, training is offered only once every two years for each city employee (New York City Conflicts of Interest Board, 2014b; there has been no update to this requirement). There is little reason to believe that training compliance rates have shifted dramatically from the small proportion actually receiving training seen in 2016 (Tcholakian, 2016). It is not so presumptuous to imagine that informal culture may hold sway when compared with formal training. Laws themselves are seen as the 'low road' to assuring compliance with ethical standards, because they outline what is considered to be illegal – not how to attain any ideal of public service ethics. There is a widening gulf between not violating a law and seeking to fulfill a duty of ethical service to the public. One can remain within the boundaries of legal approaches and perhaps not ever act in a way that is purely moral.

The compliance approach speaks more to a need to show the public that violators of the public trust, criminals, and transgressors of common sense will be punished; a system has been created to investigate these cases, and that should be good enough for the public. It is not clear that the program makes the public service more moral or affects the actions of the rank and file, but perhaps that does not matter to the value of the program. Careful individual weighing of ethical standards and growth in such capacity is not necessarily the focus, though it is worth noting that the city has tried to normalize some of the discussions, through the use of a Twitter account, for example.[3]

Public-sector employees in the compliance approach are no different than any other type of employee. The fact that many public-sector positions are at-will just accentuates an implicit assumption that character in the public workforce is perhaps lacking, and so removal from employment at some point may be necessary, and a menu of punishments for prohibited activities needs to be available.

A jaded, suspicious, or even hostile public might wonder about the exceptions in the Blue Book, if the document were more widely read. Special considerations are obviously being made in the design of the law, and the surrender to the particular affects not only the universality of the rule, but the credibility of the regime. The difference between a $49 gift allowed under the rule and a $51 unacceptable *valuable gift*, leading to a violation of the rule, is $2; however, it is arguable that there is any real distinction between the two from an ethical perspective. What is more distressing is that a compliance approach based on prohibitions, exceptions, and reviews rests almost exclusively on thinking of this sort. The system threatens to become a self-fulfilling prophecy: another agency with a budget to protect, reports to file, low-hanging fruit to snatch up, and credit to take for supposedly uncovering lapses or criminality that should be fairly obvious, ethics aside. We trade public service ethos for an opportunity for public servants to turn each other in for failings real and imagined, and for citizens to further stoke the fires of their outrage.

We now turn to concluding thoughts on public-sector ethics regimes, service, and the nature of the consent in the public sector.

Concluding Thoughts

In his illumination of the categorical imperative, Michael Sandel mentions false promises in the context of lying about paying back a loan. If no one ever paid back a loan, no one would loan money. Consider for a moment the premise that everyone suffers from ethical fading now and then – everyone has lied, even if the incidence is infrequent. The ethical problem is that a promise has been made, and not kept. To use Sandel's explanation, making a false promise puts the interests of the individual above those of everyone else, and that is what makes such assurances objectionable (Sandel, 2009).

In the case of New York City's code, the attention to prohibitions is at the expense of broader ethical development of city employees – a goal difficult to distinguish in either document. There are no attempts at carefully weighing ethical questions with means-ends tests, let alone discussions of the categorical imperative or the deontological nature of public service to serve the public interest. Instead, the system roughly states: The following behaviors are to be avoided, with some exceptions; if one has questions about a specific instance, the employee should request a review from the board which looks narrowly at the specific case. Ethical capacity is like any skill worth having, in that it requires work to develop; people with a strong motivation to succeed will seek out opportunities to grow their skills and align their goals with those of their organization (Hill, 2016). Nowhere in such a response is ethical development, the higher ideals of public interest, or individual-organization alignment a focus; we are left with punishment avoidance and a minefield of exceptions.

There seems to be some evidence of symbolic value above consistency and growth of individual ethical performance beyond simply abiding by prohibitions. Use of the word *shall* in law has been criticized as imprecise; because shall does not *necessarily* mean the same thing as must or will, use of the term undermines the structural integrity of any rule, and particularly an ethics rule, because it is counter to common wisdom, not to mention dodgy.

Applying this thinking to ethical codes, governments use the vehicle of polished, symbolic, and assuring words to pacify a public that is perhaps no longer listening or prone to believe the story being told anyway. A reason that the public is not willing to hear it is because government is privileging its "needs and desires...over everybody else's" (Sandel, 2009, p. 121) in creating such codes in the first place. This is a subject debated in the literature for decades in public management, and will not be resolved here or anyplace else for that matter, but public-sector employees mostly do not do things because they are purely right or purely wrong. They do things because of the presence or absence of consequences for their actions, because of the presence of systems which ignore ethical capacity building in favor of simple compliance. The imperative is not categorical as much as it is hypothetical; even codes that include ideals resist successful application in the increasingly strained, resource-driven existence of the public sector. They are derided as intellectual exercises in a time when neither the vast majority of the public sector nor the public itself is particularly engaged. Compliance-based approaches are comparatively ignoble and play into the public's desire for punishment of wrongdoers – for *panem et circenses*. Rather than deal directly with the public's dissatisfaction with its government, or address possibly mistaken notions of what government does or does not do, and the attendant rationale, compliance-based approaches wear the veneer of accountability and transparency, and do so at a considerable cost.

Ethical codes act may act as an assurance to the public of integrity and striving for ideals in the public interest; codes lend an air of professionalism to the fields of endeavor. Public administration as a split field of theory and practice has its codes and can be proud of them. Seeking to serve ideals beyond oneself is a noble calling, but the presence or absence of a code may have little to do with the seeking an individual does. As an example, the American Society for Public Administration (ASPA) code of ethics, other than serving as a reminder to ASPA members (a unique professional group – it may be suggested *not* representative of the rank and file of the public sector at large, because they are distinguished by their membership as caring about the future of the field), has little impact on overall public-sector worth or quality.[4]

For future research, it may be worthwhile to evaluate outputs of the system through an analysis of enforcement case studies posted on the New York City website. How ethical capacity of individuals, including those not directly involved, is affected by enforcement actions under the program is of great significance. This is more important to the future of public service in the city than, for example, the fine for an instance of moonlighting.

In closing, perhaps it is articulated best as Ayee wrote, that "the promotion of ethical behavior and professionalism…[depends on] optimism, courage and fairness…codes of conduct miss the mark because they are usually directed at the wrong target – the good public servants who follow them, not the corrupt who ignore them" (1997, p. 374). The doubt felt by citizens about the nature of the public service is nothing new, but is a matter requiring our attention. It is a symptom of a more complex disease of disaffectedness and double-standards. The fault lies not with a disobedient public service that needs to be reined in, but at least in part with an understanding that corruption is no more escapable for some prone to such means in the public sector than it is in private industry. It is an individual matter. Codes of ethics will not solve this and possibly may only reinforce the questioning of an otherwise diligent, capable, and perhaps most importantly, manageable public sector, full of hard-working and loyal citizen-employees.

Notes

1 An example of a use of *shall* that is not absolute: "Each member shall serve for a term of six years" (Blue Book, Sec. 2602, c); membership is not a mandatory requirement; rather, members may or should serve for that term.

2 See also Andy Mergendahl's blog post about sloppy use of the word shall, "Thy Legal Writing Shall Not Include 'Shall'." http://lawyerist.com/thy-legal-writing-shall-not-include-shall/; and Bryan Garner's "Shall We Abandon Shall?" on the American Bar Association's ABA Journal, http://www.abajournal.com/magazine/article/shall_we_abandon_shall/. Use of the term has been increasingly avoided at the Federal level. The ambivalent use of the term does not indicate a great potential for clear understanding between sender and addressee of the message.

3 Per the Board's education page: "The Board's Twitter handle, the COIB DailyDose, has been called 'the best twitter account ever.' Stop missing out and Follow us." Puffery aside, the account is located at https://twitter.com/nyccoib and seems to be updated regularly; the account had 3,911 followers as of September 27, 2018, and 4,593 on February 1, 2019. There were 362,881 employees in the city workforce in 2015 (NYC Government, 2015). If every follower is a city employee, the percentage of coverage for the board's Twitter account is about 1%, though that does not include users that may just visit occasionally and are not followers.

4 ASPA Code of Ethics: https://www.aspanet.org/ASPA/Code-of-Ethics/ASPA/Code-of-Ethics/Code-of-Ethics.aspx. Numbering about 10,000, ASPA members represent a small percentage of all public sector employees.

References

Adams, G. B., & Balfour, D. L. (2010). Market-based government and the decline of organizational ethics. *Administration & Society, 42*(6), 615–637.

Anechiarico, F., & Jacobs, J. B. (1992). The continuing saga of municipal reform: New York City and the politics of ethics law. *Urban Affairs Review, 27*(4), 580–603.

Anechiarico, F., & Jacobs, J. B. (1996). *The pursuit of absolute integrity: How corruption control makes government ineffective.* Chicago, IL: University of Chicago.

Atkinson, M. M., & Bierling, G. (2005). Politicians, the public and political ethics: Worlds apart. *Canadian Journal of Political Science / Revue canadienne de science politique, 38*(4), 1003–1028.

Ayee, J. (1997). A code of conduct for public officials: The Ghanaian experience 1992–96. *International Review of Administrative Sciences, 63*, 369–375.

Bashir, S., Nasir, M., Qayyum, S., & Bashir, A. (2012). Dimensionality of counterproductive work behaviors in public sector organizations in Pakistan. *Public Organization Review, 12*(4), 357–366.

Bazerman, M. H., & Tenbrunsel, A. E. (2011). *Blind spots: Why we fail to do what's right and what to do about it.* Princeton, NJ: Princeton University.

Bergsten, G. S. (1985). On the role of social norms in a market economy. *Public Choice, 45*, 113–137.

Berman, E. M., & West, J. P. (1994). Values management in local government. *Review of Public Personnel Administration, 14*(1), 6–23.

Bertram, C. (2004). Routledge philosophy guidebook to Rousseau and the social contract (e-book). Retrieved from: http://www.amazon.com/gp/product/B0013PTA7K/.

Beyer, W. C. (1922). Ethics in the public service: Proposals for a public service code. *The ANNALS of the American Academy of Political and Social Science, 101*, 152–157.

Boucher, D., & Kelly, P. (1994). *The social contract from Hobbes to Rawls.* New York: Routledge.

Brady, F. N. (2003). "Publics" administration and the ethics of particularity. *Public Administration Review, 63*(5), 525–534.

Brooke, R. (2003). Ethics and the role of regulators. *Teaching Public Administration, 23*(2), 1–19.

Chen, C., & Bozeman, B. (2014). Am I a public servant or am I a pathogen? Public managers' sector comparison of worker abilities. *Public Administration, 92*(3), 549–564.

Cooper, P. J. (2009). *The war against regulation: From Jimmy Carter to George W. Bush.* Lawrence: University Press of Kansas.

Dubnick, M. J., & Justice, J. B. (2006). Accountability and the evil of administrative ethics. *Administration & Society, 38*(2), 236–267.

Edelman, M. (1964). *The symbolic uses of politics.* Urbana: University of Illinois.

Eskridge, R. D., French, P. E., & McThomas, M. (2012). The international city/county management association code of ethics. *Public Integrity, 14*(2), 127–150.

Fassin, Y., & Buelens, M. (2011). The hypocrisy-sincerity continuum in corporate communication and decision making: A model of corporate social responsibility and business ethics practices. *Management Decision, 49*(4), 586–600.

Freeman, M., deMarrais, K., Preissle, J., Roulston, K., & St. Pierre, E. A. (2007). Standards of evidence in qualitative research: An incitement to discourse. *Educational Researcher, 36*(1), 25–32.

Garner, B. A. (Editor). (2014). *Black's law dictionary*, 10th edition. St. Paul, MN: Thomson Reuters.

Glor, E. (2001). Codes of conduct and generations of public servants. *International Review of Administrative Sciences, 67*(3), 525–541.

Greenball, B. B. (2003). A brief overview of New York City's conflicts of interest board: A model government ethics law. *NYSBA/MLRC Municipal Lawyer, 17*(3), 26–27.

Hamilton, A. (1787, December 25). The same subject continued: The idea of restraining the legislative authority in regard to the common defense considered. *New York Packet*. Retrieved from http://avalon.law.yale.edu/18th_century/fed27.asp.

Hill, P. (2016). Teaching through leadership: Lifelong lessons from the podium. *School Band & Orchestra, 19*(11), 32–35.

Kant, I. (1785, 2002 Trans.). *Groundwork for the metaphysics of morals (edited and translated by Allen W. Wood)*. New Haven, CT: Yale.

Kaptein, M. (2010). The ethics of organizations: A longitudinal study of the U.S. working population. *Journal of Business Ethics, 92*(4), 601–618.

Koh, H. C., & Boo, E. H. Y. (2004). Organisational ethics and employee satisfaction and commitment. *Management Decision, 42*(5), 677–693.

Kuckartz, U. (2014). *Qualitative text analysis: A guide to methods, practice & using software*. Thousand Oaks, CA: Sage Publications.

Locke, H. G. (1995). Ethics in American government: A look backward. *The ANNALS of the American Academy of Political and Social Science, 537*, 14–24.

Maletz, D. J., & Herbel, J. (2000). Beyond idealism: Democracy and ethics reform. *The American Review of Public Administration, 30*(1), 19–45.

Meine, M. F., & Dunn, T. P. (2013). The search for ethical competency: Do ethics codes matter? *Public Integrity, 15*(2), 149–166.

Miles, M. B., Huberman, A. M., & Saldaña, J. (2014). *Qualitative data analysis: A methods sourcebook*, 3rd edition. Thousand Oaks, CA: Sage.

New York City Conflicts of Interest Board. (2010). New York City Charter, Chapter 68, §2600–07 (Blue book). Retrieved from https://web.archive.org/web/20140403012534/http://www.nyc.gov/html/conflicts/downloads/pdf2/books/blu_bk.pdf.

New York City Conflicts of Interest Board. (2014a). Ethics: A plain language guide to chapter 68, New York City's conflicts of interest law (Orange book). Retrieved from https://web.archive.org/web/20140814201232/http://www.nyc.gov/html/conflicts/downloads/pdf2/books/orange_bk.pdf.

New York City Conflicts of Interest Board. (2014b). Training. Retrieved from https://web.archive.org/web/20140219214801/http://www.nyc.gov/html/conflicts/html/units/training.shtml.

NYC Government. (2015). Workforce Profile Report. Retrieved from http://www.nyc.gov/html/dcas/downloads/pdf/misc/workforce_profile_report_fy_2015.pdf.

Park, H., & Blenkinsopp, J. (2013). The impact of ethics programmes and ethical culture on misconduct in public service organizations. *International Journal of Public Sector Management, 26*(7), 520–533.

Pelletier, K. L., & Bligh, M. C. (2006). Rebounding from corruption: Perceptions of ethics program effectiveness in a public sector organization. *Journal of Business Ethics, 67*(4), 359–374.

Perry, J. L. (2011). Federalist No. 72: What happened to the public service ideal? *Public Administration Review, 71*(s1), s143–s147.

Pesch, U. (2008). Administrators and accountability. *Public Integrity, 10*(4), 335–343.

Richardson, W. D. (1997). *Democracy, bureaucracy, and character: Founding thought.* Lawrence: University Press of Kansas.

Saldaña, J. (2013). *The coding manual for qualitative researchers*, 2nd edition. Thousand Oaks, CA: Sage.

Sandel, M. J. (2009). *Justice: What's the right thing to do?* New York: Farrar, Straus and Giroux.

Schutt, R. K. (2012). *Investigating the social world: The process and practice of research*, 7th edition. Thousand Oaks, CA: Sage Publications.

Storberg-Walker, J. (2012). Instructor's corner: Tips for publishing and reviewing qualitative studies in applied disciplines. *Human Resource Development Review, 11*(2), 254–261.

Svara, J. H. (2007). *The ethics primer for public administrators in government and non-profit organizations.* Sudbury, MA: Jones & Bartlett.

Svara, J. H. (2014). Who are the keepers of the code? Articulating and upholding ethical standards in the field of public administration. *Public Administration Review, 74*(5), 561–569.

Tamás, D. (2012). On the issue of ethics codes legitimation. *Acta Universitatis Sapientiae. Social Analysis, 2*(2), 229–235.

Tcholakian, D. (2016, February 9). Meet the team behind conflict of interest board's hilarious twitter feed. *DNAinfo.* Retrieved from https://www.dnainfo.com/new-york/20160209/civic-center/meet-team-behind-conflict-of-interest-boards-funny-twitter-feed/.

Thoms, J. C. (2008). Ethical integrity in leadership and organizational moral culture. *Leadership, 4*(4), 419–442.

von Kriegstein, H. (2016). Professionalism, agency, and market failures. *Business Ethics Quarterly, 26*(4), 445–464.

Webley, L. (2010). Qualitative approaches to empirical legal research. In P. Cane & H. Kritzer (Eds.), *The Oxford handbook of empirical legal research, 926–950.* New York: Oxford.

6 Symbol and Substance in Local Government Workforce Development
'First Source' Hiring Programs

Most representative of progressive policy movements in the 1970s–1980s, First Source (FS) hiring programs "required private-sector employers operating under public contracts or receiving public subsidies for economic development to work with publicly sponsored employment and job training programs serving disadvantaged and long-term unemployed workers" (Schrock, 2015, p. 650). From a public administration perspective, these programs, born in the New Public Administration period, err on the side of value rationality, as an efficiency perspective is not the primary focus. Instead, ideas of universal benefit and legitimacy are at the fore; participation, public interest, and social fairness are all central features, along with a belief in humankind's inherent altruism (Dong, 2015).

The FS programs are belief-based; they depend on equality of opportunity and the value of diversity as matters of considerable normative importance. 'Doing good' is typically a laudable rationale in the public sector, and FS programs are values-driven, in that they reflect the interests and belief systems of elected officials enacting the programs, and the community that lobbies for such programs.

Policy choices in the public sector have increasingly been constrained by a belief in systems and processes above the guidance of normative values of the public interest, in the name of increasing legitimacy, even though instrumental rationality may ultimately fail to serve broader societal/contextual interests (Ventriss, 2012). It would, therefore, be expected given the creation of bureaucratic structures to run such programs that an instrumental rationality would begin to inform service provision increasingly over time, given larger shifts within public administration, perhaps even supplanting the original rhetoric rooted in belief. Providing opportunity to disadvantaged workers in original rhetoric may yield to private sector firms as failing to comply with directives and thus becoming subject to penalties and other enforcement measures (Dong, 2015).

In Washington, DC, First Source began as a broad mandate, but was revisited on a number of occasions to refine expectations and more carefully delineate program operations. The program has gone from a relatively simple pronouncement of legislative intent, to a much more complex, detailed matter. Because the DC First Source program and other initiatives like it, such as the Providence, Rhode Island First Source program instituted in 1985, indicate an intent on the part of the government to pursue means and ends toward the larger public interest, evaluating the language of such programs and their impacts is worthwhile.

"Continual inquiry," as an ethical obligation, should saturate public life (Ventriss, 2012, p. 285); there is a need to analyze the programs themselves relative to the ideologies that led to their creation. A lack of substantive program impact is not only a practical matter in the public sector – it is an ethical matter. There is potential for community benefit in such programs, but ambiguity in detailing expectations and program processes might lead to underwhelming results, even though passage or existence of the program might be enough for advocate groups. This may be attributed to differences in problem definition. Further, these programs can exhibit intricate connections of public and private sector interests – from government agencies to public-sector employment partners, to the private sector itself as the engine of employment and implementation of the initiative. Programs may suffer from a general misunderstanding on the part of clients, businesses, and the public, implementation problems, and ineffective evaluation of outcomes.

As larger issues, the matters of legitimacy and accountability are important to government's role. Public perception of governmental quality may be impacted by problem definition and program announcements, if not actual program success or failure, and this affects legitimacy. A willingness to evaluate programs frankly allows at least a measure of responsibility for the public enterprise to its citizenry (Ghere, 2011). Put another way, "what is legitimate is what is authorised" (Clegg & Gordon, 2012, p. 418). An ethical government implements policies as authorized and evaluates program performance as a matter of accountability. Otherwise, it is difficult to tell whether government has a positive impact: if programs are working, and if elected officials' policies are leading to the outcomes desired by a given community.

This chapter will examine workforce development programs, specifically, First Source programs that engage in activities to spur interviewing/hiring of hard-to-hire or disadvantaged individuals on local government contracts. First Source programs from the District of Columbia and Providence, Rhode Island are compared and contrasted. The research question is: What does the language of First Source programs say about semiotics (symbol and meaning) in public policy, and what have these programs led to in outcomes for workforce development? For First Source programs, evaluation triangulates on employment outcomes compared with the intent and language of enacting legislation as sign.

It is determined that even given the great symbolic value that goes with instituting programs that seek to benefit hard-to-hire and disadvantaged individuals, the establishment of such programs requires significant attention to fundamental elements of policymaking, as well as to the complexity of cultural impacts and change within the institution and in the surrounding community. Further, the First Source program as a policy response oversimplifies a complex societal issue, while the roles and rhetoric of both elected officials and public administrators may leave us with many questions about the function of government in comparison with public expectations. The belief in the importance of the concept of helping the underprivileged may act as a serviceable cover for ineffectual policy.

Conceptual Basis: Evaluation of Symbolic Programs and Their Ill-Defined Problems

Evaluation

Ayer (1952/1946) characterized induction as a fictitious problem, "since all genuine problems are at least theoretically capable of being solved...." He goes on to write that "we are entitled to have faith in our procedure just so long as it does the work which it is designed to do – that is, enables us to predict future experience, and so to control our environment" (p. 50). With public policy, particularly the imposition of public policy frameworks from other contexts, induction can be a serious problem because solutions that worked in one place, for one group/clientele, may not necessarily work in all contexts. As an additional evaluation question, one is left to discern whether a program worked at all, and to what extent it caused certain desirable or undesirable impacts. Even when a problem it is possible to solve a problem through a certain policy, one is not entitled, to borrow the concept from Ayer, to have faith in it when it fails to do intended work or have an intended effect. It is not ethical to favor a program choice unless it contributes to the legitimacy of the public enterprise and its accountability to the public.

A considerable portion of public policy is based on belief and the values of individuals. When individuals bring their views to elected office, or to administration through civil service, personal views take on additional power to direct the creation of law, or subsequently the fashioning of administrative provisions and structures. As an example, speaking of the value of diversity in government, Mary Guy asserted that "diversity advances the quality of our democracy...makes for more sustainable decisions," and that it "does make a difference – that is *why* it is resisted" (2010, p. 176). As beliefs, one may agree on these points as a normative matter. However, many programs are developed in furtherance of diversity, and these programs may not yield expected or even desirable results. The normative belief in diversity must be made to translate into outcomes through carefully developed programs and diligent evaluation processes. If the outcomes of a program are not acceptable, the values and beliefs that led to program choices might be questioned as a matter for ethical assessment (Stout, Tower, & Alkadry, 2015).

It follows then that evaluation research has had an evidence-based focus; officials want assurance for engaging in certain policy endeavors. They look to evaluation to provide them evidence for or against government intervention through programs and services, but it is not always clear what sort of, or how much, evidence is needed. At the same time, there is a need for evaluators to be culturally competent, aware of stakeholder needs and contexts of public programs (Newcomer, Hatry, & Wholey, 2015). For lawmakers, legislative intent and the message of policy to constituents can be more important than the form of implementation and measurement of its impact (Patton, 1987).

It is at least possible that policymaking does not set out to resolve problems in some cases; even well-intended policymaking may fail because of inadequate evaluation and feedback of program results. This should not be surprising, as a lack of time and money may lead to very few decisions being made with a strong analytical basis. Policies that make little sense or result in a few favorable outcomes may yet stay part of a government's spate of program offerings (Guess & Farnham, 2011). As an ethical matter, social policy, originally deployed in the interest of democracy, maybe "conceptually separated from the broader struggle for social justice and equality" (Ventriss, 2012, p. 288), with grave ethical implications.

The tendency to focus on variables other than mandate-specific outcomes is profound. Problem definition is a complex obstacle; problems in policy are sometimes ill-defined, and policy solutions may not be tailored (Guess & Farnham, 2011). A desire to implement what is thought to be an effective program from some other locale can be emblematic of this tendency; it may be unclear how problems and solutions influence one another. The ideal-type policymaking approach of agreeing upon a problem's definition, then choosing amongst an array of possible solutions, is subverted by expedience or worse. Whether or not necessitated by the lack of time and resources, policy choices that oversimplify and ignore the inimitability of place may short-change unique publics. Even the client to be served is potentially defined by the constructs of other communities; they are made foreign in their own community, through policy colonization, when definitions of poverty, persistent unemployment, or other needs do not consider local realities. Criticism exists for heedlessly transplanting even *best practices* because of the tendency to become too passionate about an approach without an evidentiary basis (Bardach, 2009).

The ability of policies to achieve intended aims is made less likely by the tendency of political processes to construct social problems in oversimplified ways, and to then devise manners of support that are largely ineffectual. People in living their lives have precious little time for comprehensive discussions on the nature and resolution of, for example, persistent unemployment amongst underserved members of a community. Any time people give to such a discussion, absent their being directly affected by the concern, is fleeting.

Semiotics and Symbol in Policy

The existence of the symbolic in policy necessitates utilization of methods to better understand policy meaning. Because humans are aware that signs exist, they have a responsibility for them, in a general and ethical sense. This is why Eco's definition of semiotics is worth consideration: "semiotics is the study of everything that can be used to lie" (Deely, 2010, p. 87). From this, the notion extends the thought that "common people [cannot] tell the difference between truth and manipulation" (Danesi, 2010, p. 141). Closely associated with the above is the Sapir-Whorf hypothesis, which suggests that "the language one speaks influences the way one thinks" (Randviir & Cobley, 2010, p. 119).

The attempt for a human being to communicate is essentially an effort to create a system: to speak (or otherwise communicate) in a way where the intended meaning is understood, and where whatever is spoken/written/gestured stands in for what is meant. Certain words can be used in ways that suggest a greater meaning that the words themselves contain, as placeholders for larger concepts. As Eco inferred, just because the words are used does not necessarily mean that the concept being referenced even exists at all, in any appreciable form.

The rhetoric of the political is intended to instill certain beliefs that favor ruling parties while reducing or eliminating popular concerns about the sufficiency of policies. The language of a policy is code for larger concepts: of promises of social equality and opportunity, for example. One may use a word like justice, and mean the word a given way, and others may discern the code system and hear the word as it is intended. As Ghere (2015) suggested, there are thick (particular) and thin (pervasive and widely shared) views in advocacy language; those advocating positions as agents of change may seek to place the unacceptable past against the promise of a bright future, but implicit in taking such a stand is some contextual agreement about meaning and ideology. Others not aware of a particular coding may apprehend the communication differently. In public policy, it is possible that as long as the meaning is transmitted and received as intended – that policy is intended to work a certain way, to provide given benefits desired by a community – then the communication is successful and serves the political purpose. However, following Eco (1976), the thing being referenced – justice of a preferred definition – may not exist at all. Public policy is not a natural sign, like the sound of raindrops on a house's roof. People are instead dependent on a connection between an expression and content; these nonnatural signs are given their meaning by context and experience (Eco, 1976).

Grave injustice may exist in society but if softened by rhetoric in pleasing tones, the greater population may be willing to tolerate evils without such problems being fully resolved. To this end, policies may be proposed that appear to do something, popularly defined as sufficient, but fail to get at the root concern. The policies themselves, stated as law, are groups of signs that, in the minds of their authors, hopefully overcome a natural barrier of belief and legal sufficiency, that the complex system of codes solves a problem once implemented. The formalization of law is itself communication of a semiotic nature: The governmental entity has instituted this rule to serve a given purpose. For public administration, the alibi for having done enough comes from how words are used in the public discourse (Feldman, 1995). Even the people directly involved in such programs may believe that they are doing what is right and to the greater benefit of all concerned; in the absence of conflicting views or data to the contrary, the Sapir-Whorf hypothesis allows comfort and consonance (Petrilli & Ponzio, 2010).

From a semiotic perspective, referencing and code creation may not actually yield a referent; as an interpreter one is left with symbol and must decide what "condition of truth" may exist (Eco, 1976, p. 59). A given sign may be so thick with layers of meaning invested upon a policy term, that not only is there no referent to discern, but the aim in policy may be seen as purely symbolic. What is most important then is that "the sender subscribes to a given ideology, whereas the ideology itself, the object of the presupposition, is an organized world vision" (Eco, 1976, p. 289). To put this another way, "the labor of sign production releases social forces and itself represents a social force" (p. 298). Figure 6.1 illustrates conceptually the relationship between reference (sign), symbol, and referent, with

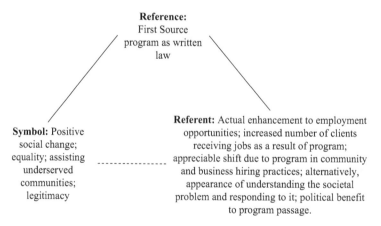

Figure 6.1 Relationship between reference, symbol, and referent in First Source programs, using Eco model (1976, p. 59).
Source: Created by C.A., based upon Eco (1976).

a dotted line indicating that symbol need not necessarily be accompanied by perceptible content, using the model proposed by Eco (1976).

Jean Baudrillard included the idea of alienation in discussion of consumption and this fleeting relationship of sign and referent; in this view, the sign exchange value is more important than the object itself. The value of a program may principally be in its existence as a product to be consumed and as a political object. The programs reviewed here even have a sort of *brand name* in that they are called *First Source* (Baudrillard, 1981); they are made law and implemented in different places but they reflect a common ideology. Levin wrote that "the arbitrary relation...permits the signified or referent to stand in, as it were, for 'meaning,' while the signifier plays" (1981, p. 19), acting as if it is some sort of guarantee of quality.

The larger concern is that consumption of the brand name item may act as a veneer for "the technical imperative of functionality...it is necessary to witness objects that are operating...the 'thing' must serve a purpose" (Baudrillard, 1981, p. 55). The brand-name program may exist more as an off-the-shelf product than manifest public will. Worse, brands can short-circuit logic and exist primarily or exclusively on emotion. "Brands are meant to create cognitive shortcuts...sometimes the idea is to have people avoid rational decision-making processes based on the brand" (Zavattaro, 2018, p. 97). Some people will buy an expensive car, using Zavattaro's example, and drive it as an outward expression of their accomplishments; however, conspicuous consumption may show insecurity or overcompensation. Branding of government policies is a step or two removed, but possibly more foolish and costly.

Edelman suggested that "government presents itself as protector against a gamut of dangers... Eagerness to believe that government will ward off evils and threats renders us susceptible to political language that both intensifies and eases anxiety..." (1977, p. 4). The poor are sometimes defined collectively as *victims* in political rhetoric, in furtherance of expansive policy; this fails because it lacks focus on personal choices that have been made or the specific assistance needs of individuals. Besides being an unfair construction of a varied, dissimilar grouping of people, defining a problem with such a broad stroke may only serve elite interests in societal stabilization. "Public policies rest on the beliefs...of those who help make them, whether or not those cognitions are accurate" (Edelman, 1977, p. 9). The problem with this is that one is meant to believe that a problem like poverty can be resolved "without drastic social change" (Edelman, 1977, p. 16). This increases *othering* of already disadvantaged groups, and does little about exclusion (Guy, 2010). Given a comforting vision of the future, a population may not only fail to resolve the factors that lead to poverty or other knotty problems, but also exacerbate such issues and become part of the maintenance of unjust, elite-favoring structures.

With accountability being the "obligation to give an account of one's actions to someone else, often balanced by responsibility of that other to seek an account" (Scott, 2006, p. 175), a government that fails to give an account may rely upon a public that likewise fails to seek it, and an ineffective or even injurious system may thus be maintained. This echoes E. L. Normanton, who wrote of the obligation for public agencies "to show that they make good and efficient use of the public contribution... this is the least that should be asked, yet in a large number of instances even this is not asked" (1966, p. 121). On the other hand, as Kamarck deliberated on this point: "Most of the time, nothing much in US government changes – even after national elections. This is good. Stability, continuity, and the rule of law are the hallmarks of modern successful government" (2013, p. 9). Predictability aside, persistence in failed policy, whether or not it assists in achieving societal stability, may speak to a fundamental misunderstanding about the public interest.

With the paper rooted in a conceptual basis of evaluation, symbolic meaning in politics, and semiotic approaches, attention is turned to the First Source programs themselves.

'First Source'

First Source programs continue to be enacted and utilized in municipalities in the United States. Their persistence as a public intervention based in the attainment of some social ideal may be reflective of broader considerations, including the recognition of barriers that may exist for some individuals in obtaining employment and a belief in the compelling interest of government to become involved to reduce or eliminate such obstacles, the use of policies that afford preference as a matter of justice, and the notion of compensatory discrimination – where government intervenes to afford specific and additional benefit to a group of people not allowed to the entire population (Nagel, 1977). The existence of FS-type programs is perhaps also evidence of "social policy innovations during periods of national conservatism" (Balducchi & Wandner, 2008, p. 112).

The existence of FS suggests a willingness to view the underlying concern as first, definable as a problem, and second, able to be addressed by government through policy. First, to the issue of FS-related concerns as problems, FS exists in a variety of forms throughout the country, from simple programs that seek to provide the first opportunity to local residents, to programs that preference disadvantaged workers over others. The matter of affording first look to local residents can be construed as a simple issue of economic development; if residents are given jobs, their employment and subsequent spending might support the local economy and help strengthen and stabilize it in a way desired by government. As suggested by Rochefort and Cobb, perception of a phenomenon as a problem might rest in reality as it is socially constructed, or through the creation of a sense of a problem through rhetoric – that the concern was triggered by some cause that can be defined; that it is severe enough to deserve our worry, in an applied way through policy; that it is proximate to our daily lives; or even that the concern constitutes a crisis demanding government intervention and attention. There may be a significant afflicted group, with powerful allies; the ready availability of a policy solution may drive rhetoric toward some desired policy outcome (1994).

Schrock refers to FS programs as part of the targeted opportunity category: "policy instruments that increase the likelihood that the benefits of publicly funded or publicly subsidized job creation activities will accrue to economically disadvantaged individuals and groups within the labor market" (2015, p. 652). In speaking of the compelling interest of government to respond proactively to such barriers, governments might enact a targeted opportunity program like FS based on demonstrable evidence of inability of certain segments of the labor force to achieve fair consideration for available job opportunities in a municipality. The program would at least initially *prefer* the group thought to be unfairly excluded, for employment consideration.

Depending on how formed, a targeted opportunity program may assume that the business community on publicly funded contracts has not already taken the appropriate and requisite steps to afford all interested employee candidates a fair opportunity for consideration. This framing of the problem may set government at odds with the business community it is depending upon to achieve a public benefit, in implementing FS. The underlying thought process behind the program may be indicative of a fundamental attribution bias – that the normal machinations of hiring in business are unjust, due to the disposition of 'business' and those hiring, and therefore business interests must be called to account, through prioritization of (assumedly) excluded groups in corporate recruiting. This approach also minimizes the need to speak directly to the circumstances of particularly affected groups – the unemployed, for example, or ex-convicts – when doing so may be politically unpalatable.

Like programs to alleviate disparity in award of contracts in public procurement or that require firms pay a 'living wage' to employees on public contracts, FS programs can represent a government's interest in achievement of a public purpose through private contracting means. As opposed to active efforts on the part of government to hire disadvantaged workers directly, FS programs may offer a useful, largely passive alternative for governments, whereby a stated public interest (*leveling of the playing field,* placement of hard-to-hire workers in jobs as a result of government intervention and requirement for referral and consideration of candidates) becomes the implementation responsibility of the private sector, as a result of taking a government contract. This additional requirement may impact the bottom line of business – adding to their burden in terms of staff costs for working the contract, and depending on the program structure.

Speaking of justice, FS programs possibly raise the question of desert, and what just distribution might entail for job opportunities on public contracts. This brings to mind the Rawls difference principle. People may have a tendency to reject preferential hiring as a principle, but government, in seeing a clear instance where otherwise equally qualified individuals are being treated differently for some reason – may wish to intervene to effect change. The countering argument to government intervention is personal responsibility and potential for growth and self-actualization (Holton III & Wilson, 2002).

As a separate matter, ex-offenders present unique circumstances and context for government intervention through policy, in the form of prisoner reentry programs. Programs that seek to assist ex-offenders may paint all such persons with a broad brush, when individual characteristics (like drug addiction or mental health concerns) may present challenges for success (McNichols, 2012). Even when there is a general agreement in the population that reentry programs are important and that training, treatment, and various types of support are essential for such programs to work, paying more in taxes to support such programs, supporting people with multiple offenses, or favoring an ex-offender over a non-offender are all less supported. There are clearly limits on public goodwill and willingness to help is balanced with other values, not least of which is a belief in hard work and retribution for past wrongs (Garland, Wodahl, & Schuhmann, 2013). However, because reentry and recidivism is ultimately society's problem, awareness of and attention to the needs of ex-offenders may foster positive states of mind and ownership of a future without crime. This thinking is more representative of the restorative justice movement, which means to address the stigma of ex-offenders, address homelessness and other disadvantages, and work toward a reintegrative identity transformation (Hass & Saxon, 2012).

There remains the idea of compensatory discrimination. The outcomes afforded by an FS program may place, through preference, a candidate who meets eligibility criteria for the program ahead of a candidate who has no need for such a benefit, because the non-preferred candidate has not been convicted of crime, or has maintained steady employment and is presently employed elsewhere, and might otherwise, all things being equal, apply, be interviewed, and offered a position.

Evaluation of First Source Programs

A standard evaluation question of program effectiveness is whether the program has succeeded in positively affecting the intended population, in a manner that would not have occurred absent the policy intervention.

Given such criteria, it would be essential to include in the analysis of any larger society-wide processes that might also contribute to the noted effect, so that the true impact of the policy itself may be discerned. For FS, policy selection is perhaps not well informed by widespread agreement and understanding of unemployment and its causes.

It is often thought that unemployment is cyclical, and duration of unemployment and differing reasons for unemployment (quitting, layoffs, etc.) are important variables to consider (Campolieti, 2011). Shimer (2012) disagreed with conventional wisdom on the subject and wrote that the probability of finding a job explains most of the unemployment cycle, rather than 'job destruction' or cyclical explanations. Beyond this, Schumpeter's work suggests an understanding of normal levels of unemployment, or system-wide adaptations due to new technologies (Boianovsky & Trautwein, 2010). Mouhammed (2011) emphasized the importance of providing accurate data about the market for jobs, the value of spending for education, and the importance of training centers in assisting the unemployed. Job-seeker personality may also be an issue related to employment outcomes (Uysal & Pohlmeier, 2011).

In program evaluation, discernment of original legislative intent is essential to measuring whether or not a given program is achieving what have been found to be worthwhile societal benefits. In terms of measuring the impacts of FS-type programs, it would be reasonable to assume that success of the program is dictated by the connection of qualified candidates to available jobs on government-funded contracts. FS programs, such as those studied here in Washington, D.C. and Providence, Rhode Island, and others elsewhere (Miami, Florida; Chicago, Illinois) are constructed to benefit individuals of a given locality, and in showing geographic preference, may run afoul of state or Federal-level rules, such as 2 CFR §200.319(b), which disallows geographical limitations when nonlocal monies are used for contracting.

The evaluation of FS candidates may become a pro forma maneuver, where those knowledgeable about the nature of the program, and the lack of penalty for failing to create positive outcomes in terms of hiring, do only what is required by rule. In such instances, there may not be a meeting of the spirit of the law, but efforts might well meet the letter of the law. Even as governments wish to send a positive message through programs that level the playing field, they may nevertheless be shy about intervening too deeply in the affairs of the private sector, given potential liability for hiring decisions and the close connection that the elected officials may have with major business interests in communities.

Beyond fundamental evaluation questions that face program designers, there are implementation questions. As with grantees facing with evaluation requirements, implementing staff may see an evaluation of programs as onerous (Sobelson & Young, 2013). Evaluations take time away from regular work, may lead to organizational instability, and the resultant reports are sometimes perceived as hostile or dismissive of staff efforts in the implementation of programs. Responsible agencies may not fully implement programs, if implementation exists at all. It may be disingenuous to depend solely on the altruism of the private sector to support FS and similar social policies.

Methodology

This work focuses on two FS programs as units of analysis. Washington, D.C.'s program was chosen because it is a critical case – the city could be seen as having a difficult operating environment in that there is a great need (Patton, 1987). The city has a complex relationship with the Federal government; Federal oversight at once informs District government and counters it. Arguably, what happens in the District is relevant for other programs and the use of this policy design. The Providence, Rhode Island program was chosen because it represents an extreme or deviant case; consideration of this case may lead to learning relevant to policies like this elsewhere (Patton, 1987).

Because these programs are ostensibly in place to positively impact trends in unemployment, unemployment statistics since the programs were founded must be examined, looking for variations that are unusual and that may be attributed to the impact of programs when compared with general unemployment trends nationally. Such indicators are tentative because of the existence of "considerable misclassifications from unemployed to not-in-labor-force and from unemployed to employed... [and assuming that] the official US unemployment rate significantly underestimates the true level of unemployment..." (Feng & Hu, 2013, p. 1069).

Given the complexities involved in program evaluation, it is not reasonable to assume that, even given unusual outcomes in local unemployment, quantitative data analysis would provide a full accounting of variation that would allow for a demonstration of effect. There are simply too many other variables that may also be impacting unemployment levels to attribute the change to one program. Changes attributable to programs may be minuscule relative to societal shifts, changes in industrial needs, and preparation of workforce. In order to better understand original intent and how what has occurred with programs either has or has not aligned well with legislative intent, qualitative analysis of legislation and, where they exist, documents taking note of program performance over time, provide an additional point of reference that may suggest something to us about program outcomes, serving as triangulation (Martinson & O'Brien, 2015). Common themes across programs, alignment with larger trends, or inconsistencies requiring further evaluation may exist. As this is an exploratory and even formative look at these programs, the intent is to provide a basis for further evaluation, rather than a summative review of programs or outcomes.

To this end, textual analysis of legislation is utilized. The method employed involves two cycles of coding: the first being a combination of descriptive coding and in vivo coding, and the second being a cycle of elaborative coding. Descriptive coding involves summarization "in a word or short phrase...the basic topic of a passage of qualitative data" (Saldaña, 2013, p. 88). In vivo coding refers "to a word or short phrase from the actual language found in the qualitative data record" (Saldaña, 2013, p. 91). Elaborative coding is "the process of analyzing textual data in order to develop theory further" (Auerbach & Silverstein, quoted in Saldaña, 2013, p. 229); here the method is to evaluate programs consistent with the understanding of intended outcomes and theoretical basis in semiotics.

Results and Discussion

Evaluating Shifts in Employment (1984–2015)

Figure 6.2 considers changes in the unemployment rate over time. It is clear that differences in employment shifts in the two cases are unlike one another, even though both communities have FS programs. While DC has shown increasing levels in employment since about 2003, adding about 100,000 workers between 1996 and 2014, with a dip between 1996 and 1999, Providence showed a gradual rise from about 1995 to 2008, with a dip of about 75,000 post 2008 (Bureau of Labor Statistics, 2015).

The United States does not have a national FS program, so local variations on some level could be attributed to the presence or absence of this

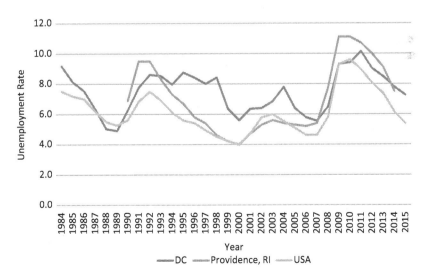

Figure 6.2 Comparison of unemployment rates, District of Columbia, Providence, RI, and USA.

Source: Created by C.A., Data from Bureau of Labor Statistics (2015).

factor, to the extent that a difference is significant. Absent more involved and direct research methods, this analysis is limited to using a t-test, to determine whether means are statistically different. If one conducts a two-tailed t-test on the unemployment rates, comparing yearly averages for the USA and District of Columbia, one finds a t-value of 3.686654 and a p-value of 0.00048. The result is significant at $p < 0.05$. The t-test for the USA and Providence, Rhode Island, for years 1990 to 2014 results in a t-value of 1.671824 and a p-value of 0.101067; the result is *not significant* at $p < 0.05$. The DC unemployment levels are clearly dissimilar from the national averages, with unemployment staying high in the period from 1992 to 1998, while the Providence, Rhode Island levels more closely approximate the unemployment cycles experienced by the country as a whole.

Ultimately, the above does not suggest the impact of FS with any clarity. Our exploratory analysis thus moves to the evaluation of language in legislation, and how these mandates have shifted over time.

The DC First Source Program

Table 6.1 outlines the major laws and themes of the District of Columbia First Source Program. Of interest is the initial version of the law in 1984, which seemed to depend heavily on altruism since it did not include any enforcement provisions. It also seems tied to the New Public Administration mindset which informed original First Source programs (Dong, 2015). In effect, this is a brand item, so it is not necessarily in-step with then-current moves toward greater instrumental rationality. This is an ideology-based program.

The Way to Work Amendment Act of 2006 seems to indicate a move toward Democratic Administration. There is a focus on public administrators as *balancers* of various interests in policy. Some additions were likely political decisions, but the program as a whole was still heavily focused on social equity (Dong, 2015). The creation of the Living Wage program in this act is representative of a balancing effort – the program appears to define away young people working part-time as not needing such protection; this may be because the imposition of such a program would reduce employment opportunities for young people (total extant opportunities, no matter the wage), and on balance decision-makers felt this could not be defended.

The Workforce Intermediary Establishment and Reform of First Source Amendment Act of 2011 continues the shift toward instrumental rationality. This was enacted after a program evaluation that found a variety of faults with the program, and focuses more heavily on accountability and enforcement, but not without maintaining a strong equity consideration. This program still seems to have as a root an idea of serving the public – and so is representative of a New Public Service orientation (Dong, 2015).

Table 6.1 Major laws and themes of the District of Columbia First Source Program

Name of law	Provisions (first cycle)	Elaboration (second cycle)
District of Columbia First Source Program		
First Source Employment Agreement Act of 1984 (DC Law 5-93)	Creates First Source program for DC; applies to entry-level jobs on 'government-assisted projects'; applies to 'unemployed District residents.' Direction for Mayor to compile First Source Register and contact community organizations for names of unemployed residents. No stated means of enforcement.	Values; Change; Government projects present opportunity for social change; implies strong client focus; 'public interest.' Altruism.
To amend the First Source Employment Agreement Act of 1984 to include leasing agreements (DC Law 5-175).	Amends act to include leasing agreements of real property for one year or more.	Change, refocusing rule to account for additional opportunity to support public interest. Still NPA.
First Source Employment Agreement Act of 1984 Amendment Act of 1992 (DC Law 9-210)	"a contract...which involves any District of Columbia funds..." as well as inclusion of targeted jobs: "All Jobs" means any managerial, nonmanagerial...[lengthy list]...and any other occupations as the Department of Employment Services may identify in the Dictionary of Occupational Titles, United States Department of Labor." No longer a focus on entry-level jobs. Includes projects funded in whole or part by DC, including funds administered by DC. Includes a requirement for "number of...residents actually employed in government-assisted projects"	Takes an expansive view of the participation of District on projects. Everything is included, even when DC part is potentially miniscule relative to other funding sources. Actual employment numbers tends toward greater accountability.
Way to Work Amendment Act of 2006 (DC Law 16-118)	Creates a "Job Opportunity Bank to increase job opportunities for low income, skills-deficient District residents" with many groups defined as served under the program; creates living wage requirement, excluding utilities, emergencies, where additional training is being provided, or where the person is less than 22 years of age working less than 25 hours/week. Provides for waiver by Mayor. "The Mayor may enter into agreements...for increased hiring in specific job categories. Displaced security workers protected, except for those that work for Board of Education or at private schools.	Program now includes ex-offenders and veterans. Eligibility. Mayoral discretion. Possibly moving toward Democratic Administration.

(Continued)

Name of law	Provisions (first cycle)	Elaboration (second cycle)
Technical Amendments Act of 2008 (DC Law 17-353)	Changes language for First Source from "this title" to "this act." (This is part of an omnibus clean-up of code)	Legal terminology.
Workforce Intermediary Establishment and Reform of First Source Amendment Act of 2011 (DC Law 19-84)	Language changed to "government-assisted project or contract", meaning "any construction or non-construction project or contract receiving funds or resources from the District of Columbia, funds or resources which, in accordance with a federal grant or otherwise, the District of Columbia government administers, including contracts, grants , loans, tax abatements or exemptions, land transfers, land disposition and development agreements, tax increment financing, or any combination thereof, that is valued at $300,000 or more"; beneficiary changed to recipient; value of subsidy increased to $300,000 for program to apply; Real estate requirement changed to: "5 years following the commencement of the tenant's initial lease date of the real estate"; Hard-to-employ "means a District resident who is confirmed by a District of Columbia government agency as… an ex-offender who has been released from prison within the last 10 years…a participant of [TANF or SNAP]…with a permanent disability…unemployed for 6 months or more in the last 12-month period; homeless…a participant or graduate of the Transitional Employment Program…[or] an individual qualified for inclusion in Work Opportunity Tax Credit Program."; 7 days' notice for program required; between 300,000 and $5 million contract, "at least 51% of the new employees hired to work on the project or contract shall be District residents." Double program credit for hard-to-hire but only for 15% of total hours worked. "potential community outreach partnerships with universities and job training partners; allows for 'good-faith effort to comply"; failure to comply leads to "imposition of a monetary fine of 5% of the total amount of the direct and indirect labor costs of the project or contract, in addition to other penalties provided by law,' or other penalties including debarment up to five years. Requires modernization of recordkeeping.	Instrumental rationality in evidence; more focus on definitions; enforcement provisions and remedies; accountability/transparency through reporting; broad/inclusive eligibility for program, expands notion of public interest and client base of program; more heavily representative of public, private, and nonprofits; detailed definitions reduce discretion (New Public Service).

Source: Created by C.A., original work.

Providence, Rhode Island First Source

The original program was enacted in 1985, but Providence "only began to implement the Ordinance in 2005 when the City Council first allocated money and passed amendments to strengthen the ordinance" (First Source Commission, 2011, p. 1). The city was then sued in 2006 for what local groups felt were inadequate measures to implement the program, through the 2005 update. The lawsuit led to the program finally having a full-time staff member for implementation. It was not until 2012, after the issuance of the "First Source Commission Report," that this program had a director. The evaluation further suggests making hiring the focus of the renewed program, and to make training a secondary matter (First Source Commission, 2011) (Table 6.2).

New Public Administration thinking exists in the original program language, but in an applied way this is akin to privatization, "engaging the private sector to assist the government and cover the shortage areas of the government in the delivery of public services in order to deliver [them]...more effectively" (Dong, 2015, p. 104). This does not constitute a direct government service but is rather a private sector hiring to solve community problems in a way that serves a definition of public interest.

While the program has two major shifts after its institution, the enactment of the original program essentially went nowhere because of the lack of implementation. The program then existed *only* as a symbolic gesture, a reference without a referent, if it had any effect at all. It appears, given the closeness of the unemployment experience of Providence compared with the nation as a whole, the program was most characteristic in its absence. The 2012 act is a protest of legitimacy for instituting the First Source program as much as it serves as operating direction for the program. To Baudrillard's argument about brand naming and the triumph of the sign over the referent, the program now has a modified name: "First Source Providence | Hire Providence." There are nominal shifts in program language that compare to DC's program changes, but the Providence program, despite the 27 years that past between first enactment and an update with some level of legitimacy, had no real implementation or effect. To this point, the Mayor of Providence was sued in 2014 for failure to enforce the program (Beale, 2014; McGowan, 2014). While the program is still nascent in many respects, reports posted on the website for this program are limited and do not suggest a great deal of activity, even with these changes (City of Providence Economic Development, 2015).

While additional research would be necessary, it does not appear that the First Source program in Providence is impacting overall unemployment in any significant way. The DC unemployment rate is different from national averages, but this may be because of a variety of factors that are associated with the community's unique experience; the program in DC

Table 6.2 Outlines the major laws and themes of the Providence, Rhode Island First Source Program

Name of law	Provisions (first cycle)	Elaboration (second cycle)
Providence, Rhode Island First Source Program		
Establishing a First-Source List (1985, Ch. 85-62)	Establishes 'first-source list…an approach that will put people to work with a minimum of government involvement…a means to encourage the retention of working, homeowning families, who will live and work in Providence…effective tool to persuade employers to come to Providence with the assurance that a trained and motivated work force will be in place to fill their requirements"; applies to recipients of city business in-cash or in-kind & projects funded whole or in part by city funds. Applies to non-supervisory positions. Agency refers "trained and qualified employees…until the employer has filled" jobs. List contains 'any bona-fide Providence resident seeking employment who wishes to register"; agency responsible for recruitment and training, establish training and referral programs. Agency 'shall place proportional share of women, minorities and handicapped persons in all job and training opportunities…goals will be 50% women, 25% minorities and 5% handicapped. Funding: "no less than 250,000 for recruitment, training, referral and maintenance of…list." Allows for enforcement: "Sanctions shall include…termination of aid or funding, termination of contract, [and] recovery of any benefits which accrued to the business during the period of violation." List establishment required within three months.	Values; positive spin on program as public-centered; role of program as a tool to attract business to Providence; some definitional outline. A start to instrumental rationality in enacting language.

Establishing a first source list, as amended (No. 288, Chapter 2005-44)	Adds compliance with Federal EEO policy on nondiscrimination for those with prison records. "Convictions should only be considered by the employer to the extent that they related to... suitability for employment." Employer required to given written notice to city implementing agency. Requirement for "at least one full-time employee... assigned to work exclusively on implementing, and ensuring compliance with, the First Source Agreement." Goals of program changed to 50% minorities, other aspects of goal left the same.	Changing idea of public interest to include those with prison records; effort to understand/serve clients; social equity. Expanding eligibility, equity.
First-Source Agreements (2012, Ch. 2012-27), Article 3 1/2.	"It is the intention of the city council to preserve the health, safety and welfare of the citizens of Providence and their property by ensuring that all significant public investments of taxpayer dollars require that employers utilize the Providence First Source List for jobs created as a result of the public investment"; "unemployment and underemployment remain serious and important problems"; city faces deficit and hardship because of foreclosure crisis; high unemployment impacts ability for citizens to pay rents/mortgage; city cannot raise fund for public works or social programs; property crime has increased; result: all of this will continue unless citizens are given opportunities on city-funded/enabled projects. Program applies to any form of aid over $25,000 in one year; doesn't apply to firms of 4 employees or less; includes all subcontractors, tenants, and sublessees; city to audit relevant records; creation of the position of director of program; more detailed process of review of efforts and exemption from program; definition of acceptable training programs; Requirement for record-keeping and reporting.	Values; government as defender; policy failure; inclusion of instrumental rationality; accountability/transparency through reports; enforcement provisions; restating of remedies with additions.

Source: Created by C.A., original work.

is more robust and has the virtue of effort to implement the initiative. More analysis would be necessary to find out what portion, if any, of the overall difference is attributable to the FS program.

The enactment and failed implementation of FS in Providence could be a strong example of blame avoidance, a concept taken up by Howlett (2012). FS was possibly seen to be successful elsewhere or at least a reasonable answer for the problems facing Providence at the time of passage in 1985. This would constitute an "attempt to construct policies so that decision-makers may, if not always claim credit for policy successes, then, at least, avoid blame for their failure" (p. 541). In Providence, due to litigation and community activism, the city was called to more make more substantive efforts to implement the program.

First Source in Providence has continued to be a target of criticism. A 2018 review of reporting for tax breaks in the city, which require "developers to comply with the city's First Source ordinance and have an apprenticeship agreement in place with local laborers," suggests that monitoring and communication in the program are still concerns (McGowan, 2018). The setting of formal criteria, again, does not equal attainment of an outcome; monitoring and enforcement are required. If tax breaks can be given late in a process, after decisions are made and opportunities to encourage employment are gone, the result is not incentivization, but corporate pay-offs masquerading as help to disadvantaged groups.

Conclusion: First Source as Symbol and Questions of Intent in Public Policy

While FS does at least in stated intent focus on increasing probability of finding a job in a locale, an employment focus highlighted as positive by Shimer (2012), outcomes are nonetheless limited. This may be because of business sector noncompliance with FS rules, failure to implement the programs in line with legislative intent, or a relatively small impact of government contracting relative to all employment-production in an area.

FS programs also assume much about the existence of labor markets and relationships between businesses and potential new hires. Implicit in the approach of FS is a mandate upon the private sector, to resolve a perceived societal problem through publicly funded or publicly enabled projects; these programs might say more about the policy context of their founding, than about sensible market-based responses to employment needs. The worry with this approach is that the accompanying bureaucratic structure can be dizzying to both government and industry, such programs lead to minimal or underwhelming outcomes, and, being based on a misunderstanding between business and government, potential relationship-building between industry, government, and the target client population is limited. The work of government falling under the authority of these programs is most probably a relatively small portion of all work in an economy; even in full compliance and implementation, the solution to society-wide problems through government-required action alone would be a small part of the change necessary to solve the larger problem. Government cannot dictate social responsibility to the market when the market has no interest, and it is possible that where government lacks capacity to positively influence business, programs founded to achieve social ends will work less well.

The ethical implications of FS for accountability and legitimacy in government deserve attention. It is possible for officials to become so focused on a well-intended, though flawed, conception of the public interest that policy implementation may become destructive, yielding moral inversion, and leading to even greater problems than what might have existed had nothing been done at all (Ventriss, 2012). Programs based upon beliefs that do not lead to intended outcomes deserve to be challenged as an ethical matter (Stout, Tower, & Alkadry, 2015).

Horkheimer and Adorno wrote that "clever people have always made things easy for barbarians" (2002, p. 173). FS wears sheep's clothes and suggests it acts in the best interests of all concerned. However, in reducing people to arbitrary definitions and prescribing mechanisms that ignore the real problem – a problem of inequality that can only be resolved through societal change – the system in place to protect the public interest may ultimately harm the most vulnerable among us. In effect, such a system might argue that

> there is no difference between a person and that person's economic fate. No one is anything other than his wealth, his income, his job, his prospects... All are worth as much as they earn, and earn as much as they are worth.
>
> (Horkheimer & Adorno, 2002, p. 175)

Categories mask themselves as knowledge of the problem; government might espouse potential and possibility for stability's sake. What is worse, law and process might stand between the people and their government, with instrumental rationality serving as a largely unchallenged substitute for legitimacy, "without the need to engage with social or ethical concerns" (Preston-Shoot, 2011, p. 187). The saving grace of these programs is in related structures focusing on training and attention to individual needs – aspects that bring government to the level of the individual.

Because such programs may take the sign for its notional value as a public good, rather than paying adequate attention to program outcomes over a lengthy period of time, a low -quality referent may result in the program itself. Worse, this may not be a noticeable until attention to the issue is forced and tough questions asked – through the economic crisis, increases in crime, or foreclosures leaving cities as barren wastelands. In these cases, symbols and good intentions, when people are out of work and hurting, are simply not enough.

References

Ayer, A. J. (1952, orig. 1946). *Language, truth and logic.* New York: Dover.

Balducchi, D. E., & Wandner, S. A. (2008). Work sharing policy: Power sharing and stalemate in American federalism. *Publius, 38*(1), 111–136.

Bardach, E. (2009). *A practical guide for policy analysis: The eightfold path to more effective problem solving,* 3rd edition. Washington, DC: CQ.

Baudrillard, J. (1981). *For a critique of the political economy of the sign.* St. Louis, MO: Telos.

Beale, S. (2014, July 10). Investigation: Companies taking millions in tax breaks, loans stiffing city for jobs. *GoLocalProv News.* Retrieved from http://tinyurl.com/q6ech52.

Boianovsky, M., & Trautwein, H. (2010). Schumpeter on unemployment. *Journal of Evolutionary Economics, 20,* 233–263.

Bureau of Labor Statistics. (2015). Economy at a glance. Retrieved from http://www.bls.gov/eag/home.htm.

Campolieti, M. (2011). The ins and outs of unemployment in Canada, 1976–2008. *The Canadian Journal of Economics/Revue canadienne d'Economique, 44*(4), 1331–1349.

City of Providence Economic Development. (2015). First source | Hire Providence. Retrieved from https://www.providenceri.com/economic-development/first-source.

Clegg, S. R., & Gordon, R. D. (2012). Accounting for ethics in action: Problems with localised constructions of legitimacy. *Financial Accountability & Management, 28*(4), 417–436.

Danesi, M. (2010). Semiotics of media and culture. In P. Cobley (Ed.), *The Routledge companion to semiotics, 135–149.* Abingdon, Oxon: Routledge.

Deely, J. (2010). Realism and epistemology. In P. Cobley (Ed.), *The Routledge companion to semiotics, 74–88.* Abingdon, Oxon: Routledge.

Dong, L. (2015). *Public administration theories: Instrumental and value rationalities.* New York: Palgrave Macmillan.

Eco, U. (1976). *A theory of semiotics.* Bloomington: Indiana University Press.

Edelman, J. M. (1977). *Political language: Words that succeed and policies that fail.* New York: Academic Press.

Feldman, M. S. (1995). *Strategies for interpreting qualitative data.* Thousand Oaks, CA: Sage.

Feng, S., & Hu, Y. (2013). Misclassification errors and the underestimation of the US unemployment rate. *American Economic Review, 103*(2), 1054–1070.

First Source Commission (Providence). (2011). First source commission report. Retrieved from https://www.providenceri.com/efile/2855.

Garland, B., Wodahl, E., & Schuhmann, R. (2013). Value conflict and public opinion toward prisoner reentry initiatives. *Criminal Justice Policy Review, 24*(1), 27–48.

Ghere, R. K. (2011). Network legitimacy and accountability in a developmental perspective. *Public Integrity, 13*(2), 163–180.

Ghere, R. K. (2015). *Rhetoric in human rights advocacy: A study of exemplars.* Lanham, MD: Lexington Books.

Guess, G. M., & Farnham, P. G. (2011). *Cases in public policy,* 3rd edition. Washington, DC: Georgetown.

Guy, M. E. (2010). When diversity makes a difference. *Public Integrity, 12*(2), 173–183.

Hass, A. Y., & Saxon, C. E. (2012). From the inside/out: Greene county jail inmates on restorative reentry. *International Journal of Offender Therapy and Comparative Criminology, 56*(7), 1037–1062.

Holton, E. F. III, & Wilson, L. (2002). Delivering workforce development programs and services. *Advances in Developing Human Resources, 4*(2), 167–179.

Horkheimer, M., & Adorno, T. W. (2002). *Dialectic of enlightenment: Philosophical fragments.* Noerr, G. S. (Ed.) & Jephcott, E. (Trans.). Stanford, CA: Stanford.

Howlett, M. (2012). The lessons of failure: Learning and blame avoidance in public policy-making. *International Political Science Review, 33*(5), 539–555.

Kamarck, E. C. (2013). *How change happens – or doesn't: The politics of US public policy.* Boulder, CO: Lynne Rienner.

Martinson, K., & O'Brien, C. (2015). Conducting case studies. In K. E. Newcomer, H. P. Hatry, & J. S. Wholey (Eds.), *Handbook of practical program evaluation, 4th edition, 177–196.* Hoboken, NJ: Wiley.

McGowan, D. (2014, July 15). Mayor Taveras sued over Providence hiring law. *WPRI.* Retrieved from http://tinyurl.com/o5qddrd.

McGowan, D. (2018, January 9). Report: Providence tax deals lack compliance, transparency. *WPRI.* Retrieved from https://www.wpri.com/news/dan-mcgowan/report-providence-tax-deals-lack-compliance-transparency/1082542097.

McNichols, K. B. (2012). Reentry initiatives: A study of the federal workforce development program. *Federal Probation, 76*(3), 37–42.

Mouhammed, A. H. (2011). Important theories of unemployment and public policies. *Journal of Applied Business and Economics, 12*(5), 100–110.

Nagel, T. (1977). Equal treatment and compensatory discrimination. In M. Cohen, T. Nagel, & T. Scanlon (Eds.), *Equality and preferential treatment, 3–17.* Princeton, NJ: Princeton University Press.

Newcomer, K. E., Hatry, H. P., & Wholey, J. S. (2015). Planning and designing useful evaluations. In K. E. Newcomer, H. P. Hatry, & J. S. Wholey (Eds.), *Handbook of practical program evaluation, 4th edition, 7–35.* Hoboken, NJ: Wiley.

Normanton, E. L. (1966). *The accountability and audit of governments: A comparative study.* Manchester: Manchester University Press.

Patton, M. Q. (1987). *How to use qualitative methods in evaluation.* Newbury Park, CA: Sage.

Petrilli, S., & Ponzio, A. (2010). Semioethics. In P. Cobley (Ed.), *The Routledge companion to semiotics, 150–162.* Abingdon, Oxon: Routledge.

Preston-Shoot, M. (2011). On administrative evil-doing within social work policy and services: Law, ethics and practice. *European Journal of Social Work, 14*(2), 177–194.

Randviir, A., & Cobley, P. (2010). Sociosemiotics. In P. Cobley (Ed.), *The Routledge companion to semiotics, 118–134.* Abingdon, Oxon: Routledge.

Rochefort, D. A., & Cobb, R. W. (1994). Problem definition: An emerging perspective. In D. A. Rochefort & R. W. Cobb (Eds.), *The politics of problem definition: Shaping the policy agenda, 1–31.* Lawrence: University Press of Kansas.

Saldaña, J. (2013). *The coding manual for qualitative researchers,* 2nd edition. Thousand Oaks, CA: Sage.

Schrock, G. (2015). Remains of the progressive city? First source hiring in Portland and Chicago. *Urban Affairs Review, 51*(5), 649–675.

Scott, C. (2006). Spontaneous accountability. In M. W. Dowdle (Ed.), *Public accountability: Designs, dilemmas, and experiences, 174–194.* Cambridge: Cambridge University Press.

Shimer, R. (2012). Reassessing the ins and outs of unemployment. *Review of Economic Dynamics, 15*, 127–148.

Sobelson, R. K., & Young, A. C. (2013). Evaluation of a federally funded workforce development program: The centers for public health preparedness. *Evaluation and Program Planning, 37*, 50–57.

Stout, M., Tower, L. E., & Alkadry, M. G. (2015). Reframing workplace spirituality to reduce career and social costs to women. *Public Integrity, 17*(2), 143–164.

Uysal, S. D., & Pohlmeier, W. (2011). Unemployment duration and personality. *Journal of Economic Psychology, 32*, 980–992.

Ventriss, C. (2012). Democratic citizenship and public ethics: The importance of civic stewardship in an era of public distrust and cynicism. *Public Integrity, 14*(3), 283–297.

Zavattaro, S. M. (2018). What's in a symbol?: Big questions for place branding in public administration. *Public Administration Quarterly, 42*(1), 90–119.

7 By Soil, Blood, and Administration

A Narrative Analysis of German Immigration Law

Assimilation has been a public policy concern as long as émigrés have set their sights on new lands. Citizenship itself is a concept that is increasingly fraught with murkiness; it cannot be assumed to be automatic or irrevocable. Further, citizens must make sense of a new environment that may be increasingly different to them, possibly leading to destabilization of self and the larger society. "What we do and think changes our environment. A changed environment changes us. We are co-dependent" (McIntyre-Mills, de Vries, Christakis, & Bausch, 2008, p. 315). While assimilation is not new, immigration policy has become a primary issue of concern for many governments in recent years. The plight of migrants and the adjustments made by host countries are frequently discussed in the news media; sometimes images associated with the circumstances of migrants are burned into our collective memory, as they were with photos of Alan Kurdi, a three-year-old Kurdish boy who drowned in the course of being smuggled into the European Union from Syria (Barnard & Shoumali, 2015).

Immigration has been a daily dilemma and source of concern in the EU, especially, as it has struggled with the complexity of a system of member nations' autonomy and attention to common values throughout the union. Even in the EU, the problem of integrating new immigrants is not new, though it has become more aggravated. As recently as 2004, the European Commission wrote that "Lack of access to employment has been identified as the greatest barrier to integration and thus the most important political priority within national integration policies" (quoted in Kesler, 2006, p. 743). On the one hand, immigration may be desirable because of the constraint placed on an economy by low or negative population growth. On the other hand, the disparity in immigrant pay can present a host of socio-economic issues, and cause strains on existing social services within the host nation. For example, if immigrants are unable to gain and keep employment, they may seek social services or other forms of assistance, including payments to support their families while looking for work. While host nations are obligated to a certain extent to do what is right to take care of people that would otherwise starve, as they flee what are sometimes horrid situations and look for a better life, this drain on resources can continue for extended periods. The help given to the newly arrived also draws away support from citizens, who might claim, because of the taxes they pay and their citizenship jus soli (by soil – born in the nation) and/or jus sanguinis (by blood), that they are the ones being underserved. When new immigrants are seen as taking advantage of the goodwill of the host nation, their stay may be short-lived; there is an assumption that allowance of entry and right to participate in the economy is not a one-way bargain. The individual has rights, but so does the society; some nations, like Germany, have been more pointed about requiring immigrants to work, and less comfortable with allowing public support, even with contextual factors in mind (Kesler, 2006).

Germany is a critical case (Ignatow & Mihalcea, 2017), deserving of additional analysis, because of Germany's economic strength, its approach to immigration policy since the end of World War II as defining for both itself and the larger European community, and the strategic significance of Germany within the EU as regards immigration policy in the larger context. This chapter considers Germany's recent constructions of immigration policy. A narrative analysis of Gesetz über den Aufenthalt, die Erwerbstätigkeit und die Integration von Ausländern im Bundesgebiet (the Act on the Residence, Economic Activity and Integration of Foreigners in the Federal Territory), facilitated by the AutoMap text mining tool, was conducted. Efforts to encourage integration through administrative approaches are based on a thin conception of what it means to be German, and lack the richness that is afforded by efforts that afford migrants their identities. Even if signaling in the political environment is the reason for such an approach, the outcome is not one that should be acceptable to either German citizens or migrants.

Semiotics, Meaning-making, and Immigration

In policy, there is work being done by officials to define what meanings are recognized, endorsed, and made real in policy terms, and what meanings or ways of thinking are left largely invisible within the process (Bezemer & Kress, 2016). The various guises of policy and program seek to translate or mirror the valuations that have been made by others, and how they see the world. To the extent that a special interest group has the recognition of officials and their processes, this worldview may become preferred and actionable. When a preferred viewpoint is selected, a problem identified, and a way of solving it devised, it becomes a matter for others involved to fall in line with the prevailing viewpoint as a selected mode. Correctness is less an issue than momentum at this point – choices have been made, the potential for error or groupthink aside, and those communicating and making a host of signs to support the prevailing view, process, and eventual outcomes are engaging in a dynamic, even transformative approach to making meaning. The language of policy provides a particularly sophisticated form of meaning-making; through the introduction of legal language, the sense of finality of the discussion and distant nature of law from most people is heightened. There is a focus upon aspects of administration and implementation that is foreign to the makers of meaning in conceptual terms. There is a making of the concept, but then a 'doing' of the work in creating the reality of a process or program, not to mention any discussion of intended outcomes and whether they are achieved. Importantly, the concept has to be placed into the context of its operating environment, and all the official and unofficial actors, program clients, and members of the public that may be encountered there (Bezemer & Kress, 2016). The meaning being made is not final – but made, constantly reshaped, and reformed long after the ink on the paper is dry.

Semiotics, aside from being about signs, is also about the relationships that connect signs, and so texts – like policy documents as "cultural products" in addition to their legal-governmental standing – are also useful for analysis. Policy documents are especially appropriate to analyze in the semiotic tradition because they are coherent – 'rationally organized' – and 'communicative'– in that, they carry a message that means something to someone (Bergström & Boréus, 2017, p. 5). These texts also have internal references that are helpful to greater certainty in identification of concepts, so the ideas being represented have perhaps a better chance of being understood well enough to be implemented as a program, leading to some outcome, desired or otherwise.

When we analyze language, we are considering reality and how closely a text reflects our understanding of reality, but at the same time, we must also consider that the concept of reality as portrayed in a text is being constructed not only by the text but also by our reading of it, and our understanding of the context in which the text exists, as well as our own background. We can focus on what the text tells us, or our response to it, or a combination. We can consider how the text may be read by different groups, with diverse circumstances. We may also wish to understand better the position of the author of the text, and the text itself as an outcome of a process of compromise, where some groups have been represented but not others, or others less so (Bergström & Boréus, 2017).

It has been observed that "all social structures and forms, including policies and policy regimes, are the product of political decisions, and though these acts of power are often forgotten and sedimented, they leave institutions, relations and policies vulnerable to reactivation and contestation" (Howarth, 2010, p. 329). In a society increasingly polarized, evidencing "a multitude of functionally differentiated social systems without a centre defining the supreme sources for the validity and enforcement of social norms" (Priban, 2009, p. 193), appeals to political lowest common denominators are similarly more common. The connection to immigration policy is clear. Problems have been defined in a particular way, which necessarily serves some interests over others. What views and perspectives are valid are associated with those that have access to the policymaking process. Other viewpoints, no matter how compelling, become less actionable the further removed they are from written law, and the ability to influence the formalization of policy and programs through law. The reality of the situation is heavily influenced by the choices made, even as those that stand to lose from law attempt to find ways to survive within new regimes.

Naming, Narratives, and Tenuous Links between Sign and Signified

Baudrillard's model of simulacrum sees "the link between sign and signi-fied...severed, eventually cycling to links between signs and signs" (Gar-rett & Storbeck, 2011, p. 532). In this model, what is real comes from no apparent origin, breaking down barriers between real and imagined, true and fake. Invoking Peirce, Marsen wrote that

> Thirdness is...evoked in organizational discourse in references to elements of authority (e.g., management requires, company policy states, company regulations permit). In this respect, thirdness acts like a cognitive schema, that is, a cognitive frame or point of refer-ence for the actions that take place in an organization,
>
> (2014, p. 304)

and that organizational failure might be accounted for inconsistent un-derstanding by various parties in an organization.

Selg and Ventsel described naming strategies as not only labels within the political sphere, but functional as grounds for discourse (or even ac-tion beyond that). Consider 'the war on...' in public policy, whether that be drugs, gun violence, or other public policy flashpoints. These wars are not actual wars, in most respects, but large-scale activities on the part of government interests, and symbolic moves with considerable forces be-hind them. Nevertheless, the tone of war remains as a marker of severity of action and firmness in public purpose. Perceiving the term might fur-ther evoke an emotional response in the public, as they hear, understand, and possibly believe that the 'image schema' (general shape) of a war mindset is being grafted onto a public policy priority (Eubanks, 2009, p. 44). In such instances of analysis, we take notice of the source, path, and goal of the statement (p. 48). This relates to the concept of pending narrative – that if certain events occur, a better outcome will be enjoyed at some point in the future (Tarronen, 2000).

Historically, Selg and Ventsel point out that the "name 'Stalin' in the Soviet Union of 1940s did not just stand for the 'Soviet people' – in the official discourse, it was the Soviet people" (2008, p. 179). The naming convention had essentially subsumed the individuality of the entirety of the nation under one person's name, in a particularly strong statement of hegemony.

Like naming, the ascendance of certain myths may force out of the discussion the viewpoints of minority or underserved groups, or leave such groups vulnerable. "Peircean semiotics renders the new a priori unintelligible even as it facilitates the analysis of the object" (Lee, 2011, p. 274). The tearing away of sign from signified does not only have theoretical ramifications, but objectively the impact to impacted groups of people, finding themselves marginalized and defined unfairly as 'opponents' in a narrative storyline, may be great. "A narrative is a story with a temporal sequence of events unfolding in a plot that is populated by dramatic moments, symbols, and archetypal characters that culminates in a moral to the story" (Jones & McBeth, 2010, p. 329).

Narrative analysis depends on how stories are related by people – a story being "what happened" (Eubanks, 2009, p. 34). The narrative or telling of the story may be grand, spanning the entirety of a culture, or more ephemeral, limited to a given organization or even an interaction between people. Grand narratives are considered to have "broad social power" (p. 36). The stuff of narrative analysis itself is as it is with other forms of qualitative analysis, frequently involving writing notes and classifying them into like groupings. Narrative analysis brings in concepts like metaphor and the 'alien name' of Aristotle, where a word is brought from its initial place to a new location, where it develops new associations in context while retaining some of its old overtones (Eubanks, 2009).

As an example of narrative analysis, a story that is often encountered in the public sector is regulatory constraint of industry. A common narrative of regulation is that it is constraining to industry and results in industry being inefficient and less competitive. A competing, and as Stone (2012) would have it, paradoxical consideration of this narrative is that sometimes industries actually favor regulation because reigning-in foreign competition levels the playing field across an industry, including competitors that might otherwise not follow domestic regulations. This story could be, in turn, framed as a different narrative – as national policy hostile to international trade.

The way we make sense of what happens to us is in telling stories about it. Stories can be complete, through denouement, or lack a subject (as in a narrative program). In narrative-semiotic analysis, in addition to senders, objects, and receivers, we also may encounter opponents and helpers that fight against or encourage the story protagonist. The placement of actors/roles and course of the storyline may be illustrated via an Actantial model (Marsen, 2014).

It seems valid on its face that a strong narrative can overcome quite a lot, including a strong evidentiary basis for a contrary or countering position. Public attention to a given narrative and how this can influence opinion, and ultimately policy choices, is a matter worth additional study. Especially when stories are easy to tell, and meaningful enough for people who know them to tell others, the public may be removed from reality and brought into the narrative world, long enough to play a decisive role in a public policy matter; poorly wrought stories or stories that fail to relate to the public may result in no appreciable impact on discourse. The presence of a hero, or a story that is artfully crafted, may lift an otherwise ordinary concern into the realm of compelling narrative (Jones, 2014).

Jones and McBeth (2010) highlighted how ideas that may not rationally relate to a policy debate can nevertheless shape public sentiment and, therefore, influence government action, for better or worse. Even with more scientific information of higher quality becoming available, context of policy debates and the prevalence of other non-evidentiary factors may lead to a poor reception for the transmission of such knowledge (Lawton & Rudd, 2014). It may be suggested that "evidence is one of a set of equally important inputs into societal decisions" (p. 855), and that policy actors engaged with scientific research must also have compelling narratives ready to counter other possible inputs into the decision-making process. It is important to bring science into the discussion, from a stakeholder standpoint, but the use of such information must be tailored to the audience to be effective (McBeth, Lybecker, Stoutenborough, Davis, & Running, 2017).

In practice, portrayals are not always so simple or obvious. An industrial concern may portray itself as a victim or a hero. An advocacy group may depict itself as acting in a heroic way, even as it is demonized by its detractors (Heikkila et al. 2014). Others working with stakeholders have found that pointing out 'worthy victims' and illustrating the heroic nature of champions in a policy area are much more conducive avenues to positive movement forward than the assignment of blame and identification of villains, although characters are important in stories, and stakeholders do pay attention to them. It is reasonable enough that business interests, too, could be victims in a policy environment – this highlights the rush-to-judgment that could result from a need to identify a villain (McBeth, Lybecker, Stoutenborough, Davis, & Running, 2017).

Narratives deeply influence understanding, and storytelling is a fundamental human endeavor, closely related to personal identity. Symbolism and discourse carried out through narratives create meaning, but also serves to persuade groups instrumental within the policy process, not only of the validity of certain outcomes, but of their expected roles within the narrative. The statement of a problem within policy, for example, provides an example of storytelling – this problem exists, therefore something must be done, and upon that outcome, the situation will either be resolved or improved. Competing discourses within a narrative analysis show multiple ways of resolving a policy problem, potentially, including not seeing it as a problem, and therefore engaging in no activity to resolve the supposed difficulty. Within study of narratives, it is possible to identify larger strategies, as well as credibility issues of communication, persuasiveness of an argument consistent with existing beliefs; the outcomes of a policy debate are such that even when one side 'loses,' the loss may lead to greater organization membership, or other long-run strategic goals (Jones & McBeth, 2010).

Through narrative inquiry, one may gain insight into how people involved in an experience make meaning of what has happened. One may understand better the perspective of people who have been relegated within the policy process, or have not been able to fully express their viewpoints. Narratives (from interviews, for example) can be analyzed to note themes that may intersect with the perspectives of other participants; this can enlighten us about the lived experience of an event, or the impact of policy over time (Blustein, Kozan, & Connors-Kellgren, 2013). We may also identify the meta-narrative in a debate: "the major oppositions to a controversy without in the process slighting any of that opposition" (Roe, 1994, p. 52).

Boucquey (2016) employed a method of examining vignettes to gain insight into narrative development, interactions between policy actors, and the function of scientific information, in the case of North Carolina fishery policy. Human values play a role in decision, beyond simple reliance on scientific input as a source of authoritative information. The analysis evaluated commission meeting minutes, management plans, among other texts. This analysis was considered alongside interviews and content analysis of newspaper articles. The intent was to provide a reading of phenomena associated with interactions in the policy process, rather than an intent to arrive at some far-reaching truth applicable generally. Maiello (2014) categorized informants' stories in a case study on the Iguacu Project, by plot/structure; meanings, knowledge, the nature of participation and engagement of the public, local environment circumstances, and what the participants learned through the experience. Archetypal narratives may be identified through narrative analysis; identification of these archetypes can be important because, as with normalizing and implementing a contested concept like sustainability, surmounting existing barriers "requires the learning from different narratives' most useful interventions, leaving behind the battleground of potentially contested pathways and their controversies" (Luederitz, Abson, Audet, & Lang, 2017, p. 404).

Interpretive policy analysis is necessarily invested in context, and tests assumptions about business-like government and wholly rational decision-making processes (Yanow, 2007). This approach gets at why, for example, best practices applied lacking their original operating context, programs, actors, and organizational relationships and connections, may fail or underperform relative to the marketing of such methods at their outset. In fact, it is quite difficult to regularize and rationalize the public space, creating the best program options once and for all, applicable to all organizational contexts. The positive outcomes of public administration occur because administrators and staff are able to make sense of their organizational context, deploy resources, and do so with due attention to the broader public interest, how their agency fits in context with other agencies, and understanding of the prevailing political climate. A trust in instrumental rationality and removing the human component from the equation betrays a lack of understanding about how government works, because forms and processes that inform the bureaucratic mindset are only part of the operation of the machinery of public institutions. Understanding of law, programs, systems, and clients, so essential to quality public service, is tragically undervalued. Sense cannot be imposed upon public programs; it must be cultivated in light of client needs as well as larger trends. This requires discourse and discussion, rather than orders and villainization of public-sector employees and government institutions.

Imposition of government onto a physical space can lead to creation of a Foucaultian heterotopia, where land is removed from common use and made other. For example, a 'border wall' becomes a manifestation of a long process with causes and effects, and is symbolic, perhaps falsely so, of safety and security from the unknown (Garrett & Storbeck, 2011), even as it is increasingly disconnected from the discourse that led to the concept in the first place. Such concepts are echoed in Vaughan-Williams (2015).

Policy Constructions of Migrant Assimilation in Germany

As recently as 2011, German population growth was negative, though it has rebounded to 1.2% in 2016, outpacing both the United Kingdom and Japan, and the highest rate since 1960 (World Bank, 2018); over the period, German population growth was consistently lower than world population growth, and generally lower than that seen for Europe and Central Asia over the period, except for a period from 1989 to 1996, and again in 2001. At times, Germany has been very restrictive in its allowances for citizenship beyond ancestral links (Kesler, 2006).

The views on migration in the EU continue to evolve. In Germany, how migration is seen has been aggravated by inequality, as society has transitioned from a manufacturing base to knowledge-work. At the same time, Germany's important role as an economic powerhouse has been possible because of immigrants. The German focus has increasingly shifted to one of integration, in alignment with a larger shift in the EU. In the German case, the object of integration has been "to ensure that re-settlers can participate quickly and sustainably in social, vocational and cultural structures in Germany" (Kohlmeier, Heine, Mananashvili, & Hecht, 2006, p. 11). However, when integration policies do not work as

intended, migrants may further withdraw into inward-looking communities, breaking down the potential for assimilation that is the stated
purpose of such policies. The view has been that migrants bring 'other'
cultures, which by nature of their very existence threaten the existing
culture, either through a competition of ideas or re-writing the text, so
to speak, upon which society operates. To avoid this, it is thought that
migrants could increasingly check their religious and cultural leanings,
which inform their own personal identity and sense of meaning, at the
national border, to encourage the pursuit of some common elements of
nationhood. A goal is to see migrants learn to speak the language of the
host country, but also become aware of, and embrace, national symbols
and viewpoints (Yurdakul & Bodemann, 2006). The intended result of
inclusion, framed as integration, is replaced in some sense by some attainment and display of the outward trappings of integration, while the
more substantial goal of inclusion is, at least from the policy perspective,
less important, if present at all in policy.

Such approaches do not put as a primary goal the maintenance of individual identity. The consequential roots of migrants in their experiences,
transitioning from home to host country, are valuable in achievement of
integration more broadly, as a maintenance of personhood and embrace
of the host country, its values, and becoming fully part of the nation and
its public sphere as a citizen (Sassen, 2006). Integration is potentially a
suspect word; integration implies a set of priorities and expected outcomes, which may be undercut or circumscribed by the language of policy. There is an active 'othering' of migrant identity, or expressed another
way, an acknowledgment that migrants possess experience and awareness that is consequential to who they are, but which may not align with
what is expected to attain acceptance.

One meaning of citizenship (from the top of the policy structure, given
prevailing sentiment that has met with electoral victory), may be quite
different from the various, not necessarily competing visions of citizenship that are held and expressed by migrant communities. Membership
implies conferring of a value based upon acceptance – meaning attainment of some formalized set of terms deemed consequential. However,
the rules and baseline for such an achievement do not and cannot look
inside the mind of the migrant, their experience, and speak to the com-
bining of past experiences and matters of personal identity that might
make citizenship more meaningful than a basic integration policy. This
larger goal is replaced by the rhetoric of the moment, which is tied to the
maintenance of power and exclusion for the sake of stability. Ironically,
this maintenance approach is subject to failure, as it ignores emerging
forces and the complexity of the environment within which public organizations operate.

Schönwälder and Triadafilopoulos suggested that "discursive constructions of immigrants as threatening or otherwise unworthy of

membership act as symbolic obstacles to their integration" (2012, p. 62). Much of the complaint rested with the divide between so-called German values and adherence to the Muslim faith. In this discourse, the othering of migrants became a distinction between Germans and non-Germans; non-German migrants were considered by some as liabilities, or untrustworthy. If given an opportunity in such an environment to choose adherence to the ways of one's former home, or to one's host country, where the residents are not so welcoming, one might reasonably take a longing look back to one's roots, or create parallel environments that avoid association with the mainstream (2012). The result, though, is that the divide widens, and distrust increases on both sides.

Where there have been restrictions on the flow of foreign workers from newer EU nations into Germany, the rationale has sometimes been that an unchecked flow would cause increased unemployment and a trend toward lower wages. Felbermayr, Geis, and Kohler (2010) disagreed with this assessment, indicating that such constraints were actually harmful over the long term.

Mocan and Raschke (2016) found an inverse relationship between the extent of xenophobic and racist feelings and an individual's perception of their economic circumstance. It is possible that some feel like they have a lack of opportunity to gain better (or just other) work, and that migrants are standing in the way of these opportunities, which should be 'rightfully theirs.' Foreigners and migrants are vague-enough categories for blame that the frustration can be displaced without causing undue drama to one's daily life. If one does not know any of these people, so much the better. Believing that one's opportunities, economic are otherwise, are limited is easier to take if it is through no fault of one's own, and is rather due to some outside force. Unfortunately, this leaves open a blind spot, which can be used politically to gain power for an elected leader, but does not offer much in return to the individual or to a nation.

The existence of such ongoing cultural matters fuels the persistence of certain factors as a crutch, when rational discussion and engagement might lead to different, perhaps more tolerant and appropriate, outcomes. If a tendency exists toward xenophobia, then a primary option in an instance of trouble may not be level-headed understanding and patience, but more probably xenophobia. If the sole tool one has is a hammer, then everything looks like a nail. Migrants who are already endangered by their circumstances, and sometimes cruel exits from their home countries, are especially at-risk if an economic downturn occurs (Mocan & Raschke, 2016). They may not receive the benefit of the doubt, as to their goodness, capacity, or potential to be able countrymates in their host nation.

Germany, with its language presenting a possible barrier to outsiders, is not entirely welcoming to would-be immigrant workers. Research has suggested that non-native workers face significant barriers to access employment in the nation (Kesler, 2006). From a narrative perspective, part of the story of the evolution of Germany's immigration policy had to do with healing social rifts. Otto Schily, an Interior Minister, even evoked a visual linkage to migrants by describing a legal change as a "bridge…that will allow us to incorporate [migrants] into our society" (Schönwälder & Triadafilopoulos, 2012, p. 53). In practice though, Germany's immigration policy has not entirely healed old rifts, or fully assimilated migrant groups into the larger society. This is to be expected, because policy in this area has an incredibly difficult task ahead of it. The need for a bridge implies that the two shores would not otherwise be connected; no bridge of fixed span can address a widening gulf.

Materials and Methods

Immigration laws in Germany are explored in this analysis. As mentioned at the outset, Germany is a critical case for immigration policy in the EU. For this study, I selected a major German law, Gesetz über den Aufenthalt, die Erwerbstätigkeit und die Integration von Ausländern im Bundesgebiet (the Act on the Residence, Economic Activity and Integration of Foreigners in the Federal Territory).[1] This law provides an official German government perspective on the ideas it presents. Through the analysis, I sought to understand the discourse position of the German government as it has concerned immigrants. The content of these legal texts was analyzed for major themes, and further evaluated for underlying (semantic-level) meaning (Ignatow & Mihalcea, 2017). Each law forms an official moment wherein the considerations of the German government may be considered to have manifested and been made official.

The law reviewed here is available online in the original German and in an official English translation. I conducted the analysis mostly using the translation, provided "solely as a convenience to the non-German-reading public," even though "discrepancies or differences that may arise in translations of the official German versions of these materials are not binding and have no legal effect for compliance or enforcement purposes." The fact is that they are provided officially.[2] German official documents have no copyright protection, per German copyright law (§ 5 Abs.1 UrhG), and are public domain.

Narrative policy analysis is appropriate for studying the language of immigration policy because these types of policies confront complex issues, which through a challenging process lead to a text (in this case, a law or series of laws). The analysis allows an opportunity to draw out meaning embedded in the text, which can lead to recommendations to improve policy and its outcomes. The process starts with the identification of stories (narratives). It proceeds with the recognition of *counterstories* that compete with the principal narrative; a comparison is then conducted of the prevailing storyline and its refutation. Finally, one may consider "if or how the metanarrative recasts the problem in such a way as to make it more amenable to...conventional policy-analytical tools..." in practical circumstances (Roe, 1994, p. 156). The analysis can consider for a moment the value and flaw that may be present in both the primary and countering storylines, and see a way forward where common ground can be seen.

I used AutoMap 3.0.10.42 (Carley, 2017), a text-mining application developed by Computational Analysis of Social and Organizational Systems (CASOS) at Carnegie-Mellon University, for the textual analysis. AutoMap "enables the extraction of information...using Network Text Analysis methods...from unstructured documents."[3] In addition to the more obvious content analysis of word usage, I also used the software to conduct an analysis of semantic network data.

Analysis and Results

I used the Word Cloud Generator by Jason Davies[4] to create a tag cloud, to show a basic content analysis, based on word count information about this law in English translation (Figure 7.1).

Figure 7.1 Word cloud for Act on the Residence, Economic Activity and Integration of Foreigners in the Federal Territory (translation).

Source: Created by C. A. from https://www.gesetze-im-internet.de/englisch_aufenthg/ englisch_aufenthg.html using https://www.jasondavies.com/wordcloud/.

I then entered the translated text of the Residence Act into AutoMap, engaged the preprocessing tools available for cleaning and readying of the text, and generated a semantic network (viewable with ORA-LITE). The light version of the Organization Risk Analyzer (ORA) application provided various measures of centrality for describing the network, highlighting, for example, the Total-Degree Centrality, "the normalized sum of [a node's] In-Degree and Out-Degree." Table 7.1 highlights identified concepts, all found to have a value higher than the mean. There was significant overlap of these concepts on other views of centrality.

We can see the major concepts of the law through these nodes – that this law covers the matter of foreigners, that employment is a significant matter, and that deportation is a possibility.

While integration is focal as a node, the concept is not ranked as highly, even though the law itself requires an integration class to obtain a temporary or permanent residence permit. There is a provision that an applicant may otherwise prove integration: "extension may be refused unless the foreigner furnishes evidence that he has achieved integration into the community and society by other means" (Sec. 8). For foreigners with considerable qualifications, "there is reason to assume that integration into the way of life in the Federal Republic of Germany and the foreigner's subsistence without state assistance are assured" (Sec. 19). Section 25b

Table 7.1 Total-Degree Centrality, ORA, of Residence Act

Rank	Concept	Value	Unscaled	Context
1	has_been	0.038	76	49.592
2	Foreigners	0.036	72	46.903
3	Foreigner	0.031	62	40.182
4	Data	0.021	41	26.067
5	Authorities	0.017	34	21.362
6	Deportation	0.016	32	20.018
7	German	0.016	31	19.346
8	Authority	0.015	30	18.674
9	Federal	0.015	30	18.674
10	Measures	0.014	27	16.657
11	Permit	0.014	27	16.657
12	Concerned	0.013	26	15.985
13	in_particular	0.013	26	15.985
14	Legal	0.013	26	15.985
15	Persons	0.013	25	15.313
16	Integration	0.012	24	14.641
17	Procedure	0.011	22	13.297
18	Employment	0.010	20	11.952
19	Law	0.010	20	11.952
20	Administrative	0.010	19	11.280

Source: Created by C.A., from ORA analysis of Act on the Residence, Economic Activity and Integration of Foreigners in the Federal Territory (translation).

provides us more information about what is required for integration: The applicant "is committed to the free democratic basic order of the Federal Republic of Germany and possesses a basic knowledge of the legal and social system and the way of life in the federal territory." Chapter 3 of the law discusses the integration course itself, a

> basic package of measures to promote integration... The aim of the integration course shall be to successfully impart the German language, legal system, culture and history to foreigners. In this way, foreigners are supposed to become acquainted with the way of life in the federal territory to such an extent as to enable them to act independently in all aspects of daily life, without the assistance or mediation of third parties.[5]

In addition to the expected frequent references to the government entity (Federal), there was a significant presence of the term foreigner (ausländer). The Collins German dictionary defines ausländer, in addition to foreigner, as a non-German alien (2007). Worth mentioning is the supporting definition of ausländerfeindlich, one "hostile to foreigners," as well as references to racist crime and xenophobia. When looking up for the word 'foreigner,' the dictionary clearly indicates ausländer, and "(neg!)" (2007, p. 311), meaning a word that "may be considered offensive" (2007, p. xvi). The word may be used to simply mean *not German* (see, for example, this Wikipedia discussion of the use of the term and how Germans may claim it means foreign and not from Germany).[6] However, this Wiki page also suggests that the word does not mean *alien*, which contradicts the dictionary definition. Even if the intention is not negative, Hackett (2013) noted that the ausländer suggested otherness, which is (minimally) not inclusive. Howell (2011) navigated the problematic terrain of using a broad term to describe people with a variety of experiences, as guest workers, or those seeking asylum, as well as the differentiation between native and non-native Germans, further complicating matters. Räthzel took up citizenship and belonging in the German nation, and broached the potential belief that only Germans "by birth belong to the nation" (2006, p. 166). German-ness might be viewed popularly as a matter of lineage, rather than a trait that can be given through administrative action, even if a law or rule is passed to suggest otherwise (Figure 7.2).

Given that the term foreigners is potentially problematic, and at least suggestive of a need for additional discussion, I used ORA-LITE to generate a 2-D network map highlighting use of the term, in Figure 7.2.

The network analysis map highlights the relationship between foreigner and other associated terms. Of note, forms of enforcement and authority play a significant role (allocated, passport, circumstances, enforceable, for example). Related works like application, competent, lawful, and dependents show a significant bent toward administrative-speak.

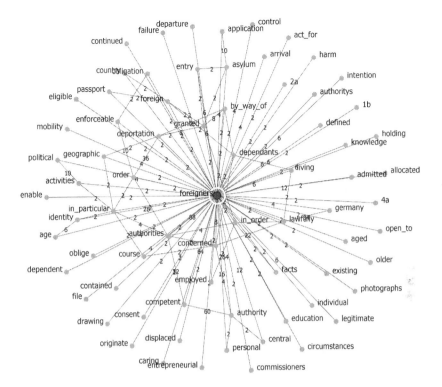

Figure 7.2 Network analysis map, use of term foreigners in German Residence Act.
Source: Created by C. A., visualized with ORA from AutoMap output, using Act on the Residence, Economic Activity and Integration of Foreigners in the Federal Territory (translation) (source for text as above).

Ascendant in this network is a general notion of the governmental apparatus enforcing a rule that refines an unclear concept – German-ness – through what it is not, and administratively imposes standards and sanctions that might be construed as arbitrary relative to the desired outcome (German citizens espousing German ideals). Assessments of eligibility or ineligibility for programs are based on standards, but these seem related to creation or bringing into being of the desired outcome in, at best, an ineffectual fashion.

Hanewinkel and Oltmer (2018) observed that integration became a stated objective of government with immigration law changes in 2005; integration programs have been seen positively, relative to other nations. They have been based on a principle of 'support and demand,' meaning that the program facilitates

> access to the labor market for asylum seekers and allows those with leave to remain to complete an education program they may have

started. But it also stipulates that benefits will be cut for those who do not participate in integration measures.

(Hanewinkel & Oltmer, 2018)[7]

Demand for integration effort means participating in courses and learning the German language. Even with an integration course, though, "people with a migration background still do not have the same participation opportunities in central social areas, such as education, employment market, residence and political involvement" (Hanewinkel & Oltmer, 2018).

This discussion may be constructed in view of narrative policy analysis. The story arc is a transition, and the order of events is ostensibly chronological. The migrant comes from their prior experiences to Germany, undertakes a series of tasks and challenges (an integration course, learning the language, and adapting to culture), and in doing so is transformed on some level into a German, worthy of recognition, initiation, and citizenship. The following of procedure, in the primary story arc, produces a German. However, there is a counternarrative, in that German-ness is produced through the creation of shared identity, rather than the completion of administrative tasks; indeed, the successful completion of an integration course does not actually integrate the migrant into German society, though it might be helpful in making the eventual transition easier. Integration in practice is difficult, and so the narrative is not necessarily chronological; more likely the arc of the story is fractured, with difficulties to overcome, and the ever-present danger of failure. Identification, particularly in situations where one group is pitted against another, is surprisingly easy. As Koestler suggested,

If our imagination can produce all of the physical symptoms of emotion in reaction to the perils of personae, which exist merely as printer's ink, how much easier, then to have the experience of belonging, of being a part of a group, though it is not physically present.

(1967, p. 255)

The 'group' need not even exist in reality, for a person to feel as though one is a part of it, in a meaningful way – whether it is a 'nation' of fans of a sports team, or a loose affiliation of people that agree with a few broad statements or general feelings and claim an identity with people they barely know. In a semiotic way, though, it is clear what the purpose is – that the identity is formed by what it is not – they are not 'us.' Even administrative completion of the assigned tasks may lead to a result considered inauthentic.

How might these countering narratives be squared? Programs that consider integration to be an administrative process are potentially unreasonable given the lived experience of migrants and the shaping of integration that must occur for migrants to become full, involved, included residents of a nation. The administrative aspect poses the idea that completing a series of tasks affords integration, but in reality, the completion does not afford recognition from fellow citizens. In addition to not being realistic about the nature of recognition in practice, the approach is disingenuous because it promises something it cannot deliver to migrants. At the same time, it undermines the real and valid concerns that citizens have about newly arrived migrants, particularly when there is a great volume of new residents over a short period of time. The administrative process cannot fully integrate these new arrivals, and the existing citizens feel like their concerns – about consistency in culture, willingness to be a host but requiring a need for mutual respect, and the like – are not being addressed. An integration process that exists in an administrative vacuum seems like a valid solution, but it actually undermines the dignity of both migrants and existing residents, with migrants receiving a fake bill of goods for their activities to become integrated, and citizens having little part in the recognition and acceptance of their new neighbors. It is a simulation, when the real process of integration is difficult, but much more rewarding.

The archetypal German people as a group – the collective self in need of protection – is put forward in this thin description as having a consistency that does not speak to the richness and beauty of modern German society; this description is unfair. There is nothing villainous or harmful about a migrant community – an archetypal, ill-defined shadow, from the story perspective (any more than individual bad actors and their activities, the tendencies of which exist in native residents on par with new residents), but it can be useful from a political standpoint to create a storyline that places migrants in this role. If these people would simply complete an administrative process, and contribute to the economy, there would be no problem; it becomes a matter of pushing the shadowy migrant out into the supposed light of accepted, recognized German citizen, even though the line between the two is not as bright as may be claimed in policy. The teacher of the integration course, the government, becomes an arbiter of German-ness, as if it were possible for government to dictate a bottom-up, closely held, evolving, community-driven definition of this sort. What is worse, there are indefensible assumptions being made: If people are wealthy and have jobs, they are more likely to be acceptable for purposes of German citizenship. One does not necessarily follow the other, and yet it is presumed as given, perhaps because quality of citizenry and integration are not driving forces at all.

Discussion

One significant barrier to understanding German immigration law is finding the text of the law in the first place. Google searches for German immigration law bring up a variety of websites for would-be residents, and even references to Germany being an 'immigration country,' but there are also references to new laws being proposed, as well as coalition efforts to redraft immigration law.[8] There is immediately a feeling of uncertainty given this lack of clear, easy to locate communication. The ground is shifting in immigration policy in Germany, and the press is mirroring this. McAuley and Noack (2018) refer to the immigration concerns in Germany not as a migrant crisis, per se, but as a political crisis for German President Angela Merkel and her coalition, in an article that appeared near the top of the search list (on September 11, 2018). It is obvious from searching for information that discussions continue and these matters are not settled business.

A major criticism of official texts is that they do not appear to have an author. If a law or policy document seems to malign or discriminate, and there is no clear author, there might be no obvious character to blame for an affront. The text might suggest it is a solution for a problem – that it serves as an official answer or statement on a matter – and fail to acknowledge that it is merely a stopping point along the way of a larger storyline, where the assumptions made and their formal solutions are potentially in dispute. Raising a societal concern to the level of crisis requires an assumption to be made – an assumption taken for purposes of the discussion to be valid, whether or not it is valid outside the narrative. If immigration disputes in policy are a crisis, then crises demand attention; this allows actors to proceed with a level of certainty about what they are doing, whether or not it is appropriate. In immigration, if 'they' (migrants, in this case, termed as ausländers) are seen as a problem, what is it that 'we' will do about it, once they get here, and disrupt stability or normalcy, whether or not those existed in the first place? (Roe, 1994).

Policy assumptions signify a view of the problem and presuppose a solution of some kind. The solutions proposed may themselves mirror fears (unfounded or not) through their identification of culprits for larger societal failures and a host of issues where the relationship between cause and effect is marginal or unclear. It is politically advantageous to put forth a simple story about how ill-effects are caused by something, someone, or some group, even if the case cannot be made formally or with evidence. The telling of a story is a form of meaning-making, which can even rise to the level of myth-making, escaping the confines of a particular scenario (Roe, 1994). Stories help an audience dispense with concerns, about how the problem as identified and the proposed solution do not align, or how the context surrounding a policy debate may suggest intellectual shortcuts to avoid the inherent complexity. Working directly with complexity in a public setting is difficult, and may have the potential to disrupt allotment and use of power in political settings; why bother with that, when a story, with heroes, villains, a climax, and a denouement can wrap everything up in a convenient, consumable package?

In immigration policy, emergent conditions, which include experiences that cause a shift in cultural standpoints, can shift governmental positions in shattering ways. Ignoring emergent conditions can lead to disturbance of hierarchies. In a rush to confirm existing judgments and ways of knowing from a top-down perspective, there is a tendency to avoid conflicting information, or reject competing viewpoints for fear that inclusion will confound method or possible, and desired, outcomes. The more that 'existing hierarchies' are given as a rationale for acting in a certain manner, organizationally or from a policy selection standpoint, the more that emerging details are likely to be ignored (Desouza & Hensgen, 2005).

If immigration policy in Germany portends a crisis, it may do so in the respect that the occurrences are of "such magnitude that [they] alter the strategic or tactical plan for an organization," (Desouza & Hensgen, 2005, p. 113), but not because they are unanticipated. It is increasingly difficult to defend the position that Germany is not aware of the role of migrants in German society, their importance to an economically sound, successful Germany, or how popular viewpoints of immigration may be at cross-purposes to the very foundations of German life. There is likely signaling going on in statement of German immigration policy, but it is a signaling of sameness – where the present that allows for change and inclusion is disallowed in favor of a notion of German-ness that is increasingly difficult to define in a narrow way. The policy language seems of another time and place, out of touch with the world it confronts. Defining the concern of immigration is made more difficult from an administrative perspective, as these top-down rules are devised and public servants seek to implement them. If the rules are out-of-touch with the clients of administrative practice, the outcomes from such rules will necessarily be of little positive consequence, and may increase divisiveness and blaming when set in motion.

In Germany, these phenomena raise interesting questions and are problematic for a variety of reasons. Integration rules could assume a certain standard of what it is to be German, but the mythical concept of German volk, or of oneness of German people, betrays the fullness of the nation as it exists currently and the profound impact migrants have had on the nation, not only recently but over the course of many decades. Questions designed to assess how German one is may seek to gauge alignment with German ideals, but actually fail in this respect because the ideal is cartoonish. Instead of encouraging new residents to learn about, embrace, and even come to love their new home, the process of inclusion is diminished to assuming or even impersonating a preferred character (Mandel, 2006). Migrants might be confronted with an uncomfortable circumstance – that they are being asked to adopt a thin representation of who they must become, to gain acceptance and citizenship, while leaving behind the thick and value-laden material of their background and experience, in and from which their real identity flows. Policy, written as a coherent whole (German-ness, viewed in a narrow way by a certain few) competing against a coherent whole (foreigners) pits false representation against false representation. There is not one experience of migrants (Korteweg, 2006). The cause of supporting national identity, attained through thin processes, is weakened by an assumption of a unified opposition opposed to it.

Conclusion

As Cornelia Wilhelm eloquently put it, in concluding her historical examination of diversity in Germany,

> A broader discourse on the social reality of Germany and patterns of the construction of diversity, cultural difference, memory, and German identity would...not only allow those who were or are immigrants to identify with the nation, but also help Germans...understand their...identity as far more diverse and culturally different....
>
> (2013, p. 26)

Germany has remarkable strength, and draws no small part of that from the rich diversity that exists within the nation. Exclusion of new would-be Germans has done Germany or its larger interests no useful purpose; it has possibly created a self-defeating cycle with migrants feeling alienated when they might have otherwise embraced with immense pride German culture, work ethic, and influence. The most obvious concern about the othering of migrants is that there is no one German pattern or identity. Germany is made up of many identities, as would be reasonable given its size and incorporation of regions that have unique historical and cultural influences of their own.

It is evident in this evaluation that the story being told in law is part of an ongoing narrative arc – the recognition and creation of citizens through some imagined, administrative transformation, but the work on paper does not solve the challenge of making real inclusion and involvement in the public sphere of contemporary German society. Instead of resolving issues and creating strong, resilient communities, policies that seek to simplify the complexity of integration in immigration short both citizens and migrants – neither side is well served by a pretension to an easy answer in such instance, though the conceptual fuzziness may serve some limited political purpose. Humanitarian concerns and economic needs compete for space in defining what is desired in German immigration policy (Bauder, 2008); instead of addressing these issues more forcefully, what seems a priority in policy is responding to narrative extremes of inclusion and fear. This is a searching after a false hegemony, attempting to convince groups that one imagined way is the best way; instead of reducing conflict, the potential for struggle is increased (Scott, 1990).

Effective immigration policy requires a balancing of considerations. It is unreasonable to assume that a nation will accept migrants with no change in their manner or behavior in their new context, but it is also unreasonable to assume that migrants will leave behind the root of their identity to take on the guise of a national identity that has been criticized as largely mythical (Williams, 2014). Integration and subsequent evolution of a new inclusive society does not happen quickly or sustainably through administrative prescription. Underneath the machinery of governance, there are people, those who have lived in the nation for a long or short time, or somewhere in between. They all bring their own views, informed by experience. It would be better if immigration reform did not proceed through a muddling, incremental process, but rather as a more coherent approach, which "highlights the advantages of migration for German society as a whole. This is important if policymakers wish to avoid or at least take the wind out of hostile knee-jerk responses and attempts to mobilize against immigration" (Kösemen, 2015). Immigration policies frequently fail, and the context of migrants and the reasons they move are not well portrayed in policy (Czaika & Haas, 2013). Without an effort to reduce gaps between intent and implementation, immigration policy writ as integration risks seeming disingenuous to both migrants and citizens, while yielding unsatisfactory results.

Notes

1 https://www.gesetze-im-internet.de/englisch_aufenthg/index.html.
2 https://www.gesetze-im-internet.de/Teilliste_translations.html.
3 The AutoMap website is located at http://www.casos.cs.cmu.edu/projects/auto map/. The ORA program, for viewing network analysis output, is located at http://www.casos.cs.cmu.edu/projects/ora/.
4 https://www.jasondavies.com/wordcloud/
5 Text of the translation is located at: https://www.gesetze-im-internet.de/englisch_aufenthg/englisch_aufenthg.html.
6 https://web.archive.org/web/20180912132150/https://en.wikipedia.org/wiki/Talk%3AAusl%C3%A4nder.
7 The principle may also be referred to as promote and demand (Wegmann, 2014); the tone of both support and promote is essentially encouraging and positive, though the program, with its demands of attending courses and meeting baseline standards, with the alternative being to leave the country, is more coercive.
8 An August 2018 article from *Deutsche Welle* titled "Germany's planned immigration law – what you need to know" (https://www.dw.com/en/germanys-new-immigration-law-what-to-expect/a-44556016), for example, references the potential for a point system for immigration admission, but quarrels with calling it a point system. The article refers to the lack of skilled workers being a pressing concern for lawmaking in this area.

162 *Analysis of German Immigration Law*

References

Barnard, A., & Shoumali, K. (2015, September 3). Image of drowned Syrian, Aylan Kurdi, 3, brings migrant crisis into focus. *The New York Times.* Retrieved from https://www.nytimes.com/2015/09/04/world/europe/syria-boy-drowning.html.

Bauder, H. (2008). Media discourse and the new German immigration law. *Journal of Ethnic and Migration Studies, 34*(1), 95–112.

Bergström, G., & Boréus, K. (2017). Analyzing text and discourse in the social sciences. In K. Boreus & G. Bergstrom (Eds.), *Analyzing text and discourse: Eight approaches for the social sciences, 1–22.* Thousand Oaks, CA: Sage Publications.

Bezemer, J., & Kress, G. (2016). *Multimodality, learning and communication: A social semiotic frame.* Abingdon, Oxon: Routledge.

Blustein, D. L., Kozan, S., & Connors-Kellgren, A. (2013). Unemployment and underemployment: A narrative analysis about loss. *Journal of Vocational Behavior, 82,* 256–265.

Boucquey, N. C. (2016). Actors and audiences: Negotiating fisheries management. *Journal of Environmental Policy & Planning, 18*(4), 426–446.

Carley, K. M. (2017). AutoMap 3.0.10.42. Retrieved from http://www.casos.cs.cmu.edu/projects/automap/software.php.

Collins German Dictionary, 7th edition. (2007). Glasgow: HarperCollins.

Czaika, M., & Haas, H. D. (2013). The effectiveness of immigration policies. *Population and Development Review, 39*(3), 487–508.

Desouza, K. C., & Hensgen, T. (2005). *Managing information in complex organizations: Semiotics and signals, complexity and chaos.* Armonk, NY: M. E. Sharpe.

Eubanks, P. (2009, orig. 2004). Poetics and narrativity: How texts tell stories. In C. Bazerman & P. Prior (Eds.), *What writing does and how it does it: An introduction to analyzing texts and textual practices, 33–56.* New York: Routledge.

Felbermayr, G., Geis, W., & Kohler, W. (2010). Restrictive immigration policy in Germany: Pains and gains foregone? *Review of World Economics / Weltwirtschaftliches Archiv, 146*(1), 1–21.

Garrett, T., & Storbeck, J. (2011). The DHS border fence in the Rio Grande Valley. *Administrative Theory & Praxis, 33*(4), 530–548.

Hackett, S. (2013). *Foreigners, minorities and integration: The Muslim immigrant experience in Britain and Germany.* Manchester: Manchester University Press.

Hanewinkel, V., & Oltmer, J. (2018, January 12). Integration and integration policies in Germany. *Bundeszentrale für politische Bildung.* Retrieved from http://www.bpb.de/gesellschaft/migration/laenderprofile/262812/integration-and-integration-policies-in-germany.

Heikkila, et al. (2014). Understanding a period of policy change: The case of hydraulic fracturing disclosure policy in Colorado. *Review of Policy Research, 31*(2), 65–87.

Howarth, D. (2010). Power, discourse, and policy: Articulating a hegemony approach to critical policy studies. *Critical Policy Studies, 3*(3–4), 309–335.

Howell, T. (2011). The caricatured eastern German: Complicating the east-west binary in Eulenspiegel cartoons and Osman Engin's Kanaken-Gandhi. In J. E. Twark (Ed.), *Strategies of humor in post-unification German literature, film, and other media, 28–54.* Newcastle upon Tyne: Cambridge Scholars.

Ignatow, G., & Mihalcea, R. (2017). *Text mining: A guidebook for the social sciences*. Thousand Oaks, CA: Sage Publications.

Jones, M. D. (2014). Communicating climate change: Are stories better than "Just the Facts"? *The Policy Studies Journal, 42*(4), 644–673.

Jones, M. D., & McBeth, M. K. (2010). A narrative policy framework: Clear enough to be wrong? *Policy Studies Journal, 38*(2), 329–353.

Kesler, C. (2006). Social policy and immigrant joblessness in Britain, Germany and Sweden. *Social Forces, 85*(2), 743–770.

Koestler, A. (1967). *The ghost in the machine*. New York: Macmillan.

Kohlmeier, M., Heine, J., Mananashvili, S., & Hecht. H. (2006). 2005 Policy analysis report on migration and asylum. Retrieved from https://ec.europa.eu/home-affairs/sites/homeaffairs/files/what-we-do/networks/european_migration_network/reports/docs/annual-policy/2005/germany_policy_report_20-3_en.pdf.

Korteweg, A. C. (2006). The murder of Theo van Gogh: Gender, religion, and the struggle over immigrant integration in the Netherlands. In Y. M. Bodemann & G. Yurdakul (Eds.), *Migration, citizenship, and ethnos, 147–166*. New York: Palgrave Macmillan.

Kösemen, O. (2015). Implementing migration policy reform: An outline for Germany. *Bertelsmann Stiftung*. Retrieved from http://aei.pitt.edu/74111/1/Implementing_migration_policy_reform.pdf.

Lawton, R. N., & Rudd, M. A. (2014). A narrative policy approach to environmental conservation. *AMBIO, 43*, 849–857.

Lee, K. (2011). The semiotics of Singapore's founding myths of multiracialism and meritocracy. *The American Sociologist, 42*, 261–275.

Luederitz, C., Abson, D. J., Audet, R., & Lang, D. J. (2017). Many pathways toward sustainability: Not conflict but co-learning between transition narratives. *Sustainability Science, 12*, 393–407.

Maiello, A. (2014). The organizational view of public participation: A narrative analysis. *Systemic Practice and Action Research, 27*, 499–522.

Mandel, R. (2006). Being German and Jewish in Kazakhstan and Germany. In Y. M. Bodemann & G. Yurdakul (Eds.), *Migration, citizenship, and ethnos, 95–102*. New York: Palgrave Macmillan.

Marsen, S. (2014). "Lock the doors": Toward a narrative-semiotic approach to organizational crisis. *Journal of Business and Technical Communication, 28*(3), 301–326.

McAuley, J., & Noack, R. (2018, July 3). What you need to know about Germany's immigration crisis. *Washington Post*. Retrieved from https://www.washingtonpost.com/news/worldviews/wp/2018/07/03/what-you-need-to-know-about-germanys-immigration-crisis/?noredirect=on&utm_term=.8db837110a6b.

McBeth, M. K., Lybecker, D. L., Stoutenborough, J. W., Davis, S. N., & Running, K. (2017). Content matters: Stakeholder assessment of river stories or river science. *Public Policy and Administration, 32*(3), 175–196.

McIntyre-Mills, J. J., de Vries, D., Christakis, A., & Bausch, K. (2008). How can we break the mould? Democracy, semiotics and regional governance. *Systems Research and Behavioral Science, 25*, 305–321.

Mocan, N., & Raschke, C. (2016). Economic well-being and anti-semitic, xenophobic, and racist attitudes in Germany. *European Journal of Law and Economics, 41*, 1–63.

Priban, J. (2009). Symbolism of the spirit of the laws: A genealogical excursus to legal and political semiotics. *International Journal for the Semiotics of Law, 22*, 179–195.

Räthzel, N. (2006) Aussiedler and ausländer: Transforming German national identity. In R. A. Starkman (Ed.), *Transformations of the New Germany. Studies in European culture and history, 157–179*. New York: Palgrave Macmillan.

Roe, E. (1994). *Narrative policy analysis: Theory and practice*. Durham, NC: Duke University Press.

Sassen, S. (2006). The repositioning of citizenship and alienage: Emergent subjects and spaces for politics. In Y. M. Bodemann & G. Yurdakul (Eds.), *Migration, citizenship, and ethnos, 13–34*. New York: Palgrave Macmillan.

Schönwälder, K., & Triadafilopoulos, T. (2012). A bridge or barrier to incorporation? Germany's 1999 citizenship reform in critical perspective. *German Politics & Society, 30*(1), 52–70.

Scott, J. C. (1990). *Domination and the arts of resistance: Hidden transcripts*. New Haven, CT: Yale University Press.

Selg, P., & Ventsel, A. (2008). Towards a semiotic theory of hegemony: Naming as a hegemonic operation in Lotman and Laclau. *Sign Systems Studies, 36*(1), 167–183.

Stone, D. (2012). *Policy paradox: The art of political decision making*, 3rd edition. New York: Norton.

Torronen, J. (2000). The passionate text. The pending narrative as a macrostructure of persuasion. *Social Semiotics, 10*(1), 81–98.

Vaughan-Williams, N. (2015). *Europe's border crisis: Biopolitical security and beyond*. Oxford: Oxford University Press.

Wegmann, K. M. (2014). Shaping a new society: Immigration, integration, and schooling in Germany. *International Social Work, 57*(2), 131–142.

Wilhelm, C. (2013). Diversity in Germany: A historical perspective. *German Politics & Society, 31*(2), 13–29.

Williams, H. (2014). Changing the national narrative: Evolution in citizenship and integration in Germany, 2000–10. *Journal of Contemporary History, 49*(1), 54–74.

World Bank. (2018). World development indicators. Retrieved from https://tinyurl.com/y7cp46zf.

Yanow, D. (2007). Interpretation in policy analysis: On methods and practice. *Critical Policy Studies, 1*(1), 110–122.

Yurdakul, G., & Bodemann, Y. M. (2006). Introduction. In Y. M. Bodemann & G. Yurdakul (Eds.), *Migration, citizenship, and ethnos, 1–12*. New York: Palgrave Macmillan.

8 Reforming the Affordable Care Act

A Semiotic Analysis of Tweets Using LIWC

Symbolic uses of language in policy may be strongly indicative of certain outcomes to the public, but the actual consequences realized may be far different. The purpose of this research is to better understand Twitter use in a specific policy context, using signs and symbols that align closely or loosely with written policy – in this case, policy actions related to a particularly contentious recent policy issue: reform efforts for the Patient Protection and Affordable Care Act (also referred to as the Affordable Care Act, ACA, but also as Obamacare, meant positively if accepted by the speaker or in a snide or choleric fashion if meant derisively). The ACA was intended to make health insurance available to more Americans; the program included the introduction of health insurance markets and expanded Medicaid coverage. While a goal was to reduce the cost of health care, premiums paid, and the high cost of pharmaceuticals remained dilemmas. Complaints about the program rose, especially from Republican quarters, and calls grew to 'repeal and replace' the law, or just repeal it altogether (Obama, 2017).

Public officials may use social networks like Twitter to encourage support for their particular views, which are taken by them to be emblematic of what is needed for the larger society, but the communication on social networks is not one-way. Users of the social network are responding to elected officials and to each other, and airing their feelings. Key officials thought to be able to swing a vote toward one result or another are particularly prone to receive social network responses in great volume. The research question asked is: What can tweets about ACA to key senators during a critical policy period tell us about signs and symbols employed in the discourse? As a corollary, what can we know from an exploration of the tweets about the thinking and interaction patterns of Twitter users, with regard to this policy debate?

Tweets were scraped to form the corpus for analysis, covering the period before and after the Graham-Cassidy amendment (Senate Amendment 1030 to the American Health Care Act of 2017, HR 1628, September, 2017); from this, I derived a subset to focus on tweets to Senator John McCain, who became a focus of intense discussion on Twitter during this period. I used LIWC2015 (Linguistic Inquiry and Word Count) to conduct a comparative analysis of the tweets, from a computational linguistics perspective. I have found that tweets about ACA during this period were more analytic and less authentic that what are typically found on Twitter; the tweets have a more negative tone than usual, and show a considerable division between positive and negative responses. As a group, the tweets used many negating words, showed higher than expected incidence of death-related words, and high levels of anger. More subjectively, I was struck by the nastiness of discourse exhibited on Twitter in the context of the policy debate; network users seemed to speak past not only each other, but the policy issue itself. Efforts made to understand the policy or Senator McCain's vote were not evident; Twitter was instead a place to vent emotions of all sorts, while predictably splitting into camps along party lines. McCain's presence became less about his status as a senator and person, and more symbolic – about his saving ACA or standing in the way of President Donald Trump's agenda. Social networks are especially relevant given recent discussion about their role in shaping public opinion and acting as a virtual public square, but this research casts serious doubt about the efficacy of these platforms for those public purposes.

The Enabling and Entitlement of the Popular Sentiment as a Profit-Center

George Berkeley made the exaggerated claim of siding "in all things with the Mob" (Pappas, 2000, p. 209). There is a sense in the public sphere that it is possible to grasp the prevailing wisdom, where one might think as others do, without the burden of learned thought or lenses of critical inquiry to throw one's senses out of focus. In reaching out for this common sense, one might avoid "the prejudices of a learned education...be represented as one who trusts his senses, who thinks he knows the things he sees and feels, and entertains no doubts, of their existence" (p. 211). Berkeley embraced being of simple "vulgar cast" (p. 212), banishing skepticism and abstract ideas that exist independent of perception. But, even the evocation of the public as a group as a mob is a selection of terminology that favors elite interests (Scott, 1990) – fair or not, it involves the imposition of a value judgment that reduces the potential for discourse.

Some in public spaces have no interest in hearing what challenges them, whether it is taxing on their core beliefs or simply differs in a minor way with an idea they have. The defiance that exists must be defended, and demands a quick, snarky comeback, so that the imagined oppressor will be made aware that they do not own the discourse. Not only is the opposing version of reality not appreciated, but it is also rejected outright, along with any worth the opponent might have as individuals. It is far easier to rubbish a person and what they believe in than to consider carefully their perspective and any value it might have, let alone come to a consensus. This unfitting behavior is not unique, unfortunately, to any specific political party, and is spurred along by individuals who hide behind screen names and have virtual lives. The failure is real – people value each other less. We have shared values, and common threats against our quality of life, but those are ignored for the light entertainment of identifying and destroying differences in thought.

Writing about political advertising, Holtz-Bacha and Kaid (2006) made a distinction between mediated and non-mediated forms of communication, dependent on the level of control a candidate maintains over the message. The message itself is persuasive and may be recognized as having that purpose, which may result in a countering effect from the receiving audience. Considering the path of social networks as a communication channel, an initial post may be a controlled statement, but the fact that the public can respond to it how it wishes, subject to some constraint on behalf of the service provider, can lead to a mediated, shaded perception of the original post. Further, the larger media, having taken to reporting on official tweets and other controlled messages as news, without a transparent, open discourse on policy issues with those sending the message. The centrality of individual instances of social network communication and retorts to direct official messaging, along with other societal shifts, have supplanted more traditional approaches to meaning-making.

Expressions of anger and even outright wickedness have found their way into the common on social media sites. Rather than serving as a venue for the meaningful exchange of ideas, social networking sites may become a forum for public beatings and the spectacle of destroying people professionally and personally. A poorly considered or misunderstood tweet might lead to a public haranguing or worse – threats against the poster or their family. Discourse regularly skips several steps ahead, missing disagreement, discussion, and acceptance of ideas that may differ significantly from one's view, to an inferno of victimization, posturing, and verbal violence.

The academy has not been safe from such targeting. The toxic environment of regular shouting-down has ramifications for the free exchange of ideas in a scholarly environment; rather than remaining involved and weathering the storm, there is a disincentive for even bothering to engage the broader public. Professors as public voices who can assist in creating shared understanding and leading public discourse out of darkness may not try to accomplish such lofty goals, because they do not wish to upset an already boiling pot (Lieberman, 2017). Over the long term, we all are the less for such silence, but it is useful to admit the futility where it exists. Also, professors being human, some have posted silly, even ignorant comments that fail to engage their public role in a positive way. Because the discussion and understanding that could be available has been downplayed, the counting of examples that reinforce metanarratives, strongly informed by bias, becomes the rule. Anyone who errs is left to accept heated protest from random strangers sniping from the darkness; those strangers are not called on their own speech or personal behavior, or made to explain why they believe as they do. This cruelty is increasingly taken for public exchange of ideas, but what it actually does is further isolate. The public is becoming paranoid, with due reason – it has exchanged its common interest in civic engagement for a pastiche, in the form of a virtual public square with little real accountability. It is a public with a proclivity for watching people who are different, and believe differently, hurt, in addition to the usual stream of new memes. It may be recognized that social networks are aware that they currently provide what is perhaps the most efficient, targeted access to active voting communities, but it is important to guard against the sale of public engagement for nefarious purposes, or to parties that may serve to do harm to the public generally.

Social networks themselves are not the entirely altruistic entities that they appear. Of Facebook, for example, Bustillos (2018) denied its primary role as a community, and argued that it was instead "a wealth-creation machine built from private messages and friendships and cat videos and other publications' journalism, mixed up, wrung out for salable information, plastered with ads, and otherwise corrupted for money on its way to your 'news' (ha!) feed." In the same piece, Facebook CEO Mark Zuckerberg's initially disdainful attitude toward the site's users was recounted. The backdrop of the article was the ongoing deepening of understanding about how social networks were utilized during the 2016 US election cycle to manipulate voter inclinations, favor certain candidates over others, and otherwise interfere with transparent and sound practices appropriate for a social sphere based on truth and reason (Kelly & Bowman, 2016).

This has important implications for the public sphere, and the meaningful exchange of ideas between the public and representatives. Social networks are not, in the simplest sense, public fora, even as they may occasionally seek to act in that matter. It could be said that we can easily lose our way in the frenetic world of online networking, individually and collectively. As much as social networking platforms can be considered a platform for social change, they have had a foul underbelly that is antithetical to the better angels of our humanity. Users might be encouraged to check some of their humanity at the door, so to speak, when they enter an online format. There is no requirement that people remain who they are in real life when they sign up. It has been accepted that foreign powers have sought to affect the outcomes of political races through psychological operations in social networking environments, where doubt in candidates is created with little need for evidence in a willingly led public. What is most important, it might seem, is that the social network tell us something about ourselves that we like, or a tidbit that we agree with, whether or not it is true. The preferred role is to make one feel knowledgeable about larger issues. Barring that, a goal can be to make one use the system more, tell something salacious about someone one does not like, and then point them toward others who share those views. They can then feel involved and connected, to support some preferred and, in their view, necessary aspect of their identity.

We study language and how it is used so that we may gain insight into how it works and perhaps even replace these processes with structures and systems that work better for more people (Hylton, 2004). It might be tempting to act as if language is stable, meaning the same thing for everyone, once and for all, but we must admit at some point that this simply is not true. It is critically obvious in policy circles, where past errors are held in high relief as signs of incompetence on the part of the public sector. Quine suggested that translation required discernment, and consistent with Peirce, meaning extends from what counts as evidence (Gibson, 1996). We should not necessarily take as given that people mean what they say, but on the other hand, they may mean exactly what they say and be precisely wrong about all of it. The result could be incomprehensible because there are potential differences in determination of even supposedly objective meanings. Many so-called facts depend for their existence on belief and possibility, leading us to modal notions and possible worlds. This is a relevant point, because social media users become pseudo-journalists, able to spread a story far and wide even if it is wholly or partially untrue. Not knowing or lacking discernment does not stop social networkers from micro-publishing anyway. Wittgenstein wrote that "the limits of my language mean the limits of my world" (2006, p. 23), and concluded that "Whereof one cannot speak, thereof one must be silent" (2006, p. 30), but this talk is groundless on Twitter; what matters most could be convincing others and maybe ourselves.

The roads of public and private purpose in social networking clearly divide. There is enabling of popular sentiment, whatever that sentiment is, wrong or not, for profit. Social networks have trappings of public interaction, but have yet to figure out the complexity of inclusion and involvement in the work of the public sector. As a matter of policy and administration, the public through social networks is a bullhorn pointed at government apparatus ill-equipped and underprepared to address such interaction. This is not just a point for discussion – it is a critical public failure in a variety of respects, as it lends pushes further societal decay, weakness in other modes of communication, and a lack of capacity in public organizations to address needs and bridge gaps that exist. Under the guise of a free-flow of information, individual voices of the tech-savvy variety may approach the 'new public square,' at least close enough to have their voices thrown into a void with all the others; others without proper equipment are simply out of luck.

What is abandoned is an opportunity for real engagement, including the valuable opportunity to find out that one's contemplated opinion is incorrect, upon consideration of additional data and knowledge. What is lost is a sense of authenticity in public policy, and a chance to confront a top-down, elite-centered approach to replace the views of the communities supposedly served by programs. What is expected, in return for online environments where users are not challenged by material that they would potentially find in conflict with their established views, is constant engagement with social networks and web-enabled devices, lest we be left behind entirely. It is at best irresponsible, and at worst, an abridgment of founding principles of how people should ideally relate to their government and its administration, and to their fellow citizens. This present work takes a slice of social networking, in a contentious policymaking issue, and considers these and related issues.

Social Networks – Contextual Issues

Social networks present data, meaning "information or knowledge about an individual, object, or event" (Purdam & Elliott, 2015, p. 27). This can include both facts and perceptions. Data that exist on a social networking site like Twitter would constitute social media data, or "data generated through some public, social process that can potentially be used for social science research with or without permission" (p. 29). Twitter data is useful for understanding public attitudes (understanding that what constitutes the public represented on Twitter may not match the general non-Twitter public), but also in breaking-news situations, to explore patterns of communication (Purdam & Elliott, 2015). This allows for time-sensitive understanding of when events occurred, how knowledge came to light, and to what extent understanding became a basis for formal action.

As of April 2017, Twitter had 328 million active users (Sparks, 2017). It has been suggested that up to 48 million Twitter accounts are not run by people, but by computers, or 'bots' (Newberg, 2017). Not everyone tweets, and of those that tweet, not everyone tweets with the same volume. Americans are generally aware of Twitter but most do not use it; between 7% and 21% of Americans are Twitter users (Aslam, 2018; Baer, 2018; there appears to be some disagreement on this statistic). Behaviors run the gambit – some users publish primary material. Others are mostly content to retweet and respond to the tweets of others. What is sometimes missing is that journalists, particularly, may refer to a tweet as indication of prevailing sentiment, without noting sample sizes (Purdam & Elliott, 2015). The Twitter-verse is not representative of the entire population, though as an increasing number of people tweet, the alignment may improve.

In the Twitter environment, the lack of real-time consistency in terms of a spatial-temporal frame is obvious. An official opinion can be aired, and platform users respond at different times and places. Responses may be entered long after the original tweet ceases to be of any active importance. Importantly, though, the site is acting exactly in the manner afforded its generic term – it is a platform for writing, or sharing previously existing writing or works (including videos and pictures) (Bezemer & Kress, 2016). From a meaning-making perspective, it is a purposeful site – users log in to read the work of others (opinions and news, for example), intending to consume, or to opine on issues themselves and create content. Within the walls of the Twitter-verse, the spectrum of views might even seem total, though the site is limited to its users, a relatively small proportion of the population, and their productive capacity. This is produced through the collective work of the users a sort of atmosphere of the virtual place. It can feel light, happy, and airy, or dark, suffocating, and angry, by the prevalence of certain types of content and general thematic elements at play.

Social media has become a venue for protest, for the airing of grievances, and support of causes. Some of the same challenges that exist in real-world protests, such as the denial of right by protestors to a public space, or their right to express countering opinions, exist in the virtual world of social network use. The transfer of various forms of freedom and rights to express oneself and one's viewpoint from the offline world to an online forum is not always clear, and internationally, it is less apparent what will be tolerated by governing institutions and what will be rejected as inappropriate. Freedom of expression through social networks allows one to 'get the word out' about one's views and preferred actions, and can be a powerful influence on policymaking circles. A well-coordinated campaign can force a government, through direct contact with legislators, administrators, and others, to hear public views and do what is preferred by individuals and their affiliated groups. The direct accountability of social networking is a double-edged sword, though – it can be effective in forcing reconsideration of decisions or influencing choices to be made, but online communication can devolve into trolling and character assassination. Certain segments of the population, such as younger people, are more likely to fully utilize social networking, and the politically savvy can take advantage of these outlets to spur involvement with users. The choice among various networks may be related to who uses the tool, usage patterns, and demographics related to specific policy areas (Willis & Fellow, 2017).

It is marketing, in so many words, in that the message and intended effect will work better through some avenues of message delivery, depending on the content of the message. Brands can be effective or not, and the value-proposition offered to the targeted market may ring true and lead to intended outcomes, or fail. Communications through social networks have led to 'tangible results' in influencing political choices. Social media can shine a light of truth on injustice, but it can also lead to threats against people operating in the public space, such as journalists (Willis &

Fellow, 2017). In the US, certain social conditions, such as economic disparity, the right role of government and options for distributional policies, and threats to civil liberties, have been standard points of discussion and debate. Privacy periodically surfaces as a factor in public debate. The goal of national security has long been a consideration in public policy, particularly since the attacks of 9/11 (Willis & Fellow, 2017). These topics are common on Twitter.

It would be a mistake to ignore the impact on social networks created by US President Donald J. Trump. Trump has been a particularly strong advocate of Twitter. In a Times interview with Michael Gove, Trump noted that he would keep his personal Twitter account as he entered the presidency, because "I'd rather just let that build up and just keep it @realDonaldTrump, it's working — and the tweeting, I thought I'd do less of it, but I'm covered so dishonestly by the press — so dishonestly — that I can put out Twitter — and it's not 140, it's now 140, 280 — I can go bing bing bing and I just keep going and they put it on and as soon as I tweet it out — this morning on television, Fox — 'Donald Trump, we have breaking news'." (2017). Tweets have taken on a different aspect – moving from communication directly into the creation of news, given the 24-hour television and internet news cycle (Ingram, 2017). The professional media has little opportunity to serve its traditional role as filter of information and arbiter of what constitutes real or 'fake' news.

Since Trump entered office, there was some disagreement on whether his tweets constituted official statements, but this disagreement was largely put to rest in June 2017, when White House Press Secretary Sean Spicer offered of the tweets – "The President is the President of the United States, so they're considered official statements by the President of the United States" (Landers, 2017). This disagreement notwithstanding, it should be apparent that public officials writing in their official capacities, even if through a social networking channel like Twitter, are indeed making official statements. Public officials, including public administrators, are sometimes cautioned that they retain their right to free speech as they too are members of the public, but must actively distance such use from the making of statements in an official capacity. The voicing of a personal opinion may be taken to mean something hostile to broadly held public sentiment, which puts both public officials and government institution at potential disadvantage.

Social Networks for Research

Social life is notoriously difficult to examine. Use of interactions through online social networks provides a record that can be explored, potentially yielding insight into individual thoughts, responses to public statements, and even declarations of intended public policy, as has been increasingly the case in government officials' use of social media. An official may tweet an idea and, from the response on a social network, make the idea into an endorsed policy or adjust the approach of the policy given the feedback received.

"Social media are web-based services that allow individuals, communities, and organizations to collaborate, connect, interact, and build community by enabling them to create, co-create, modifies [sic], share, and engage with user-generated content that is easily accessible" (McCay-Peet & Quan-Haase, 2017, p. 17). Twitter, as a prominent platform, has been used in social sciences research more and more as a window on the human psyche. It is a global public space, illustrating in real-time the mundane and the monumental, with 500 million 'tweet' messages of 140 (or 280) characters or less each being shared per day. Twitter and other social networks are not separate from daily life; they are now effectively a part of it, and fora for Weberian social action, with a great percentage of people being connected to online profiles and news feeds through smartphones during practically all waking hours (Golder & Macy, 2015). Golder and Macy opined that "Twitter stands out as by far the largest and most comprehensive publicly accessible source of online data on human behavior and social interaction...[with] billions of time-stamped digital footprints..." (2015, p. 3). Through tweets, one can see both the incidence and passion of exchanges. The usefulness of this type of data and analysis in the public policy context is clear, and the mining of such interaction, in an effort to guide formal policy processes, is as a result on the rise.

Analyses of Twitter data have included the diffusion of ideas through hashtags across a social network. One can gauge interest in a particular view from the behavior of those considered influential. A study can be made of retweets (sharing of posts) and responses to given posts, as a two-way forum rather than simply a one-way publishing medium. It has been suggested that it is possible to not only explain behavior in the public sector through examination of Twitter posts but also to predict how certain groups may react to various stimuli (Golder & Macy, 2015).

Beninger (2017) put forward a number of potential concerns in reviewing the use of social media for research purposes, noting specifically that anonymity, informed consent, and avoidance of undue harm remain concerns in social media research as they are in other forms of research. In addressing the concern about consent, the issue is raised about the nature of privacy online (notably, that it does not exist), and that most issues with consent are then addressed by courtesy and intellectual property. Whether researchers actually seek consent is another story entirely, with a tacit acceptance that consent is not sought, either because it is not required or because it cannot be obtained in any realistic or consistent way (there is seldom a need for people posting online to stand by their actual identities, let alone be responsible for their comments, some of which they would dare not make if they were using their actual names).

For that reason, social media research does well to consider the context of posting online, and that the online environment is different than other published forms (even if these sites might consider themselves a form of micro-publishing, or if public officials are using them to state policy objectives in an official capacity, or to test the waters for potential policy ventures). There are differences of opinion on whether anonymity is an expectation for research on social media posts (Beninger, 2017). For purposes of this work, which revolves around public officials, as a public official is acting in a public role, public statements are not afforded anonymity, whereas responses from the public would be afforded such anonymity. The reason for affording anonymity to public responses is that the public is being treated as a general entity (the mass of public opinion) rather than any specific grouping or individual; while the posting is public, the private individual is perhaps not acting in a public role, but as part of the voicing of concern in the public sphere. In terms of causing undue harm, social media sites are clear with users that their posts are made public and that the individual user is responsible for the use of the service.

Issues exist with the collection and use of social network data. For one, the data are voluntarily published on a privately owned website and these data are thus privately owned, even though they are made publicly available, and monetized to the company's benefit. Consistent with discussion elsewhere in this book, it has been asked whether the online world is a reflection of the real world or simply and parallel adjunct to it. Clearly, not everyone uses social networking and many voices that exist in the real world do not exist as part of a social network like Twitter, so there is no one-for-one correspondence. Nevertheless, the 'world' posed by social networks is valid on its own terms (Golder & Macy, 2015), and increasingly impactful upon the real world, given that public officials post on social networks and these posts have implications for real world behavior and public outcomes.

Methods and Materials

Johnston suggests that uncovering "various layers of symbols, styles, appeals, and content in political advertising" can be understood through "qualitative content analysis, quantitative content analysis, and critical and rhetorical analysis" (2006, p. 17). Through rhetorical and descriptive analysis, one can view critically the narratives and imagery that make up official persuasive communication. From a semiotic perspective, these attempts at persuasion are themselves indicative of larger frameworks of meaning, and should not be taken at face value alone. One may explore meaning made through such entreaties by considering structure, portions of the written/image content, or combinations of both. Variables in the analysis, such as time spent discussing certain points relative to others, and what exactly makes a persuasive effort negative (Johnston, 2006).

Viewing social media interaction, retweets and comments, and the volume of such interaction, can exist themselves as a document of communication, and also serve to show whether interactions had the intended effect. A negative advertisement has no effect if it is not seen and heard, just like the proverbial tree falling in the forest with no one to hear it. The tendency to 'go negative,' may have an impact on the public space, in increasing jadedness and negativity among those responding to initial adverse posts. If public decisions are already foregone conclusions, airs of public engagement and involvement can be seen as hollow and a waste of time.

More people are writing and publishing than ever before, and this gives social scientists and others great prospect for understanding decision-making and behavior in a variety of contexts. A problem of social networking research is volume; too much data moves through the system at all times to make data selection and analysis choices easy. When using complex computational algorithms, transparency of method may be lacking, and sham correlations may be presented from inductive methods. Mixed method approaches can provide a way forward, and anonymization of data can help deal with ethical issues that might be associated with the use of social media data. There are concerns with using Twitter data, for example, as a substitute for conventional survey data, due to representativeness concerns (Halfpenny & Procter, 2015). Still, the traditional survey instrument imposes a worldview and potentially a bias of the researcher, in how questions are stated. Twitter data has a level of meaningfulness that is not offered by traditional surveys, in that site users actively make their own sense of reality and make statements that seek to mirror that perspective. They interact with one another, arguing in a public space, echoing sound bites and comments removed from their former contexts.

Twitter makes the following statement about ownership of tweets and subsequent use:

> This license authorizes us to make your Content available to the rest of the world and to let others do the same. You agree that this license includes the right for Twitter to provide, promote, and improve the Services and to make Content submitted to or through the Services available to other companies, organizations or individuals for the syndication, broadcast, distribution, promotion or publication of such Content on other media and services, subject to our terms and conditions for such Content use. Such additional uses by Twitter, or other companies, organizations or individuals, may be made with no compensation paid to you with respect to the Content that you submit, post, transmit or otherwise make available through the Services.
>
> (Twitter, 2017)

Twitter data are free up to certain limits, beyond which data are available for purchase from Twitter or secondary suppliers. "The coding of tweets and re-tweets and Internet search engine terms for attitudes and meaning can be of considerable value" (Purdam & Elliott, 2015, p. 44).

Text mining describes "either a single process or a collection of processes in which software tools actively engage in 'the discovery of new, previously unknown information by automatically extracting information from different written (or text) sources'" (Ampofo, Collister, O'Loughlin, & Chadwick, 2015, p. 162; Fan et al, 2006). These data sources are unstructured, and so present some analytical challenges, due to the large potential volume of text. Even with the challenges, the opportunities presented make sources of data like Twitter worth consideration. Big data methods possibly offer greater understanding of behavior, but they are not a cure-all for analytical problems. Given the consideration of semiotic approaches in this volume, how people use words and communicate with one another is not a set matter, so assumptions that are made about these phenomena, which fail to grasp at the intricacy that exists in the real world, will lead to mistaken results. Idioms, too, present real challenges for automated big data analyses (Ampofo, Collister, O'Loughlin, & Chadwick, 2015).

How *much* data is an issue. Twitter has a full public stream called the firehose, through which all published tweets flow. Lesser streams are also available for analysis. There have been concerns about the changing nature of Twitter's service agreement, with previous versions of the agreement preventing researchers from individual tweets, but not derivative data of 'positive sentiment' (Ampofo, Collister, O'Loughlin, & Chadwick, 2015).

Social media posts, such as Twitter, have been considered "relational, performative, and ephemeral," but this has changed somewhat as social media has become more fixed in the larger culture; some have become more careful with their interactions given awareness of the persistence and searchability of such communications (Veletsianos, 2016, p. 56). The question might be asked of whether context matters for interpretation; a tendency might exist for any statement to be taken out of context and used for any purpose, no matter whether the statement is made on Twitter or in an academic text.

This analysis considered tweets from key senators in the debate on repeal and replace the Affordable Care Act (ACA, also referred to as Obamacare). 2017's contentious debate found the Republican majority unable to obtain consensus and passage of the Graham-Cassidy bill to repeal the ACA. At the time, news stories tended to focus on a small group of senators, including both moderates and hard-liners, which had various concerns and issues with the proposed repeal measure. Their concerns and opinions tended to be more highly scrutinized, even magnified, because of the importance of their vote in determining the ultimate decision on repeal and replace. Shapiro and Soffen (2017) identified 11 'key senators' instrumental in defining the debate on Graham-Cassidy: McCain of Arizona, Moran of Kansas, Lee of Utah, Johnson of Wisconsin, Cruz of Texas, Paul of Kentucky, Heller of Nevada, Capito of West Virginia, Portman of Ohio, Murkowski of Alaska, and Collins of Maine. Reilly (2017) also considered Collins, Heller, Johnson, Lee, Paul, Capito, Portman, Moran, Cruz, McCain, and Murkowski, and added Cassidy. For the analysis in this chapter, I began with tweets to the 12 key senators.

For the period of study, I selected a date that showed high interest for purposes of this policy debate: September 26, 2017, was the day that it was determined that the Graham-Cassidy amendment (Senate Amendment 1030 to the American Health Care Act of 2017, HR 1628) would not be brought forward for a vote. I then extended the period of review back to August 24, 2017, and then forward to October 30, 2017, to gather additional sentiment about related decisions, and public interactions on either side of the key date. To gather the tweets, Data Miner was used; Data Miner includes a variety of 'recipes' to facilitate a variety of scraping approaches. Because the intent was that all possible tweets were being collected (as many as possible given this rather crude, but cost-effective method of scraping), I used the recipe called 'Download Tweets (Navigate to End) Full' – this allowed Data Miner to force a continual re-load of tweets until the end of the search called for in Twitter's 'Advanced Search' is completed. Through advanced search, one provides a variety of parameters, including search terms, Twitter accounts to examine (options include tweets to, from, or mentioning the account). One can also include a range of dates for searching.

Using the Twitter accounts mentioned above (option was to include a reference to any of the accounts, in any tweet), I focused on the terms 'ACA' and 'Obamacare.' The reason for including ACA was that this is a more neutral, technical reference to the law and its attendant program; 'Obamacare' was included, because it is the more difficult term used to describe the program. It has a negative association, in which program opponents use the term and it is meant derisively; however, program proponents have also used the term. Indeed, in South Florida at least, storefront operations in strip malls were set up to facilitate program enrolments. These businesses were not official government locations but rather set up by entrepreneurial sorts that were either enterprising or opportunistic, depending on one's perspective. The Obamacare term was regularly used in business signage, signaling both acceptance of the term in a branding sense and widespread understanding of its use as equivalent to ACA, not necessarily including a negative undertone.

The research question for the chapter is: What can tweets about ACA to key senators during a critical policy period tell us about signs and symbols employed in the discourse? As a corollary, what can we know from an exploration of the tweets about the thinking and interaction patterns of Twitter users, with regard to this policy debate?

This analysis employs content and sentiment analysis. This policy debate was of significant interest to the Twitter-verse. This analysis suggests a system of beliefs and ideologies among various users of the platform, which indicates the presence of larger forces at play in positioning certain points and crafting positions at a branded level. Counting is prominent in this approach, so the methodology is more quantitative, and less subject to interpretation of text. Underlying meaning, while possibly important, is less important initially in this particular approach over the breadth of the material, and figures more conspicuously in subsequent analysis of major themes and apparent symbols/brands that are used to convey beliefs or argue for certain outcomes within the reform debate (Boréus & Bergström, 2017).

The rationale for content analysis of this material is that utilization and repetition of materials via tweets to (or in some cases, more properly at) key senators in the context of a policy debate invokes aspects that are indicative of other underlying tendencies, beliefs, or concerns. The analysis may evidence patterns that exist, or show how facets of a topic, or even key people involved, are being portrayed, in a way that seeks to encourage or discourage behaviors. The recurrence of certain terms, phrases, or quasi-sentences may be illustrative of ideology or utilization of symbol toward a specific, identifiable end. Content analysis might be used in discerning how use of a concept has changed in communication over time (Boréus & Bergström, 2017).

Lindberg reminds us of Friedrich's argument, that "the truth or falsity of the ideas and ideologies is not important for their possibility of being effectual or operative. The key thing is that they are subjectively held to be true by their propagators and adherents" (2017, p. 89). In the tweet-discourse on ACA-reform, there were instances of users taking their beliefs and idealism as the larger reality applicable equally to others, and that consensus had been reached when the truth of the debate was far different. Assumptions of holism were made. As there is no requirement that posters on Twitter go by their real-life names, the agent of the messages was frequently unclear. Even when posters were retweeting the messages of large, organized interests, it is possible that they did not know of these outside interests, and were instead just agreeing with the micro statement of belief, as its own entity, rather than showing an awareness of being part of the larger platform of an outside interest group (Lindberg, 2017).

This chapter relies upon James Pennebaker's work on computational linguistics, to examine how words are used and what word frequency counts can tell us about patterns of social interaction (Pennebaker, 2011). More specifically, I used the LIWC2015 program to evaluate the corpus of tweets. LIWC works by processing written or transcribed...text files. The text analysis module then compares each word in the text against a user-defined dictionary... the dictionary identifies which words are associated with which psychologically-relevant categories. After the processing module has read and accounted for all words in a given text, it calculates the percentage of total words that match each of the dictionary categories.

(LIWC, 2018a)

The strength of the approach is in the work that has gone into the dictionaries associated with the program, which can relate a massive corpus back to not only variables that show percentage of words against the total words of the corpus, but also summary variables. These summary components include analytical thinking, meaning "the degree to which people use words that suggest formal, logical, and hierarchical thinking patterns," clout, or "the degree to which people use words that suggest formal, logical, and hierarchical thinking patterns," authenticity, meaning honesty of the writer, where they are more likely to be humble or vulnerable, and emotional tone, where a score above 50 on a 100-point scale would indicate a relatively more positive tone (LIWC, 2018b).

Sharp (1998) studied the National Performance Review (NPR) through two types of quantitative analysis: a content analysis of the NPR lead report, and a story analysis values being promoted by stories within NPR. The finding was that stories are effective in communicating, given central tenets of a need for change and the inherent value of productivity. The cutting of red tape, the creation of citizen as customer, and the supposed need for government to act like more business-like were defining characteristics of NPR stories, and the NPR effort effectively used media in many respects to sell NPR ideas. Beyond analysis of sentiment, as with Sharp's experience, I expected to see not only interesting phenomena to be identified through this analysis, but also to note the presence of storylines, perhaps involving certain senators or decisions being made within the larger debate.

Analysis

The large volume (about 290,000 tweets, including retweets) that had been collected by Data Miner for the period opened up an interesting analytical problem – there were many approaches that could be taken to analyzing Twitter data. However, given my question, which sought to identify signs and symbols, I recognized that the nature of the tweets tended to focus on certain senators, and, generally speaking, lacked nuance. Twitter had become a blunt instrument, the tweets so numerous toward certain senators that it could be suggested that as a window into the public's viewpoint on ACA, the Twitter-verse lacked the decorum for policy discourse. I did a simple 'bag of words' word count on the corpus, which led me to the realization that tweets were tending to center on Senator John McCain. I wanted to know more about these tweets and Twitter-users statements and their modes of thinking. As a result, I ran LIWC a number of times on the corpus – on the corpus as a whole, which yielded baseline results that could be compared against ambient levels for Twitter, as identified by Pennebaker, Boyd, Jordan, and Blackburn (2015). From there, I searched the corpus to identify only those posts that involved Senator John McCain; I broke this sub-corpus into nine weeks, from August 25, 2017 through October 26, 2017, so that I could note shifts in LIWC measures, as representative of tweets directed to Senator Mc-Cain and how they changed over time, as the policy issue evolved.

Figure 8.1 shows the 'bag of words' for the corpus as a word cloud. The appearance of Senator McCain's Twitter handle is evident as impactful. Figure 8.2 shows the volume of tweets about ACA/Obamacare, including Senator McCain, during the studied period; the decision point is discernible by the peak volume of tweets, though the slight uptick in tweets in October, where users were considering what had occurred and responding to it, is notable.

Table 8.1 shows the LIWC analysis, for baseline/ambient Twitter (external to this policy debate), for the corpus as a whole, and for the tweets involving Senator McCain, which are in the following columns divided into nine periods of a week each. LIWC includes a long list of categories. I have included here the four major categories of the LIWC system (analytic, clout, authentic, and tone), as well as those

Figure 8.1 Bag of Words, Word cloud for McCain tweets.

Source: Created by C. A. based upon subset of collected tweets related to the Affordable Care Act, referencing Senator John McCain, using https://www.jasondavies.com/word cloud/. I collected the tweets as described in the text.

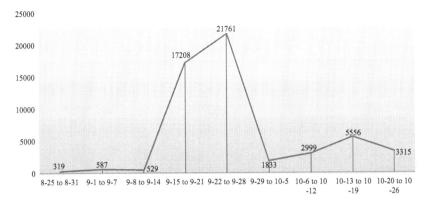

Figure 8.2 Tweets, McCain Subgroup, August 25 to October 26, 2017.
Source: Created by C. A., based upon subset of collected tweets related to the Affordable Care Act, referencing Senator John McCain. I collected the tweets as described in the text.

categories differing by more than 25% from the ambient Twitter background score as noted in Pennebaker, Boyd, Jordan, and Blackburn (2015). The levels are highlighted in light gray for 25%–49% difference from the ambient level; medium gray for 50%–74%; and black for a difference of 75% or more.

The emotional tone of the tweets tracks with the volume of tweets posted, with a peak at the decision point and an additional increase during the October 6–12 period. Emotional tone is the window on how people cope as well as react to a situation; more emotional words may indicate greater immersion in a traumatic event, for example (Tausczik & Pennebaker, 2010). As shown in Figure 8.3, analytical scores remained high through the study period, and authenticity scores were low throughout.

This output paints a worrisome portrait. For one, users clearly had some idea that their tweets would be seen and that sending a message via this medium was purposeful. The problem with that is that there were others who had the same idea, and further, elected officials are not willing (or possibly even able) to engage in this flow of discussion in a way that would make sense for discerning public opinion. The Twitter-verse is not representative of all constituents (or even constituents at all, from a hyperreal perspective; all that is required is to sign up for an account and login to post in a manner that could, conceivably, be viewed as 'public comment,' not to mention that some posts could be from 'bots' or computers). While users are passionate and employ all manner of rhetoric in a fevered effort to sway opinion and even persuade, one cannot persuade when one has no audience. It is obvious, given the timing of the greatest volume of tweets and the changing, negatively emotional tone, around a week before the eventual decision-point, that there was a sense that

Table 8.1 LIWC, Tweets on ACA involving Senator John McCain, compared with ambient Twitter background levels

	Twitter ambient background levels	8-25-17 to 10-26-17 (whole period)	8-25-17 to 10-26-17 (whole period, McCain tweets only)	8-25 to 8-31	9-1 to 9-7	9-8 to 9-14	9-15 to 9-21	9-22 to 9-28	9-29 to 10-5	10-6 to 10-12	10-13 to 10-19	10-20 to 10-26	Difference between McCain tweets and ambient twitter levels (%)
Analytical thinking	61.94	77.11	80.43	73.71	79.42	71.77	84.02	77.62	78.40	84.45	79.84	79.00	29.85
Clout	63.02	73.05	76.54	86.51	83.28	76.10	66.52	79.65	82.60	77.69	83.35	79.84	21.45
Authentic	50.39	5.17	3.39	2.82	4.56	2.83	3.53	3.28	3.26	2.99	3.77	3.27	−93.27
Emotional tone	72.24	47.02	46.71	30.62	24.46	44.29	69.12	42.95	27.00	41.20	27.10	22.00	−35.34
Other punctuation (other than periods, commas, etc.). Might include @, #, *, for example.	1.56	12.12	17.99	13.45	16.30	16.49	19.00	17.94	18.35	21.81	15.72	13.59	1053.21
Quotation marks	1.3	4.38	4.56	4.85	5.21	5.28	3.86	4.89	3.91	4.40	5.43	4.89	250.77
Power (drive)	2.17	4.29	5.04	4.88	4.65	5.01	4.33	5.37	5.85	6.75	4.96	4.35	132.26
Money (personal concern)	0.74	2.58	1.65	0.87	1.02	1.05	2.20	1.31	1.36	1.62	1.76	1.55	122.97
Dashes (punct.)	1.21	2.25	2.69	2.28	4.81	3.69	2.47	2.52	4.70	4.68	2.27	1.61	122.31

Risk focus (drives)	0.46	1.17	1.02	0.60	0.81	0.71	1.63	0.72	0.74	0.99	0.82	0.59	121.74
Health/illness (biological)	0.54	1.29	1.19	0.66	0.61	1.46	2.10	0.84	0.92	0.83	0.54	0.78	120.37
Death (biological concern)	0.19	0.34	0.37	0.30	0.19	0.24	0.53	0.31	0.23	0.26	0.37	0.30	94.74
Question marks (personal concern)	1.4	2.25	2.56	2.38	2.89	2.72	0.71	2.41	3.52	3.54	2.92	2.79	82.86
Words >6 letters	15.31	24.00	27.40	24.59	23.91	25.59	27.92	27.75	25.66	28.46	26.99	24.55	78.97
She-he (3rd person sing.)	0.64	0.80	1.14	2.04	1.43	1.89	0.48	1.27	1.07	1.24	1.73	2.28	78.13
Male referent	0.84	0.82	1.32	2.34	1.66	2.07	0.66	1.42	1.15	1.38	1.99	2.62	57.14
All punctuation	27.46	36.32	42.66	37.59	44.72	42.81	42.34	42.15	43.53	48.07	40.94	36.56	55.35
Sad (affect word)	0.43	0.64	0.66	0.67	0.60	0.51	0.52	0.72	0.53	0.76	0.86	0.65	53.49
Anger (affect word)	0.75	0.99	1.12	1.52	1.11	1.11	0.70	1.18	1.57	0.83	1.63	1.84	49.33
Numbers	1.98	2.43	2.90	2.21	3.29	3.29	2.97	2.69	3.63	3.89	2.49	2.87	46.46
Drives (inclusive of affiliation, achievement, power, reward, and risk)	7.5	10.03	10.62	9.75	10.00	10.65	10.41	10.73	11.48	12.77	10.03	9.13	41.60
Negations	1.74	2.65	2.34	1.72	1.97	2.28	3.34	2.16	1.79	1.16	1.53	1.65	34.48
Netspeak	3.23	3.06	4.29	4.18	4.88	4.91	4.07	4.31	4.58	5.53	3.87	4.06	32.82

Source: Created by C.A., using LIWC2015 analysis output. I collected the tweets as described in the text. The ambient twitter levels are from Pennebaker, Boyd, Jordan, and Blackburn (2015), The development and psychometric properties of LIWC2015.

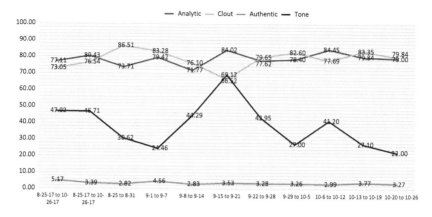

Figure 8.3 Tweets, LIWC2015 Results, ACA/Obamacare Tweets, McCain Subgroup.

Source Created by C.A., using LIWC2015 analysis output. I collected the tweets as described in the text.

communication via the platform might change things in one's favor, or affect the eventual decision. This sense, however, was most likely mistaken. The 'aftermath peak' in October further indicates a desire to discuss or understand, if not simply vent about the decision, but again, these posts lack impact on the process in real life.

Discussion

What are we to take then, from a review of about 290,000 tweets, and the still-sizable subset focused just on Senator John McCain? What became clear is that the decision-makers are not making use of feedback received via these tools, in an active and engaging way, and may only be able to do so in a way that is as equally automated and artificial as the manner in which the feedback is being received. The responses are, in many respects, dummy variables: The variable of preference is either on or off, and there is little shading. What is most helpful is the deeper understanding one can gain from discussions with individuals and small groups, but there simply is not time for a senator, with all their other obligations, to fully engage the firehose of public sentiment to be gained via Twitter. We see instead patterns and general viewpoints, and perhaps overlaps of term usage; even with machine learning, though, so much is lost. It is perhaps a positive that most users do not employ Twitter for carefully nuanced communication, but to join a battering ram of popular sentiment in favor of one action or another. This, to proponents of a repopulation of the public sphere, fuller discourse, and transparency, must seem a shame. Twitter is no place for a careful hearing of a nuanced debate.

The Twitter discussion was not 'public engagement' with potential of interacting with leaders or changing minds. On big national debates, the quality of interaction and potential for change is likely smaller than it would be on a local or even state level. In this instance, rhetoric was fiery and emotions raised, but for what real, impactful purpose?

One moves beyond the favoring of one side or another to take a closer look at the story of Senator McCain in this debate, given that he was most targeted via tweets. I could have just as easily examined him through the portraits painted by Twitter users. McCain became either a protagonist of this debate, joining his status as a highly decorated American war hero and former prisoner of war, honored senator, and a maverick of public policy, or a villain, a turncoat traitor, and enemy of 'MAKE AMERICA GREAT AGAIN!' evidenced by the frequent use of the #MAGA hashtag[1] McCain himself was a symbol for policy purposes – ill understood, taken for granted, loved or villainized on the basis of decisions made, and at times, removed in various quarters from himself and his career as a civil servant to function as the hyperreal face of either the success or failure of someone else's policy platform, as unavoidable historical evolution, or failed ambition. These portrayals, positive or negative, were simplistic and beneath him.

Concluding Thoughts

Social networking has opened up a host of issues that might involve government. The expression of free political speech on the web is, as free speech is elsewhere, not without consequence or responsibility. The minimal principle of liberty suggests that "the government should not prohibit people from acting as they wish unless it has a positive reason to do so" (Greenawalt, 1995, p. 664). Is speech harmful in a public forum? Where is a line crossed? This must be balanced with the goal of promoting tolerance. Examples of espousing a narrow, and even indefensible, view while refusing to allow that right for others abound. Speech, written and spoken, may be venting, but it is also purposeful action. If dissent is not allowed at all, because it is out of alignment with a prevailing sentiment, then the underlying assumptions and considerations that are being made, perhaps unfairly, can never be addressed positively. Or else, we have liberty as long as it is convenient; this limited liberty is provisional, and allowed only as long as it does not destabilize or threaten existing power structures. The outcome of this scenario is not tolerance, nor does it constitute equity. It does not allow for the dignity or the identity of the individual, as it sees the system *choosing the winners* absent discourse and disagreement. The creation is a thin society, perilously devoid of meaning, where acceptability of thinking and action are predetermined.

At various times in history, the commons has served as a venue for punishment as public spectacle. Wrongdoers, real and supposed, are brought before the collected citizenry, their transgressions read in the court of public opinion, and judicial enforcement meted out to the horror or delight of baying crowds. The crowds themselves become part of the spectacle, in that they function as audience, but serve no official function. They do not participate in decision-making processes, or otherwise, determine what occurs. What they do matters little to the decisions that are made for the public spectacle that will occur, because those decisions have already been made. Placing the punishment in the commons and allowing, for lack of a better way of putting it, the public to have its say, adds a layer of popular sentiment to what would otherwise be a process devoid of public involvement. Entertainment, rather than participation, is the apparent goal.

With social networks, when a public figure has crossed some real or perceived line of transgression, instead of being placed in the stocks in a public square, the individual is hoisted up and scourged via tweets or Facebook posts. There is no court – anyone with the sense (or lack of) to sign up for a social networking account can become a judge and jury for the court of public opinion. For some, the need may be vengeance, for an action taken in the public sphere, where disagreement exists, to see that person and their reputation destroyed. The extra steps of confronting opposing views and understanding complexities are deemed unnecessary. The victors on social networks are the first in, so that their views may be retweeted by others – so that their sphere of individual influence may grow. Instead of a patient, tolerant discourse, we have vile tweets and retweets, and a drumbeat of 'repeal and replace.' There is little attention to proper and respectful social discourse, because frankly that is seen as a waste of time.

When taking into account the sum of the corpus of tweets studied here, it is clear that attention became focused, both positive and negative, on Senator John McCain, the health condition that went on to subsequently end his life, and the fitness of his decision. The comments were personal and often vicious. He became a polarizing figure, reflecting the split view seen in the initial analysis of all tweets. Given his policy decisions, which were not apparently influenced by social media, the most those in the Twitter universe could do in response was seek to shame or publish him in the virtual public space, as someone that stood in the way of a promise to repeal and replace the hated Obamacare. The anger persisted and worsened after the decision was made. That he personally stood in the way of #MAGA and prevented President Trump's victory took on symbolic, even mythical proportions. Discourse devolved into either curses, or thanks from those who were proponents of the ACA and its reform. McCain probably did not spend his days reading the flood of messages on Twitter, so "the show is all actors, and no audience" (Scott, 1990, p. 59).

It is difficult to avoid the idea that, absent other narratives, the profoundly negative and even threatening posts on Twitter about Senator

McCain betrayed some very base notions of the Congress as simply a means to an end, which should have been more or less clear as a result of the election of President Trump. In this respect, any further discussion, from the perspective of the most vocal in the Twitter-verse, was a waste of time, if not wrong-acting in the face of a supposed overwhelming mandate to roll back the ACA entirely. The tone of this writing is not exaggerated – this merely reflects the tenor of the tweets from the proponents of ACA repeal. Senator McCain's 'no' votes were a slap in the face of certain vocal groupings within the Republican party, even if he had every reason to consider policy the way he did, and come to the conclusions at which he arrived. Senator McCain was persisting in serving in the senatorial role as he understood it; this simply was not well taken by proponents of ACA repeal. I would not generally suggest that Twitter users who wrote these posts would, on reflection, be this reckless or show a conscious preference for authoritarianism, given a real-life opportunity for discussion and understanding, even though some might. There is a distinct and noticeable lack of thought that goes into writing posts on social networks, in emotional policy circumstances, which goes to baser instincts and does not allow for discourse and increase of understanding. Worse, the posts are mean, thoughtless, and in many cases juvenile; posters are hiding behind Twitter handles as if there are no repercussions for their behavior, because they are right – there are probably no repercussions for often their hateful, self-serving behavior.

In a late 2017 interview with the BBC, former US President Barack Obama spoke on the use of the Internet by senior public officials. "All of us in leadership have to find ways in which we can recreate a common space on the internet," Obama said. "One of the dangers of the internet is that people can have entirely different realities. They can be cocooned in information that reinforces their current biases" (Smith-Spark, 2017). Obama went on to suggest that people should consider disconnecting from the online world more often, so that they can see the complexity of individuals in real-life; for the time being spent online, there is a poverty of allowance for diverse viewpoints.

There are problems with social networks as public forums. Ira Strauber wrote that "it is prudent to consider that in the past, (unpredictable) social forces shape and drive technologies as much as (unpredictable) technologies shape and drive society" (2004, p. 362). It is evident that social networks do not have a firm command of their services as resources, to the full extent that their eventual use in the public domain has dictated. Rather than taking to social networks incrementally, the expansion and filling up of this public forum has been one of trial-by-fire. All expertise via social networks is not sorted out by evaluation of the "qualifications, incompleteness, uncertainties, and flaws" associated with truth claims (Strauber, 2004, p. 362), and so large mistakes and misunderstandings are possible.

There are open questions to the genuineness of the discourse and the credibility of statements of fact, or pretensions to right interpretations. Villains and victims are made on social networks daily. Even with all of that, social networks have demonstrated their ability to re-involve people into discussions of public importance that otherwise may have been largely ignored. The medium, whether printed documents or communication via traditional radio and television, or new media and via the Internet, matters less than the factor of inclusion of those that might otherwise be marginalized. Particularly because it is so difficult to involve actively and meaningfully large segments of society in public discourse, there is the potential to make better use of these tools to act as a sounding board for public sentiment, but also to make the choices made by governments more representative of the public's desires, and ultimately the work of government more transparent and accountable. It is possible that the impactful and important perspective of the individual is lost among greater participation or too much regard for the meta-narrative (Tohar, Asar, Kainan, & Shahar, 2007), but it most assuredly is lost when it is not heard or acknowledged at all. The more people are made non-entities, the greater the chance that they will react in a jaded, disinterested manner in approaching public discourse. The possibility of a more knowledgeable and engaged public is worth any assumed bother associated with public participation – it is, after all, the public's government.

Note

1 *Make America Great Again*, of the Donald Trump usage, was a frequent refrain in social media from the 2016 election campaign into Trump's term in office. Trump referred to his use of social media as 'modern day presidential,' seeming to herald a new era of political usage of social media, through his own use of the Twitter platform (Graham, 2017). In short form, #MAGA indicates belief in and consistency with Trump's perspectives.

References

Ampofo, L., Collister, S., O'Loughlin, B., & Chadwick, A. (2015). Text mining and social media: When quantitative meets qualitative and software meets people. In P. Halfpenny & R. Procter (Eds.), *Innovations in digital research methods, 161–192*. London: Sage.

Aslam, S. (2018). Twitter by the numbers: Stats, demographics & fun facts. Retrieved from https://www.omnicoreagency.com/twitter-statistics/.

Baer, J. (2018). 7 surprising statistics about Twitter in America. Retrieved from https://www.convinceandconvert.com/social-media-strategy/7-surprising-statistics-about-twitter-in-america/.

Beninger, K. (2017). Social media users' views on the ethics of social media research. In L. Sloan & A. Quan-Haase (Eds.), *The SAGE handbook of social media research methods, 57–73*. London: SAGE Publications.

Bezemer, J., & Kress, G. (2016). *Multimodality, learning and communication: A social semiotic frame*. Abingdon, Oxon: Routledge.

Boréus, K., & Bergström, G. (2017). Content analysis. In K. Boréus & G. Bergström (Eds.), *Analyzing text and discourse: Eight approaches for the social sciences, 23–52*. Thousand Oaks, CA: Sage Publications.

Bustillos, M. (2018, March 8). The smallness of Mark Zuckerberg. *Medium*. Retrieved from https://medium.com/s/story/the-smallness-of-mark-zuckerberg-4e94a88bba02.

Fan, W., Wallace, L., Rich, S., & Zhang, Z. (2006). Tapping the power of text mining. *Communications of the ACM, 49*(9), 76–82.

Gibson, R. F. (1996). Quine, Wittgenstein, and holism. In R. L. Arrington & J. Glock (Eds.), *Wittgenstein and Quine, 80–96*. London: Routledge.

Golder, S. A., & Macy, M. W. (2015). Introduction. In Y. Mejova, I. Weber, & M. W. Macy (Eds.), *Twitter; A digital socioscope, 1–20*. New York: Cambridge University Press.

Gove, M. (2017, January 15). Donald Trump interview: Brexit will be a great thing. *The Times*. Retrieved from https://www.thetimes.co.uk/article/donald-trump-interview-brexit-britain-trade-deal-europe-queen-5m0bc2tns.

Graham, C. (2017, July 2). 'Modern day presidential': Donald Trump defends use of social media in Twitter storm. *The Telegraph*. Retrieved from https://www.telegraph.co.uk/news/2017/07/01/modern-day-presidential-donald-trump-defends-use-social-media/.

Greenawalt, K. (1995). Rationales for freedom of speech. In D. G. Johnson & H. Nissenbaum (Eds.), *Computers, ethics & social values, 664–677*. Upper Saddle River, NJ: Prentice Hall.

Halfpenny, P., & Procter, R. (2015). Introduction and overview. In P. Halfpenny & R. Procter (Eds.), *Innovations in digital research methods, 1–24*. London: Sage.

Holtz-Bacha, C., & Kaid, L. L. (2006). Political advertising in international comparison. In C. Holtz-Bacha & L. L. Kaid (Eds.), *The Sage handbook of political advertising, 3–14*. Thousand Oaks, CA: Sage Publications.

Hylton, P. (2004). Quine on reference and ontology. In R. F. Gibson, Jr. (Ed.), *The Cambridge companion to Quine, 115–150*, Cambridge, UK: Cambridge University Press.

Ingram, M. (2017, January 17). Here's why Donald Trump says he loves Twitter and plans to keep tweeting. *Fortune*. Retrieved from http://fortune.com/2017/01/17/trump-loves-twitter/.

Johnston, A. (2006). Methodologies for the study of political advertising. In C. Holtz-Bacha & L. L. Kaid (Eds.), *The Sage handbook of political advertising, 15–36*. Thousand Oaks, CA: Sage Publications.

Kelly, M. L., & Bowman, E. (2016, December 10). CIA concludes Russian interference aimed to elect Trump. *The Two-way (NPR)*. Retrieved from https://www.npr.org/sections/thetwo-way/2016/12/10/505072304/cia-concludes-russian-interference-aimed-to-elect-trump.

Landers, E. (2017, June 6). White House: Trump's tweets are 'official statements.' *CNN*. Retrieved from http://www.cnn.com/2017/06/06/politics/trump-tweets-official-statements/index.html.

Lieberman, D. (2017, December 28). Death threats are forcing professors off campus. *CNN*. Retrieved from http://www.cnn.com/2017/12/21/us/university-professors-free-speech-online-hate-threats/index.html.

Lindberg, M. (2017). Qualitative analysis of ideas and ideological content. In K. Boréus & G. Bergström (Eds.), *Analyzing text and discourse: Eight approaches for the social sciences, 86–121*. Thousand Oaks, CA: Sage Publications.

LIWC. (2018a). How it works. *LIWC*. Retrieved from https://liwc.wpengine.com/how-it-works/.

LIWC. (2018b). Interpreting LIWC output. *LIWC*. Retrieved from https://liwc.wpengine.com/interpreting-liwc-output/.

McCay-Peet, L., & Quan-Haase, A. (2017). What is social media and what questions can social media research help us answer? In L. Sloan & A. Quan-Haase (Eds.), *The SAGE handbook of social media research methods, 13–26*. London: SAGE Publications.

Newberg, M. (2017, March 10). As many as 48 million Twitter accounts aren't people, says study. *CNBC*. Retrieved from https://www.cnbc.com/2017/03/10/nearly-48-million-twitter-accounts-could-be-bots-says-study.html.

Obama, B. H. (2017). Repealing the ACA without a replacement - The risks to American health care. *New England Journal of Medicine, 376*(4), 297–299.

Pappas, G. S. (2000). *Berkeley's thought.* Ithaca, NY: Cornell University Press.

Pennebaker, J. W. (2011). The secret life of pronouns: What our words say about us. New York: Bloomsbury.

Pennebaker, J. W., Boyd, R. L., Jordan, K., & Blackburn, K. (2015). *The development and psychometric properties of LIWC2015.* Austin, TX: University of Texas at Austin.

Purdam, K., & Elliott, M. (2015). The changing social science digital landscape. In P. Halfpenny & R. Procter (Eds.), *Innovations in digital research methods, 25–58.* London: Sage.

Reilly, M. (2017, June 27). Here's where key senators stand on the GOP health care bill. *Huffington Post*. Retrieved from https://www.huffingtonpost.com/entry/senate-health-care-bill-whip-count_us_59528846e4b05c37bb79b921.

Scott, J. C. (1990). *Domination and the arts of resistance: Hidden transcripts.* New Haven, CT: Yale University Press.

Shapiro, L., & Soffen, K. (2017, September 26). How key senators changed their positions to bring down Obamacare repeal. *The Washington Post*. Retrieved from https://www.washingtonpost.com/graphics/2017/politics/health-care-swing-votes/?utm_term=.676008f1e4a4.

Sharp, B. S. (1998). *Expressing political and administrative values through stories: A semiotic analysis of the national performance review.* Doctoral dissertation. UMI 9905608.

Smith-Spark, L. (2017, December 27). Obama warns over divisive social media use in Prince Harry interview. *CNN*. Retrieved from http://www.cnn.com/2017/12/27/politics/obama-prince-harry-interview-social-media-intl/index.html.

Sparks, D. (2017, April 27). How many users does Twitter have? The motley fool. Retrieved from https://www.fool.com/investing/2017/04/27/how-many-users-does-twitter-have.aspx.

Strauber, I. L. (2004). Semiotics, civic education and the internet. *International Journal for the Semiotics of Law, 17*, 343–363.

Tausczik, Y. R., & Pennebaker, J. W. (2010). The psychological meaning of words: LIWC and computerized text analysis methods. *Journal of Language and Social Psychology, 29*(1), 24–54.

Tohar, V., Asaf, M., Kainan, A., & Shahar, R. (2007). An alternative approach for personal narrative interpretation: The semiotics of Roland Barthes. *International Journal of Qualitative Methods, 6*(3), 57–70.

Twitter. (2017). Twitter terms of service. Retrieved from https://web.archive.org/web/20171015022717/https://twitter.com/en/tos.

Veletsianos, G. (2016). *Social media in academia: Networked scholars.* New York: Routledge.

Willis, J., & Fellow, A. R. (2017). *Tweeting to freedom: An encyclopedia of citizen protests and uprisings around the world.* Santa Barbara, CA: ABC-CLIO.

Wittgenstein, L. (2006). *The Wittgenstein reader,* 2nd edition, A. Kenny (Ed.). Malden, MA: Blackwell.

9 Economic and Energy Development and the Goal of Sustainability in Thailand
An Argumentation Analysis

Introduction

The current state of environmental degradation in the developing world, coupled with the impact of climate change, has created a precarious state for communities and individuals. There is a clear, shared need among humans to continue long into the distant future, but just as clear is the divergence of ideas and beliefs about our interaction with this system, what role the Earth is expected to play for us as a species, and what obligations we might have to the Earth. We are within the Earth's ecosystem, part of it, and yet most likely among all species to have a role in changing the system in ways that affect ourselves and the rest of the system. Unfortunately, most of the public, understandably quite busy accomplishing the many tasks that make up their lives, do not view the system in a holistic matter. People are mired in their daily existence, so much so that the vulnerabilities that surround are not so apparent until they rear up and force a confrontation with our other priorities. The need to see the linkages and relationships between institutions, businesses, and individuals is always there (Nelson, 2012), but there is only so much urgency to spread around.

Climate change and sustainability possibly do not seem as pressing as short-term obligations – a need for jobs and shelter, for example. Nevertheless, climate change has been called "arguably the most important issue facing humanity" (Matthews et al. 2012, p. 3). Adjustments to patterns of consumer behavior and utilization of resources likely need to occur, but such change foregoes the immediate gratification of Western-styled consumerism. The assessment that climate change does not affect the present, and that current patterns of behavior do not impact our lives, is incorrect. Environmental change impacts nations around the world, even with the advance of society's technological ability to respond to concerns. The means of connecting possible environmental concerns to human activities is limited; we rely on impact and vulnerability assessments (Matthews et al. 2012), which seldom account for all detail, and do not adequately take into account the whole of the system. Assessments tend to focus on the materials and change of a project or case, and less on connecting a project with the environment, upon which the whole of the system depends. Strategic choices made may leave out critical factors, leaving fracture fissures that may rupture when a system is stressed. Even with the understanding that our means and methods are insufficient in most cases to address every eventuality, we still must find a way forward to work with the uncertainty we face (Harrison, 2012).

As a policy matter, it is difficult to connect larger, international policy issues to local action and a feeling that individual changes can lead to appreciable improvements in stemming global environmental degradation. The most fruitful efforts point to the value of the individual, and that even small changes can have large aggregate benefit (Padre, 2010). Environment policy, especially policy related to issues of environmental justice, is most impacted by clear connections between individuals and avenues of involvement, and a weaving in of citizens as part of the plot of a larger story, of localism, of protection of one's family and community, and refusing to bow to larger pressures. Collective action can make a difference in a concern being seen as an actionable policy problem. Still, policy interest in this area tends to be cyclical, and there may be times when the policy agenda is simply not open to the issue, despite fervent enthusiasm from the public. Other interests and influences may play a role in setting the agenda and prioritizing other issues, offering alternative solutions to solving the supposed problem, or possibly defining the issue as not a problem at all. Positive movement in policy requires alignment of policy actors (like businesses, the government at various levels, and individuals and interest groups), the overcoming of areas where the groups may differ in perspective, and the availability of resources, financial and administrative, to accomplish programmatic tasks (Moon & Cocklin, 2012). Lacking alignment, the policy response from the system may be "business as usual" (Barrow, 2012, p. 438), until some event comes along to change minds, a critical mass is reached in negative outcomes, or influential groups/individuals begin to make resolution of the problem a priority (Barrow, 2012).

This chapter examines the case of Thailand's energy policy and sustainable development, and how arguments for such efforts have been constructed and deployed in the Thai case. The research question is: What can we learn about Thailand's commitment to sustainable development through public and private statements on economic and energy development projects? This chapter takes up the question by comparing official state direction on development, and statements on sustainable development of the state-run energy authority and a major private-sector energy company, with an analytical approach, informed by persuasion and argumentation. Thailand has made clear its intent to increase development in areas south and east of Bangkok, including Rayong, through the Eastern Economic Corridor (EEC) project; this project, part of 'Thailand 4.0,' portends to increase economic well-being, but will require additional energy resources. The Energy Generating Authority of Thailand (EGAT), founded in 1969, is Thailand's state-enterprise for energy production, managing most of Thailand's energy generation needs and its energy supply grid. Gulf Electric is an energy company that has made statements about its commitment to sustainability even as it has encountered some difficulty with public protests against its plants and further development; the inclusion of the private-sector partner further informs the discussion by showing how signaling and symbol are abundant. The chapter concludes with discussion and considerations for further research.

Argumentation

Argumentation has a variety of definitions. One is that it is a "verbal, social, and rational activity aimed at convincing a reasonable critic of the acceptability of a standpoint by putting forward a constellation of one or more propositions to justify this standpoint" (van Eemeren, Grootendorst, & Henkemans, 2010, p. xii). At an elementary level, we may doubt expressed viewpoints, even in an official capacity, when the message and the generally accepted meaning of a concept diverge. The problem is made worse when either the concept is messy and imprecise, or the messaging about the concept is flawed from an argumentation perspective. There can be a large number of solutions to a problem, but rather than increasing comfort with what may eventually be chosen as a preferred option, this may lead to rising public uncertainty and questioning of root assumptions. When official pronouncements differ significantly, any truth argument made can be undermined. Standpoints and opinions are mistaken for facts or absolutes, narrowing the way forward in how a problem is seen, or how policy options are constructed. Because there may be no interest in resolving a difference of opinion, or setting aside the disagreement in a constructive (or at least, not destructive way), argumentation instead becomes a question of whose materials or resources are stronger, or else attrition, during an ongoing confrontation (van Eemeren, Grootendorst, & Henkemans, 2010). If the winner takes all in this venue, the winner of the debate has not actually won anything, because their problem definition and solution may be significantly lacking in important respects; the loser is angry, deservedly so, for the limitation of their viewpoint and its potential positive impact on the eventual programs.

A willful or neglectful attention to the clarity rule in making an argument is notable from a semiotic perspective; a lack of clarity may indicate that the communicator had little interest in whether the elementary aspects of the argument being presented were clearly understood by the audience. This is exclusionary, whether or not it was intentional. This lack of clarity may help along casual acceptance of logical inconsistencies in arguments, such as where statements contradict one another and demand additional discussion, or given pragmatic inconsistencies, where characterizations of a concept are positive and negative, and probably to some extent each true on their own merits. Some in the 'audience' of public work may accept a statement from a preferred party no matter what they say, and require no documentation or support of any kind. Appealing to one's authority to support nonsensical arguments is an abuse of the public's ability to comprehend and understand an issue. Where there is no reasoning or appeal to rationality, none have been needed or expected. When material is presented, it may be irrelevant on purpose. This approach clouds the issue and makes it difficult for people to discern the acceptability of a standpoint (van Eemeren, Grootendorst, & Henkemans, 2010).

Persuasiveness is a major consideration in public policy and public expressions of private business intent. Persuasion has been defined as "a successful intentional effort at influencing another's mental state through communication in a circumstance in which the persuadee has some measure of freedom" (O'Keefe, 2016, p. 4). Persuasion might lead to a change in attitude, or reinforcement of an existing attitude (that a policy works/ is effective, for example, or that a given company cares about an issue important to the persuadee). If the effort is not designed to encourage some specific action, but to inspire complacency, then a way of judging whether an effort to persuade has been effective might be to see how much the public simply goes along with a plan. This has to do with O'Keefe's inclusion of mental state: does the effort put the subject in a mood to accept the communication as offered, rather than to argue the point? What are the appeals being made? Even if they violate principles of acceptable argument, does the audience object? There can be an absence of judgment and resultant countering action, when it might otherwise be objected. Through social judgment theory, we might question how the message itself was received and processed, or via cognitive dissonance, some new information and appeals may be set aside, because they conflict with already held cognitions, so that dissonance, conflict, or regret for action or inaction may be avoided (O'Keefe, 2016).

Environment Protection: The Ideal and the Practical

If it is not clear why government should be involved in the protection of the environment, some attention to that topic is appropriate. From a purely market-based perspective, the business community has previously shown that it will *generally* not, of its own accord, put the environment first in making decisions, unless doing so makes business sense – meaning maximizing return for shareholders. A business engaged in the production of cars, for example, has its primary responsibility of making cars and selling them to consumers. It must produce supply to equal demand,

and increase wherever possible that demand through marketing activity. The fact that a business's production model contributes to externalities, such as pollution, is from a business perspective nearing an immaterial issue, unless there exists a regulatory structure to require attention to such details. Paying careful attention to compliance with regulations costs money, and affects the business's bottom line; there is a chance that full compliance may impact profits and competitiveness, especially if the business in question has competitors who do not choose to comply with regulatory requirements (free-riding). If there is lax enforcement, 'doing the right thing' puts the business at a disadvantage, and perhaps for no clear reason that it can see. This behavior might even be seen as inconsistent with maximizing self-interest, and damaging to markets as a result (Harrison, 2000). A failure to consider political and social aspects of a policy when implementing an environmental science-led program "may...increase environmental degradation and poverty by threatening livelihoods" (Forsyth, 2003, p. 2). Solutions, especially government solutions that have a desire to achieve outcomes, must always consider context.

Corporations, being artificial entities, have a right to operate in this capacity granted by government. From a behavioral standpoint, a corporation reflects the character of those involved in it, and particularly the directorship. Attention to corporate social responsibility waxes and wanes with the times. Though profits and the ability for the corporation to have its way and control its own destiny, unfettered by regulation, remain steady concerns, a corporation and its directors do, in fact, have responsibility beyond return to shareholders. Corporations that are well-led by honest individuals, who care about their communities, can have substantial added value, in addition to those behaviors helping to keep the directors and corporation out of trouble (Hamilton, 1996). When corporations tend too far away from this thinking, a marketing effort showing adherence to such tenants may be invoked to remind the public of the entity's loyalty, quality, and community values – as if the entity has realized the error of its ways, even though it is more likely that the directors are merely feeling the heat of loss revenue for having been caught out on less than honorable conduct.

From an economic standpoint, the marginal benefits derived from polluting could make sense, and provide a competitive advantage, as long as there are no especially immediate consequences. Environmental degradation may take a long while to make itself fully apparent, and for people to be held to account, if that ever happens. The blame for any trouble may be explained away by all manner of excuses: ignorance of potential effects, sharing the blame with other polluters, and the sunk costs of production models. This is not Pareto optimal, because people involved outside the decision-making process may be made worse-off, but this thought process has the advantage of keeping shareholders and one's bosses happy in the corporate world. The decision creates wealth. Certain people who are important and proximate will be better off, and that is relatively more important from a decision-making perspective. This is countered by the consideration that we do want to be fair and be seen by others as treating people fairly, even though individuals may differ considerably in their definitions of fairness (Harrison, 2000).

Of course, this is only half the story. The adverse impacts of business production have significant consequences for the environment. Giving attention to the larger, societal perspective, not only is such decision-making suboptimal, it is not even an acceptable option on a marginal basis when all costs and a consideration of wider impacts is made. Government will have to figure out a way to clean up the pollution mess at some point, and depending on the severity of the problem, the cost may be quite dear. The supposed profit disappears because the lower cost of not polluting in the first place was replaced with the false narrative of pollution being free of cost to the company and society. Even though jobs may have resulted, the people that fill those jobs may be injured by this pollution. Business may resist such impositions, because business may not actually agree that it is doing anything wrong; regulatory efforts are from a market-based view of a coercive force. Framing the problem differently may affect how people answer a straightforward question (Harrison, 2000): Would one support a decision if it offered jobs, or destroyed the air quality in a town, or did both? How might the answer change with knowledge in mind?

This is evidenced throughout the environmental protection literature, notably in cases like asbestos mining in Libby, Montana, USA (Naik, Lewin, Young, Dearwent, & Lee, 2017; Sullivan, 2007), or lead exposure at the Picher, Oklahoma Tar Creek site (Shriver, Cable, & Kennedy, 2008) A plant eventually closes, the jobs go away after all the productive capacity is gone or the market shifts, even as the larger company remains. The workers are not only out of a job – their health is harmed and their hometown devastated. But because the decision to pollute or harm the environment was not predicated on such considerations in the first place, it may be of little consequence to business, even though it is of tremendous significance to these people, their families, and society, or at least it should be as a normative matter. This is an incredibly hardship to steer, though: The Coase theorem – where "the assignment of rights by courts or legal authorities may have little to do with who eventually possesses those rights" (Harrison, 2000, p. 66) – has an impact. Government intervention may not be effective at all in stopping pollution because market forces are dominant. If business has a choice, the business choice is in effect preferred, and it is difficult for competing interest groups to overcome such a tendency in practice. Government's greatest impact might not be in regulation at all, but through reducing transaction costs, so that contracting is cheaper. The people who own the resources already will end up with great interest in keeping those resources, leaving little real opportunity for productive public discussion on projects that relate to environmental impacts.

Analysis of potential profit and harm in decisions that affect the environment gets close to a convincing argument when the rationality of such decisions is addressed in local terms, and on the real, socially conscious costs of transactions. Businesses have a need to tell a story about productivity, success, and ultimately power and competitiveness in the marketplace. These factors are different than the factors that face a town that is being polluted; the factors of personal harm make the argument much more personal. Over the short term, it matters more that desired choices are made, large production is supported, stock prices soar, and elected officials helpful to such causes are reelected. It matters in different ways over the long term, when the argument starts to fall apart – when we realize that the cost is much more than we were led to believe, that we have not been nearly as successful as we were told, or that our production model has harmed people; from a tortious perspective, those possible problems are further out in the timeline, and the harm caused may not even be direct. Regardless, these concerns are harder to square with our view of ourselves as good and virtuous citizens – that we are people that would not hurt others so that we can live more comfortably. That view also has moral and ethical consequence, and it can only accommodate so many challenges before people begin to act out, dig in and defend indefensible positions, or deflect blame that is rightly ours.

> Forest, wetlands, wastelands, coastal zones, eco-fragile zones, they are all seen as disposable for the accelerating demands of human population...to ask for any change in human behavior – whether it be to cut down on consumption, alter lifestyles or decrease population growth – is seen as a violation of human rights.
>
> (Bavadam, 2010, pp. 4–5)

When environmental issues are raised in the public space, the words used may have alternate and even opposite meanings. Development can mean building and construction, but the development may destroy what was there before, rather than protecting culturally and historically important places. Wildlife sanctuaries may not offer much sanctuary for wildlife when these places are frequented by humankind. Environment, instead of an encompassing concept, is a product to be used toward further production and wealth creation (Bavadam, 2010). Bunsha (2010) noted how pressing issues like climate change are not well understood by the public because knowledge is not being communicated, and the science 'not popularized' (p. 72). Rather than being a hindrance, the exclusion of the public has been a help to the cause of development and growth.

In Thailand, a government apparatus informed by light authoritarianism placed a priority on economic development goals, which in turn created growth and employment opportunity for many in the nation. It has been suggested that "Thailand may have been corrupt and even careless at times, but at no point was the government consciously and intentionally acting against the interests of the people or...development" (p. 11). Others have expressed a different view: "In the mouths of leaders, 'development' is either a euphemism for telling Western donors what they wish to hear or a means of providing outright disinformation: it certainly does not even periodically correspond to the noble goals laid out" (Thompson & Thompson, 2000, p. 11).

Environment as Policy Symbol

Communicating about the environment poses its own kind of difficulty. People regularly do not agree with definitions of environmental problems, or that concerns rise to the level of a crisis demanded action. There is disagreement on how much emphasis should be placed on environment policy relative to other types of policy, such as support of business and employment. Creating meanings that people share about the environment and its consequence can be difficult because underlying assumptions may be quite dissimilar. Use of language in these areas of policy study, as with the others in this volume, hinges on how persuasive it is: The intent is not merely to describe an issue, but to encourage people to do something about it that furthers a mostly particular agenda. To the extent that there is a commitment to public involvement, the public may be invited to have a say in environment-related issues, but the reality of competing priorities within the policy system may make these discursive opportunities more or less disingenuous. The voices using the space afforded to public participation are, in effect, going through the motions of involvement, because decisions may have already been reached; the engagement and story-building involved form a false narrative where the public had a say, but it is just a simulation of public involvement. Unfortunately, the people yoked the most with the problems of pollution, who stand to lose, are further marginalized by these behaviors. Instead of being seen as needed partners in a decision, the public might be painted as needing education and persuasion to accept a decision already made, treating community leaders as enemies, or making little use of the public's input in choices made (Pezzullo & Cox, 2018).

The environment as it exists in reality and as a construct created through rhetoric, positive or negative in the policymaking environment, might be very different. Take for example an assertion that a program or community is sustainable. Depending on how one is defining the term, which is appealing in its nebulousness, a community might, in fact, be demonstrably sustainable on certain set criteria, even if many aspects of its existence are fundamentally unsustainable, to the point that the diminishing elements outweigh any positive case to be made. The communicated notion of sustainability, though, succeeds or not based on the efficacy of the communication. Sustainability is afforded a place of privilege based on assumptions that it is generally good; it is unchallenged, even when people are not sure what it means in a particular case. The style of the message, and how much it resonates with the primary addressees of the message, matter much to the success of the initiative to claim sustainability. The message will exist in a rhetorical situation: an exigency, or urgent problem; the suitability of the audience to receive and act upon a message; and any attendant limitations on the situation (Pezzullo & Cox, 2018). The effectiveness of messaging is improved if the offered policy does not challenge too much what the public already knows or feels to be valid, because any natural biases present may create an untenable situation for a new policy. This can be helped along by clear statements of support from people who are assumed to know objectively whether claims being made are truthful; it matters little to the public whether the claims are actually truthful, valid, or buttressed by documentation, if supposedly objective sources support the claims.

For environment policy, actions against policymaking may incorporate the 'trope of uncertainty' (Pezzullo & Cox, 2018, p. 135), or a claim that more research is needed to make a firm decision on matters involving environment protection. This naturally favors business interests most of the time; it avoids taking up the precautionary principle, which might make more sense as prevention is cheaper than cure, and settles for appeals to scientific certainty, when absolute certainty is a concept abjured by science. Further, raw data are not helpful in improving our understanding without interpretation, and the public relies upon the interpretations of subject-matter experts and scientists in government (Harrison, 2012). If the experts that know how to interpret data fail to do this and 'tell the story' in a meaningful way, which can be understood by decision-makers and the public, then others who do not understand the data and materials are free to twist the analysis into whatever form serves them. Through these means, claptrap may be raised to the level of 'competing theory,' when such material would ideally be immediately rubbished by a public with critical understanding.

Companies may use environmental reporting as a signal to stakeholder groups – from those marginally to directly affected – that environment quality, responsibility, sustainability, or stewardship are important aspects of the corporate culture. Claims of responsibility to the environment may be legitimate, with firms setting the standard for environment protection even beyond what would be required by government regulations, or, as with policies that fail to accomplish stated outcomes, may serve as window-dressing for appeasement of vocal public segments, for marketing purposes (greenwashing), or to reduce possible barriers to intended corporate activity. The different ways a keyword like 'sustainability' is being defined by various corporate interests, or even within the same corporation, may provide a guide to semiotic analysis.

We may find that the materials of the communication are what is intended by the sender, and how the sender wants to be viewed, rather than what is. Such statements may be desires or goals, but the information contained within them may never come to pass. The signaling of commitment carries with it the trappings of promise and obligation, but because the value of these communications is in the initial telling, rather than in the evaluation, it matters less whether the reality matches with the communication. Image is what matters. A major polluter can issue reports that state that the business is a champion of the environment. The American energy company Enron, prior to its collapse, famously prided itself on its corporate code of conduct (*The good, the bad...*, 2005). With environment policy, "environmental narratives have been found to be symbolic rather than substantive messages. An implication that emerges is that genuine corporate environmental engagements and efforts may be few, but companies make use of dialectic presentation to create an emblematic panorama that provides strong significations of their environmental responsiveness" (Yusoff & Lehman, 2009, p. 240).

The Intersection of Environment and Energy Security in Thailand

In Asia, there are a number of factors that can impede sustainable development initiatives, notably "the widespread poverty prevailing in the region and inadequate financial resources," and in Southeast Asia specifically, "inadequate institutional and technical capacity and difficulty in accessing environmentally-sound technologies" (Rao, 2008, p. xiii).

Thai policy has had to balance critical aspects of energy security, environment protection, and public participation. Sustained development has long been the key component of Thai national success. Thai leadership has notably delivered on its promises in development most of the time, and the longevity in the lines of central leadership has informed ministry goals throughout Thai government. Priorities are nevertheless clear – development is about making money and environment quality, even if it is important and recognized as a worthy goal, is at best secondary to development and attendant achievement of economic power. The connection between political stability and economic growth is clear (Thompson & Thompson, 2000). Having noted this, corruption leads to sub-optimal economic outcomes, and the public, being aware of the real-world impact of suboptimal decision making, can and will respond in ways that may force reconsideration of short-sighted decisions. Civil society in Thailand has acted and could increasingly act as an excellent counter to military-based and corporately oriented policy rationales (Thompson & Thompson, 2000).

There are common interests between government and business in Thailand and the Westernized view of the need for a clear demarcation between the two is less important than economic growth, for instance. Efforts to reform the economy extend back to the 1960s and 1970s, though major liberalization efforts began in the late 1980s. There was realization that the fortunes of the nation and business were closely aligned (Ariff & Khalid, 2005). Thailand is a business-minded nation with a strong interest in international trade; this is a major reason why the economy is robust.

However, Thailand was named a source of the Asian Financial Crisis in the late 1990s (specifically, the volatility of the Thai baht), though a variety of factors, including questionable IMF decisions, are to blame. Thailand had excess reliance on foreign-currency loans, and a large proportion of bad private loans during the crisis; Thailand also experienced a real estate crisis before its crash, and a weakening in exports, specifically electronics (Ariff & Khalid, 2005). There was a thinking at the time that the Asian Tiger nations could do no wrong with their development pattern, and continue to provide incredible returns on investment well into the future without disruption, but this simply did not occur. The Thai economy has rebounded remarkably since the crisis. Still, Nordholt cautioned that "formal domains of politics and economy" in Thailand "are interwoven with illegal economic activities and criminality in which bureaucrats, politicians, military, police, businessmen and criminals maintain intimate relationships" (2004, p. 33). The closeness of these relationships perhaps does not allow for the oversight necessary to achieve a balancing of individual and societal interests, especially when it is assumed that business and government interests are in sync and that these interests represent the totality of societal interest. The ability of the Thai economy to withstand shocks rests in no small part on the capacity of the national regulatory apparatus. Figure 9.1 shows Thai purchasing power per capita; note that purchasing power is concentrated in areas around Bangkok, in Rayong province, and in the south along the coast of the Gulf of Thailand (shown in areas of relatively darker shading). Much of the economic and development focus has been to these areas that have already shown their strength.

The nature of local Thai government being directed according to the proclivities of bosses has been encouraged by intergovernmental practice on a historical basis. The state has stood out of the way allowing for power to become decentralized, and the result has been that local power brokers have been able to make arrangements with industry, for example, that serve perpetuation of the power arrangement, rather than an active attention to or serving of the public interest. Where the central government has more recently come back into the conversation, in

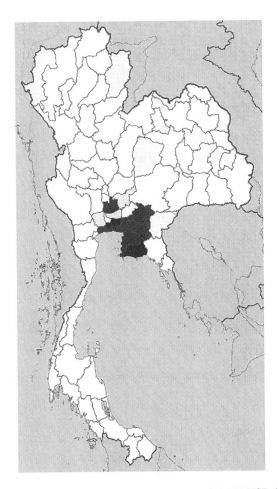

Figure 9.1 Thai provinces with GDP per capita at least $10,000 USD (328,185 Baht). Source: (Revised) Wiki map modified by C.A., from original work by NordNordWest, under CC BY-SA 3.0., Adjustments were made for highlighting areas with highest GDP, principally around the Bangkok area, and removing shading choices for the rest of the country where the GDP is low... Link to original map: https://web.archive.org/web/20171228061032/https://en.wikipedia.org/wiki/File:Thai_provinces_by_GPP_per_capita_2013.png.

the interest of pursuing environmental goals and sustainability, the web-like nature of local government power has nevertheless been persistent. When the sense of a local leader providing for a community is strong, this increases legitimacy; if services are strong, then any linked corruption might be more easily overlooked. In the Thailand case, in particular, corrupt practices like the selling of regulatory favor have been noted, and the interest of this leadership in the accumulation of wealth is a pattern that has occurred over a period of decades. These local/regional leaders used power to elect or install themselves or like-minded associates in central government power centers and agencies, as well, so the potential is that the central reflects the narrow interests of local power brokers (Sidel, 2004).

Lak Thai (Thai greatness) is a mindset that exudes confidence and belief in the nation's capacity for further development and superior achievement. Among Thai leaders, the old saw about how those that abuse leadership tend to lose it seems applicable. The succession of Thai coups belies a relatively consistent approach to governance. Even where a coup occurs, the underlying mechanisms of regulatory process and enforcement persist more or less unabated. Changes at the leadership level are less revolutionary than related to personality and clashes between elites. There has been a regularization of shifts, and Thai elites concern themselves with attainment and maintenance of power (Marshall, 2015).

Thailand's law that protects the royal family from criticism (Article 112 of the Thai criminal code) through a threat of imprisonment tends to discourage outright dissent, even though protests have increased and are allowed, to some extent. In such an environment, the truth is not as absolute as one might insist elsewhere. Societal choices favor elite interests, sometimes for quite good and honorable reasons, sometimes not, but historically, discourse on policy topics with broad segments of the public has not been a priority. Reverence for the royal family, and respect and appreciation for the elite, have been expected, because these societal forces have allowed for development and growth, and provided for the nation in that respect. Marshall (2015) posited that the outward expression of Thailand and its internal reality are quite different, and that the effort to legitimize the elite through the permeation of a preferred styling of Thai cultural identity, and marginalization of those that differ with these sentiments.

Eckersley (2013) showed how this can be examined at the national level, through a consideration of how nations present themselves on responsibility for climate change, with Norway and Australia as case examples. When the portrayal is accepted, the image created can take on a life of its own, stepping away from the reality of whatever the nation, industrial concern or advocacy group, or individual does in the future. They continue to carry a reserve of image-driven goodwill, even when actions and decisions betray some dissonance between the image and reality. At a national level, for example, the view of goodness and benevolence toward environmental interests may stand in contrast to policies on oil production; the dissimilarity is more obvious when views on positive portrayal converge as implicit acquiescence.

A major turning point for Thai environment policy was the kingdom's participation in the Stockholm Conference of 1972; the Office of the National Environmental Board was established as a result of an increased understanding of the fragmented nature of regulatory processes to that time. Nevertheless, economic priorities, population growth, and industrial development have led to an increasing amount of environmental degradation. Public protest of development efforts, including the Nam Choan Dam, began to increase in the 1980s. Citizens recognized that without protest, there was the potential that their rights for settlement and compensation in the face of development efforts might be limited (Bureekul, 2007).

Public participation became a stated objective, in the Enhancement and Conservation of National Quality Act of 1992, echoing the requirement of the constitution. The Public Hearing Regulation 1996 also supports 'open government'. The increasing inclusion of participatory-minded language in national law has led to a similarly strong growth in demand for such access. Bureekul identified a number of concerns that could adversely impact public participation, including an inadequate understanding of how to use public participation channels to address national environmental law; a lack of concern about what those involved in public participation have to say about official decisions, which ultimately leads to the public mounting more vociferous objection; a lack of awareness of problems that impact the environment; the idea that increasing trust in official action will result in increased public participation; the time, setting, and availability of public involvement opportunities; and access to information. The level of best involvement is likely more local than centralized (2007).

Public participation occurs via receipt of input from individuals and stakeholder groups; sharing of information on policy with the public; and sharing of perspectives between concerned parties, formally (through legal/administrative means) and informally (workshops, protests, other forms of involvement). Even though Thai approaches to public involvement have improved dramatically, there have been limitations on involvement, such as a requirement that individuals must use rights to participate through non-governmental organization (NGO) venues; this requires indirect participation and increases the potential for disruption of the public's intended message through alternate interpretations. A law like the Official Information Act of 1997 might not be as useful as it could be, because the public may not understand how to utilize the rule or negotiate the bureaucracy of the Thai government system to make a request. Even though Thai citizens have broad rights to information and explanations for official action, related to potential environmental impacts, the availability of a right and its effective use are quite different from one another (Bureekul, 2007).

Energy security is a concept with many interpretations, so many that, given the diversity of possible definitions, the term approaches self-referentiality. It has a purpose and use on its own as a public concept.

Energy security is closely related to energy vulnerability, in the sense that vulnerability arises from "insufficient domestic energy supply, which leads a country to become heavily reliant on imports" (Daojiong, 2013, p. 7). Keeping in mind that the development and productive capacity of East Asia generally has been informed by advance in the ability to find and use energy sources, there is nevertheless a shortage of energy supply from within the region; the accompanying dependence on outside sources of energy undermines the region's growth model, requiring choices to be made internally within the region and within nations to meet the growing need in other ways. Thailand uses 168.30 billion kWh of electrical energy in a year, or 2,438 kWh per person; the nation has to import energy from outside its borders to meet demand. Fossil fuel reliance for energy generation (76.7%) is more than the EU (48.9%), and there is less reliance on renewable energy (14.2% in Thailand) compared with the EU (16.2%) (eglitis-media, 2018). Figure 9.2 shows energy consumption in Thailand compared with the population (in millions) for the period from 2000 to 2018. While the population has seen marginal increases per year, energy consumption has jumped significantly, doubling during the period.[1]

In order for the productive capacity of business to be satisfied, a state's sources of energy must be stable; the economic needs within a society may tend to take precedence over other needs, such as public desires of sociocultural importance. In a state within this environment, the national plan for energy security must be made to align with local/regional planning, so that stability can be achieved and/or maintained. Public relations are

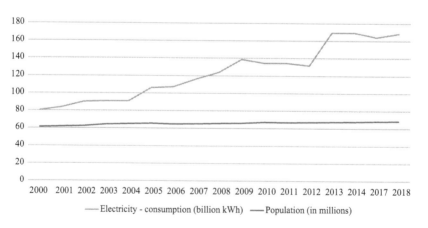

Figure 9.2 Thailand, energy consumption compared with population, 2000–2018.
Source: Created by C.A., using CIA World Factbook data, https://www.indexmundi.com/g/g.aspx?c=th&v=81.

a part of this effort, to "enhance awareness of and actions to support [energy security] policies" (Daojiong, 2013, p. 42).

The breakdown in making the public aware of projects and actually encouraging meaningful involvement in planning has been clear, particularly in megaprojects. Sovacool (2013) pointed out that consultation in some large projects in developing regions has amounted to extended presentations followed by highly abbreviated opportunities for members of the public to provide comment; the receiving of massive numbers of public complaints and addressing such matters through a legalistic framework (drowning the dissent, effectively, in a drawn-out process, for which affected members of the public lack the resources for participation); and displacement of communities for the projects, with affected individuals and families not receiving enough compensation to move on and begin their lives anew elsewhere. Not only do larger projects fail to improve living standards – Sovacool revealed that they are quite damaging, to the environment as well as to indigenous peoples and their knowledge, expertise, and potential capacity to be part of an improved livelihood for the affected area (2013).

An example of private sector energy development is the natural gas-fired Gulf Tasit 3 (GTS3) plant in Rayong province. Rayong is on the Gulf of Thailand, south and east of Bangkok. Rayong is lush with trees, mangroves, and natural landmarks, including waterfalls (vegetation areas are darker shaded areas south and east of Bangkok as shown in Figure 9.3, to the right side of the map; this contrasts with the irrigated croplands (lighter areas north and west of Bangkok) and city areas (dark grey) around Bangkok.

We now move on to the materials and methods for this analysis.

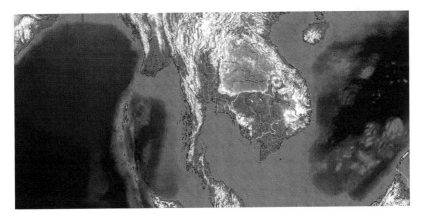

Figure 9.3 Thailand, geographical features.
Source: (Revised) Map is from https://maps-for-free.com/. MFF-maps are released under Creative Commons CC0. Maps for Free is located at maps-for-free.com.

Materials and Methods

Massik and Solomon (2012) propose addressing denotative meaning, connotative implication, signs that might be connected to the sign in question, major differences among the related signs, and probable rationalizations for the distinctions, such as larger cultural trends. If there is an intended response on the part of the sign-maker, it would be worth noting that, and whether the effort seems genuine and successful. Special attention is paid to how the sign or sign-system works, "what cultural beliefs and viewpoints underlie it, [and] what its significance is" (Maasik & Solomon, 2012, p. 29), among other factors. A system means "the code, or network, within which a sign functions and so achieves its meaning through its associational and differential relations with other signs" (p. 700).

It may be useful to note whether, as within the institutional analysis and development (IAD) framework, we would see the appearance of levels of rulemaking power, and grouping of intended actions into strategies, norms (induced), and rules (as imposed with a threat of punishment); how government defines stakeholder groups in a policy debate is also important (Nowlin, 2011). The context of the decisions made and predilections to favor certain stakeholder groups over others matters as far as policy outcomes are concerned.

This analysis utilizes a recent distribution of Computer aided techniques for process analysis and control (CATPAC) software, codenamed Pony. CATPAC software reads text and summarizes main concepts. The output is viewable through an accompanying program called Thoughtview. "Galileo's Catpac program can analyze narratives and identify key concepts and the strengths of their relationships, by means of a neural network...[producing] entity relationship diagrams, but which are determined by precise and replicable mathematics, and derived from the data themselves, not from the analyst's interpretation of the data" (Library & Archival Security, 2004, p. 63). CATPAC visually shows the clustering of concepts, and in that respect provides a serviceable simulation of how human beings might look at a text and identify its concepts and conceptual groupings. In the visualizations of what Woelfel (2018) refers to as Galileo space, concepts are situated within a three-dimensional field of meaning. Concepts and related attributes are located together, and where the concepts and attributes have little to do with one another they are farther apart. This can help us understand message focus, and from a strategic perspective, what a non-biased read of a text indicates as important conceptually. CATPAC has been used in a variety of research projects, from an evaluation of accounting standards (Samkin & Schneider, 2008) to destination image formation and the Sochi Olympic games (Potwarka & Banyai, 2016), to the perception of representation and authenticity in Vietnamese tourist souvenirs (Trinh, Ryan, & Cave, 2014), and others. Through such an approach, researchers can see how concepts and terms are related to other terms in a document (Prior, Huges, & Peckham, 2012), potentially allowing for increased understanding of the message and the efficacy of its communication. The approach can also be replicated, based upon analysis of the texts used, employing the same parameters.

CATPAC analysis supplements a review of argumentation – who is arguing for what, the viewpoints present, and what contentions are being used (Bergström & Boréus, 2017). In this chapter, Thailand's Power Development Plan (PDP) 2015–2036, as the state's chief explication of its energy policy, is examined from a semiotic perspective. Gulf Electric is a principle private energy company in Thailand; the company has made statements about its commitment to sustainability (the term is listed as a primary menu button on the company's website as of this writing, and they have developed a series of videos that proclaim how their corporate culture aligns with sustainability). EGAT is the public energy authority in Thailand. As a final point of review, the marketing positioning of the EEC and Thailand 4.0 help us to understand the development viewpoint relative to other points of view. Argumentation analysis was used to examine given the nature of this material and its appeals to logos (rational capability), ethos (disposition projected by the speaker), and pathos (passions or sentiments) through various symbolic tactics. Timing is important; picking the appropriate moment to make a compelling case, or Kairos, is essential to persuasiveness (Berger & Stanchi, 2018).

As Boréus (2017) suggested, argumentation analysis may center on various fallacies of argument, especially that people in the public sphere are not engaging in an *effective discussion*, where the goal is expanding comprehension of a particular issue. This despite the fact that an effective ploy in public discourse is to change the subject and veer from the topic, rather than take on tough issues. For purposes of argumentation, though, it is most proper that sound premises lead to reliable, firm conclusions. Claims may be made along the way that are descriptive, and that demand some action be taken. The more logical the argument, and more rooted in one's inborn values, the more the argument will seem reasonable, persuasive, and actionable (Boréus, 2017).

For this argumentation analysis, the intent was to explore linguistic topographies to reveal strategies employed to argue for a particular way of thinking on the part of the government and the energy company. The contextual factor of public counterargument is also considered. The analysis shows claims of alignment with larger themes, such as sustainability or attainment of development goals, and examples of multiple voices, given documents' need "to handle competing interests, beliefs and voices" (Fløttum & Gjerstad, 2013, p. 418). While some strategies are clear, some claims do not align well with larger narratives, such as of sustainability, and as such exist more as a symbol, functioning in a hyperreal capacity without a referent.

Analysis

Using CATPAC, I performed an analysis on four text documents, each representing one of the actors involved in energy policy in Thailand: The Thailand PDP 2015–2036, from the Energy Policy and Planning Office of the Thailand Ministry of Energy; the Electricity Generating Authority of Thailand (EGAT), through webpages devoted to sustainable development on its website[2]; Gulf Energy Development Public Company Limited (Gulf), private power generating/holding company, through its web pages on innovation & education, social responsibility, and global patronage[3]; and finally, the transcribed text of the English language video for Thailand's Eastern Economic Corridor (Thailand Board of Investment).[4] The transcription was performed by rev.com. These entities were selected because they provide a cross-section of thinking about sustainable development and energy in Thailand. Again, the research question is: What can we learn about Thailand's commitment to sustainable development through public and private statements on economic and energy development projects? (Figure 9.4).

In the CATPAC analysis of the PDP, there are two major clusters. The cluster on the left of the grid refers to cogeneration, countries, electricity/fuel, dam, renewables, natural, and Bangkok. On the right, the main cluster centers on power generation and development, and includes words like coal, gas, hydro, and capacity. If one were to characterize the clusters, the cluster on the left seems more aspirational, and the right cluster seems more related to the reality of power generation to fulfill the needs of a growing Thailand. The closeness of the concepts within these clusters and their distance from one another in three-dimensional space

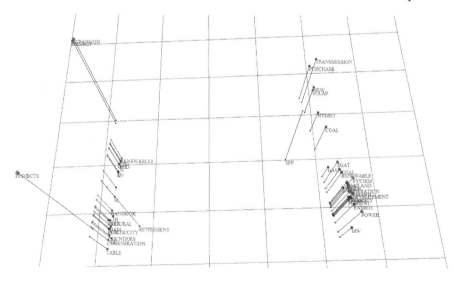

Figure 9.4 Thailand PDP network analysis using CATPAC (Pony), log transform.
Source: Created by C.A., analysis conducted using CATPAC, image created with Thought-View. Source document, https://www.egat.co.th/en/images/about-egat/PDP2015_Eng.pdf.

are notable. The practical realities could be some distance conceptually from the aspirational goals of the plan – to afford a more partnership-oriented, sustainable approach to energy provision for the nation. The left cluster is nearby to a smaller grouping on expansion projects, consistent with this being a planning document. In discerning the argument, the national focus is clearly on capacity and meeting the needs of the nation as it moves forward, from a power perspective, though the connection with sustainability and long-run considerations is not necessarily as clear. The approach, nevertheless, is rational and purposeful toward intended (development) outcomes.

In Figure 9.5, EGAT also has two tightly focused clusters, an appreciable distance from one another. The left cluster includes references to communities, universities, students, activities, dam, and plant. Near this cluster but opposite in space are references to natural gas. In the cluster on the right, safety, power, health, quality, environmental, and social appear. To characterize these clusters, one could see the cluster on the right as EGAT's larger commitment cluster, even though the left cluster is also characterized by partnerships and community-focus. What is impressive about this is message-focus in EGAT documents. EGAT is responsible for energy, but it is aware of its need to be responsible from an environmental and public health standpoint. It is arguing for the value of such

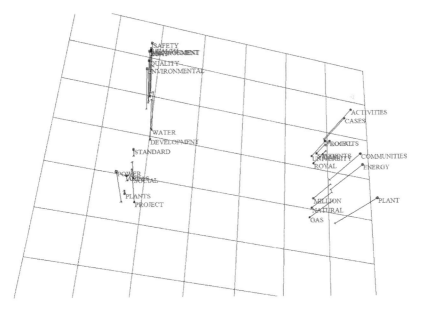

Figure 9.5 EGAT network analysis using CATPAC (Pony), log transform.
Source: Created by C.A., analysis conducted using CATPAC (Pony), image created with ThoughtView. Source webpages were the subpages under the "Sustainable Development" tab on EGAT's English language page: https://web.archive.org/web/20180405155609/ www.egat.co.th/en (Archive.org version, April, 2018).

larger considerations, from a science perspective, even as it is responsible for energy generation and transmission to serve the needs of the nation. While the PDP did not take up these issues, EGAT is doing so. As a national agency, EGAT has science-based approaches and this is being communicated to website visitors in a focused way. The reader may have a better sense of EGAT as an organization – their ethos – and the rational way they seek to balance development and environment needs.

Next, we consider the network analysis for Gulf Electric statements on sustainable development. There are general terms that appear largely rhetorical – success, innovative, cultural, and creative. There are references to initiatives. But oddly, there are also references to football, golf tournaments, and championships. While it is true that community resilience and strength are important, and perhaps a case can be made for the value of sport in the larger matter of sustainability as part of culture, there does not seem to be a case being made for that here. Instead, these associations with golf and football are placed haphazardly – their connection to sustainability is unclear. There is little text on any of the websites, and from an argumentation standpoint, the position on what we are supposed to be persuaded of, as readers, is indistinct , with such a thin argument. Any passion Gulf Electric might have for sustainable development is not well conveyed, either (Figure 9.6).

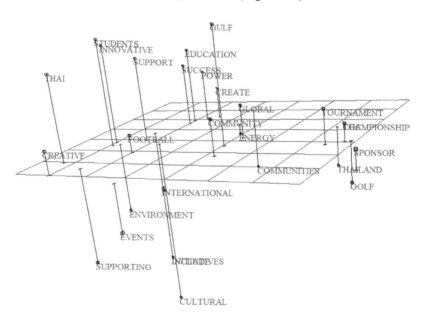

Figure 9.6 Gulf Electric network analysis using CATPAC (Pony).

Source: Created by C.A., analysis conducted using CATPAC (Pony), image created with ThoughtView. https://web.archive.org/web/20181129141009/https://www.gulf.co.th/en/sustainability/ (Archive.org version given here for consistency, though the page is still live the way it was originally accessed).

The figure for the network map of the EEC marketing material, below, shows almost no clustering. Instead, CATPAC presents an array of terms that are generally economic in nature and development-related. The material is mostly on development, Thailand's future, Asia, access to ports and airports, and other related concepts that may be considered valuable to developers. There is little discussion of environment or larger concerns about community responsibility or sustainability in development. The spread of concepts in three-dimensional space and absence of any particular focus indicated a marketing message that might have been designed to appeal to a host of different interests in a short time, through inclusion of terms that are operant as code to receivers. There is little detail given on each point, so there is no time to form a concept. Appealing to a variety of industries, on a number of levels, is the goal here. The arguments being made are obvious: "Thailand is undoubtedly the best investment destination in ASEAN" for example, and "The EEC, the most strategic area for investment for the future, the EEC, the new metropolis of the future, gateway to Asia. The EEC, the new economic hub for Asia, offering the perfect future for every investor worldwide." Sustainable development is featured in passing: "10 main industries are being promoted as the key driving forces of sustainable economic growth. This entails upgrading five existing industries with immense potentials, through the injection of technology into next-generation automotive, smart electronics, advanced agriculture and bio technology, food processing and tourism." This language is vague, and along with a reference to bio fuel and 'green,' seems more akin to inclusion of buzzwords, or a soft attempt to placate interest groups. Even the use of the word sustainable is suspect here – it seems to be used to mean 'ongoing for the foreseeable future,' rather than a call to environmental responsibility. This is strong with passion and vision, but light on substance (Figure 9.7).

Table 9.1 categorizes this analysis by focus on sustainable development, and the public or private focus of the entities involved.

Considering the different organizations and how they communicate, it is clear that EGAT has a science-based approach that allows for discussion and engagement with doubt. Others may have propositions that differ considerably from the official viewpoint, and part of science is engagement with those viewpoints, rather than simple rhetorical expressions. EGAT most successfully balances ethos, logos, and pathos to make a relatively more balanced case for sustainable development; their approach weaves technology, partnerships, and contextual awareness. The argument is stronger because the base of understanding and deployment of this understanding in messaging is more valid. Interestingly, while EGAT's approach is most optimal for public involvement, they may not be in the best position to allow for such involvement in a meaningful way – development and private interests hold great power in determining Thailand's future, and some of the larger societal considerations,

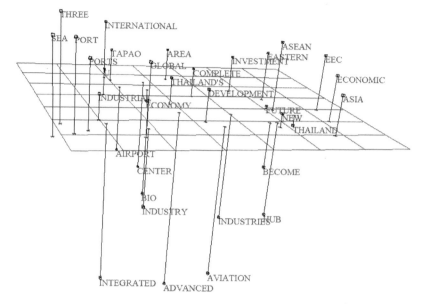

Figure 9.7 Thailand EEC network analysis using CATPAC (Pony).
Source: Created by C.A., analysis conducted using CATPAC (Pony), image created with ThoughtView. This analysis was conducted based on the transcript of the video promoting the Thailand EEC (https://www.youtube.com/watch?v=QlEHdC4WWVU). Rev.com transcribed the text for purposes of conducting the analysis.

Table 9.1 Focus on sustainable development, public-private focus, of Thailand Ministry of Energy, EGAT, Gulf Electric, and EEC

	Relative less focused on sustainable development	*Relatively more focused on sustainable development*
Public focus	Ministry of Energy Interest: Government, long-term power generation capacity, sustainable development less of a focus	EGAT – Energy Generating Authority Larger societal concerns included in materials, including sustainable development and concern about public health.
Private focus	Gulf Electric Little discernible understanding of sustainable development, which is especially concerning for an energy-generation company. Inclusion of unrelated concepts in discussion about company's sustainable development priorities.	EEC Concerned about economic development. Cursory reference to sustainable development and green technology. Largely rhetorical, with little reference to documentation or 'showing one's work' on impacts from the expansion project over the long term.

Source: Created by C.A., original work.

like environment, may, in fact, end up being secondary considerations. Whether these arguments are persuasive also depends on the audience – if the public perceives sustainable development to involve massive development projects, or football or golf sponsorships, then those messages and expectations may align.

Conclusion

Catellani (2012) wrote that production of government texts and documents may tend toward an exclusionary stance toward members of the public, due to a narrowing of the field of possible policy options, and a positioning of a preferred policy option as in keeping with larger considerations of the advance of humankind, the privileged place of science, or an optimism about future prospects. People can be manipulated through the use of power, as Lukes described; this takes place in getting people to do what they would not have done otherwise, to engage in activities that do not benefit them, or to engage in behavior that excludes people from participating (2003). The privileging of science tends to occur most readily where scientific outputs intersect with the interests of government and/or industry, with the government-industry preference being potent. The prospect of public participation is desirable only to the point that the government (or government-industry) apparatus is willing to hear public comment and make use of it in a considerable way through policy means. A variety of interactions may signal a consensus among a group of stakeholders. The invitation of their participation and any value in its content is voided by its non-receipt. Even if the signaling itself has value among the stakeholders themselves, or to an individual acting as an entrepreneur or is hopeful about leadership opportunities within that group, it has failed to affect policy in a considerable way; the horizon of options had already been limited, or an option selected, before the public was brought in. Little sentiment aired can overcome the portrayal of certain options as essential for the advancement of humankind, national interest, or of specific and, again, exclusionary notions of community. Appeals to banal nationalism might be suspect because they can curtail further discussion and incorporation of competing ideas (Bergström & Boréus, 2017).

Suwannathat-Pian described Thai democracy as "a series of documents written to ensure the power and interest of those who affected its drafting," and documentation of the battles for power among the ruling elite (2003, p. 3). In this view, Thai democracy was preoccupied with form rather than substance, and paid relatively less attention to the needs of the masses – for life, liberty, and happiness – or the sovereignty of the Thai people. "The masses would become valuable" around election time, and then typically persuaded to vote for what the elite wanted (2003, p. 7). The resulting system supported continuation of power among Thai elite, but did little to support the idea of popular will or accountability of government to the people generally. This is, of course, one view of matters. The kingdom has moved away from despotic paternalism, and has allowed increasing forms of public participation. However, these shifts are subtle, and the path dependence of the constitutional framework hinges on traditional sources of power (Suwannathat-Pian, 2003).

In Thailand, the need for growth and development, indeed a match of or return to the explosive growth rates of the past, is seen as a must for an indication of quality within the government ranks. The term of leadership is closely associated to bottom-line outcomes, in a society that has proven itself capable in business terms. Certain organizations and official actors within the nation clearly understand sustainability, but it must be noted that sustainability and the growth model employed in Thai development have not always fully united.. Maintenance of growth in economic terms is 'job one,' as it were; there are acceptable points in the debate, and an opportunity to do more, as long as this first priority is addressed fully. Projections have been for expansive growth, and estimated increases in GDP from 2010 to 2030 on the order of 299% (Logan, 2017). If sustainability is to exist at all, it has a second or lower place, but it must have some place in the decision-making apparatus, given the great potential for irreversible damage. Simply put, if Thailand is to achieve its goals, it must develop economically and cultivate international relationships at an increasing rate and impact; this is not sustainable. If sustainability is the driving factor, this characterization of Thailand's development goal is invalid; if sustainability is the goal, not development as noted above, it may achieve sustainability, only with a major shift in societal goals and consumer expectations. Pollution is less an outcome, and more a symptom of the larger rift made by attention to development priorities at a great cost to other urgencies. At the same time, we feel development is important and generally agree that it is, so it might feel wrong to suggest that it is less important than some other competing priority, like sustainability. Rather than engage the issue, it is easier to set it aside. The fallacy is that there is only one answer – unlimited, unchecked economic development is the *only way forward* – when this is demonstrably not the only option. Just because the popular standpoint is widely shared, does not mean that it is right, or that those offering other viewpoints are wrong.

Notes

1 Source: CIA World Factbook, via indexmundi.com, 2018.
2 The Thailand Power Development Plan 2015–2036. http://www.egat.co.th/en/.
3 Gulf Energy Development Public Company Limited. https://www.gulf.co.th/en/sustainability/.
4 https://www.youtube.com/watch?v=QlEHdC4WWVU.

References

Ariff, M., & Khalid, A. M. (2005). *Liberalization and growth in Asia: 21st century challenges.* Cheltenham: Edward Elgar.

Barrow, C. J. (2012). Socioeconomic adaptation to environmental change: Towards sustainable development. In J. A. Matthews et al. (Eds.), *The Sage handbook of environmental change, Vol. 2, 426–446.* London: Sage Publications.

Bavadam, L. (2010). Environment stories, among the most challenging. In K. Acharya & F. Noronha (Eds.), *The green pen: Environmental Journalism in India and South Asia, 3–11.* New Delhi: Sage Publications India.

Bergström, G., & Boréus, K. (2017). Analyzing text and discourse in the social sciences. In K. Boréus & G. Bergström (Eds.), *Analyzing text and discourse: Eight approaches for the social sciences, 1–22.* Thousand Oaks, CA: Sage Publications.

Boréus, K. (2017). Argumentation analysis. In K. Boréus & G. Bergström (Eds.), *Analyzing text and discourse: Eight approaches for the social sciences, 53–85.* Thousand Oaks, CA: Sage Publications.

Bunsha, D. (2010). Lost in the smog. In K. Acharya & F. Noronha (Eds.), *The green pen: Environmental Journalism in India and South Asia, 72–78.* New Delhi: Sage Publications India.

Bureekul, T. (2007). Access to environmental justice and public participation in Thailand. In A. Harding (Ed.), *Access to environmental justice: A comparative study, 271–288.* Leiden: Martinus Nijhoff.

Catellani, A. (2012). Pro-nuclear European discourses: Socio-semiotic observations. *Public Relations Inquiry, 1*(3), 285–311.

Daojiong, Z. (2013). Introduction. In Z. Daojiong (Ed.), *Managing regional energy vulnerabilities in East Asia: Case studies, 1–13.* Abingdon, Oxon: Routledge.

Eckersley, R. (2013). Poles apart? The social construction of responsibility for climate change in Australia and Norway. *Australian Journal of Politics and History, 59*(3), 382–396.

eglitis-media. (2018). Energy consumption in Thailand. Retrieved from https://www.worlddata.info/asia/thailand/energy-consumption.php.

Fløttum, K., & Gjerstad, Ø. (2013). Arguing for climate policy through the linguistic construction of narratives and voices: The case of the South-African green paper "National Climate Change Response." *Climatic Change, 118,* 417–430.

Forsyth, T. (2003). *Critical political ecology: The politics of environmental science.* London: Routledge.

Hamilton, R. W. (1996). *The law of corporations.* St. Paul, MN: West.

Harrison, J. L. (2000). *Law and economics in a nutshell,* 3rd edition. St. Paul, MN: Thomson West.

Harrison, S. (2012). Philosophical and methodological perspectives on the science of environmental change. In J. A. Matthews et al. (Eds.), *The Sage handbook of environmental change, Vol. 2, 37–52.* London: Sage Publications.

Library & Archival Security. (2004). Using Galileo's Catpac and Thoughtview software to analyze texts. *Library & Archival Security, 19*(1), 63–67.

Logan, J. (2017). The contradictions of US China policy: Implications for the US Air Force. In A. Lowther (Ed.), *The Asia-Pacific century: Challenges and opportunities, 93–114.* Maxwell Air Force Base, AL: Air University Press.

Lukes, S. (2003). *Power: A radical view*, 2nd edition. London: Palgrave Macmillan.

Maasik, S., & Solomon, J. (2012). *Signs of life in the U.S.A.: Readings on popular culture for writers*, 7th edition. Boston, MA: Bedford/St. Martin's.

Marshall, A. M. (2015). *A kingdom in crisis: Thailand's struggle for democracy in the twenty-first century*. London: Zed.

Matthews, J. A. et al. (2012). Background to the science of environmental change. In J. A. Matthews, et al. (Eds.), *The Sage handbook of environmental change, Vol. 2, 1–34*. London: Sage Publications.

Moon, K., & Cocklin, C. (2012). Policy and management options for the mitigation of environmental change. In J. A. Matthews et al. (Eds.), *The Sage handbook of environmental change, Vol. 2, 406–425*. London: Sage Publications.

Naik, S. L., Lewin, M., Young, R., Dearwent, S. M., & Lee, R. (2017). Mortality from asbestos-associated disease in Libby, Montana 1979–2011. *Journal of Exposure Science and Environmental Epidemiology, 27*, 207–213.

Nelson, D. R. (2012). Vulnerabilities and the resilience of contemporary societies to environmental change. In J. A. Matthews et al. (Eds.), *The Sage handbook of environmental change, Vol. 2, 374–386*. London: Sage Publications.

Nowlin, M. C. (2011). Theories of the policy process: State of the research and emerging trends. *The Policy Studies Journal, 39*(S1), 41–60.

O'Keefe, D. J. (2016). *Persuasion: Theory and research*, 3rd edition. Thousand Oaks, CA: Sage Publications.

Padre, S. (2010). Water journalism warrants better attention. In K. Acharya & F. Noronha (Eds.), *The Green Pen: Environmental Journalism in India and South Asia, 157–170*. New Delhi: Sage Publications India.

Pezzullo, P. C., & Cox, R. (2018). *Environmental communication and the public sphere*, 5th edition. Thousand Oaks, CA: Sage Publications.

Potwarka, L. R., & Banyai, M. (2016). Autonomous agents and destination image formation of an olympic host city: The case of Sochi 2014. *Journal of Hospitality Marketing & Management, 25*, 238–258.

Prior, L., Hughes, D., & Peckham, S. (2012). The discursive turn in policy analysis and the validation of policy stories. *Journal of Social Policy, 41*, 271–289.

Rao, P. H. (2008). *Greening the supply chain: A guide for Asian managers*. Thousand Oaks, CA: Response Books/Sage.

Samkin, G., & Schneider, A. (2008). Adding scientific rigour to qualitative analysis: An illustrative example. *Qualitative Research in Accounting & Management, 5*(3), 207–238.

Shriver, T. E., Cable, S., & Kennedy, D. (2008). Mining for conflict and staking claims: Contested illness at the Tar Creek superfund site. *Sociological Inquiry, 78*(4), 558–579.

Sidel, J. T. (2004). Bossism and democracy in the Philippines, Thailand, and Indonesia: Towards and alternative framework for the study of 'local strongmen.' In J. Harriss, K. Stokke, & O. Tornquist (Eds.), *Politicising democracy: The new local politics of democratisation, 51–74*. Houndmills, Basingstoke, Hampshire: Palgrave Macmillan.

Sovacool, B. K. (2013). Is bigger always better? The challenges facing international Asian energy megaprojects. In Z. Daojiong (Ed.), *Managing regional energy vulnerabilities in East Asia: Case studies, 128–149*. Abingdon, Oxon: Routledge.

Sullivan, P. A. (2007). Vermiculite, respiratory disease, and asbestos exposure in Libby, Montana: Update of a cohort mortality study. *Environmental Health Perspectives, 115*(4), 579–585.

Suwannathat-Pian, K. (2003). *Kings, country and constitutions: Thailand's political development 1932–2000*. London: RoutledgeCurzon.

The good, the bad, and their corporate codes of ethics: Enron, Sarbanes-Oxley, and the problems with legislating good behavior. (2003). *Harvard Law Review, 7*, 2123–2141.

Thompson, N., & Thompson, S. (2000). *The baobab and the mango tree*. New York: Zed Books.

Trinh, T. T., Ryan, C., & Cave, J. (2014). Souvenir sellers and perceptions of authenticity – The retailers of Hội An, Vietnam. *Tourism Management, 45*, 275–283.

van Eemeren, F. H., Grootendorst, R., & Henkemans, A. F. S. (2010). *Argumentation: Analysis, evaluation, presentation*. New York: Routledge.

Woelfel, J. (2018). *Galileo and its applications: Tools for the study of cognitive and cultural processes*. Buffalo, NY: Rah Press.

Yusoff, H., & Lehman, G. (2009). Corporate environmental reporting through the lens of semiotics. *Asian Review of Accounting, 17*(3), 226–246.

10 Bridging the Gap between Intent and Practice

In reviewing the programs of government, their attendant regulatory works, and the laboratory of rhetoric that leads to presumed innovation, one might sense an increasing division between the legitimate, authentic expression of wants and desires in the public square, and an Adorno-esque *jargon* (Claussen, 2008) of truthiness – with a public disposed to act as if one's gut feeling and the facts in evidence are unavoidably the same (Caron, 2016). Hot-aired visions of utopia and high-minded language prevail, undergirded by ill-conceived legal structures, far-removed from the citizen perspective. They prevail because they do a useful job, as "the partisan performances of the auxiliaries of the stronger" (Edwards, 2008, p. 91). The public is asked to take for granted this sport, as work on its behalf, and any outcomes as a sign of legitimate movement toward attainment of a perfect vision, if we simply instituted this or that public program, and trusted that the rhetoric of the day would save us. This laziness masquerading as hope will not serve well either the public or its government, and may hasten the demise of both. Instead of assuming we will eventually reach an ideal by letting others define the quest, we might spend more time fully defining problems, aligning intended solutions with these problems, and evaluating whether or not the expression of obstacle and resolution effectively mirrors reality. If administration and the public could be brought closer together, we might find that charity and trust are needed more than some imagined public policy fix, always just out of reach, which exists in signaling and symbol.

This chapter brings the book to a close, highlighting the methods and findings in preceding sections to bring theory and practice in public policy closer together through inclusion of a semiotic perspective. Considerations of the public sphere and lifeworld of Habermas, and the potential for realization of deliberative democracy in complex and troubled times, conclude the work.

Semiotics in Public Policy Analysis: Signs, Symbols, and Words That Fail

This book included chapters that explored an array of public policy issues, from a number of methodological perspectives. Table 10.1 highlights the policy areas, methods utilized, and terms of importance for analysis.

Table 10.1 Overview of public policy areas, methodological approaches, and general findings

Public policy area	Method(s) utilized	Words that fail	Findings/discussion
Regulation of food safety	Evaluation of import refusal system data, based upon refusal charges and source nations	Filth (Cheese, import refusal system)	The US FDA import refusal system includes a large volume of data, and portrays a rigorous, stable system of evaluation and enforcement, but from a public health protection standpoint, the system is reactionary. Cheese held on basis of arbitrary rule actually delicious, and not filthy.
Public procurement	Greimas Square; Text analysis – network visualization. Main topics and influential terms	'Green procurement'	We do not have a clear view of what 'green procurement' is, as a defined and implementable concept. Instead, we have the trappings of administrative rules and procedure. Some standards easily attained – not pushing environmental responsibility forward.
Government ethics laws	Contrast table, New York City conflicts of interest law and implementing guidance	Ethics rules as compliance	Rules draw prohibitions on behavior as proxy for ethical practice while barely speaking to the ideals of public service, placing public service in a defensive, compliance-oriented mode. This ultimately does not serve to make the public sector more ethical – only to widen the rift between the public and government administration.
Employment programs	Examination of employment rates; qualitative exploration of enacting legislation	'First Source'; workforce development	Limited employment improvement outcomes, despite obvious efforts to brand programs in a positive manner. Imposition of bureaucratic structures, or a lack of implementation depending on the case.
Immigration policy	Narrative analysis of German immigration reform debate (network analysis using AutoMap)	Support and demand; integration; foreigner/ ausländer	Integration rules could assume a certain standard of what it is to be German, taught in integration courses, but this betrays the richness of the nation as it exists currently and the profound impact migrants have had on the nation, not only recently but also over the course of many decades. Administrative oversimplification of matters affecting identity, inclusion, and citizenship.

(Continued)

Public policy area	Method(s) utilized	Words that fail	Findings/discussion
Healthcare policy	Analysis of tweets to US senators seen as pivotal on ACA reform vote, using LIWC (sentiment analysis)	Obamacare, Affordable Care Act *reform*; repeal and replace	Tweets about ACA during this period were more analytic and less authentic that what are typically found on Twitter; the tweets have a more negative tone than usual. As a group, the tweets used many negating words, showed higher than expected incidence of death-related words, and high levels of anger. Senator McCain's role in vote increasingly symbolic, incorporation of #MAGA# and implementation of Trump agenda seen as overarching issue.
Energy policy	CATPAC (Galileo) analysis of Thailand Power Development Plan, EGAT sustainability websites, Gulf Electric website for sustainable development, and Thailand EEC marketing language from development video; argumentation.	Sustainable development	Clear distinction between public and private focus for sustainable development. Scientific orientation and public-facing direction of EGAT, which shows understanding of sustainable development, does not square with ongoing economic development orientation from a national policy standpoint. Private sector orientation shows only cursory attention to sustainability, or use of buzzwords to placate/greenwash the issue.

ACA, Affordable Care Act; CATPAC, Computer Aided Techniques for Process Analysis and Control; EEC, Eastern Economic Corridor; EGAT, Electricity Generating Authority of Thailand; FDA, Food and Drug Administration; LIWC, Linguistic Inquiry and Word Count.
Source: Created by C.A., original work.

In Chapter 1, the question was asked: Does the current emphasis on instrumentality in public policy undermine the values it purports to uphold? What can be discerned from this summary table is that the use of expansive, symbolic terms with little underlying substance is fairly common across the territory of public policy. As policy debates become more agitated, the search for meaning becomes even less important than the limited basis it already has in practice. Policies might exist that have little to do with identified problems, and implementation/enforcement might not be all that important. The policies may exist for their own merit – as indicators of concern on the part of the more rhetorical/persuasive aspects of government, and markers of efforts made on behalf of populations that are underserved. Outcomes of such policies might be limited, but the effort to include symbolic terms appears to serve a different purpose – appeasement, and possibly maintenance of existing orders of doing business. This undermines public values.

In practice, programs may show little of the outcomes that may be assumed from problem definition. From a pragmatic standpoint, if the public feels like government programs might stray from their intended goals, they might be quite right about this; what is more worrisome is what the intention is in straying, and the damage that such irregular, casual attention to the relationship between intent and outcome in policy might have for the public and administration of public institutions and programs. The 'lie' of mollifying terminology begins small, but compounds over many instances; the consequence is potentially a serious wound to the public trust. From a semiotic perspective, it can be read as petite oppression on an individual basis, which eventually adds up to a "generally prevalent marginalization of many groups" and an undermining of identity (Grenberg, 1999, p. 736). It is systematic and far-reaching.

Semiotic Analysis and Public Policy: Lessons Learned

Semiotic analyses of legal documents and political rhetoric allow for review of program alignment with original policy intent, and for assessment of the level of coordination between law and enacting procedure. It is sometimes taken by the public that political intents are directly translated into laws, which then result in programs resulting in fulfillment of these laws, with outcomes being evaluated on a consistent basis. Public participation in policy circles might amount instead to simulation instead of an impactful exercise. When this 'black box' of effective policymaking is shown as false to greater or lesser extent, the positive intent of public policy is sometimes disregarded in favor of competing narratives: of governments run amok, or an incompetent public sector. The reality is often less sensational – governments are organizations of people, influencing and influenced by their environments, and seeking to create meaning on a daily basis in ways that improve their communities. Success or failure in this regard has little to do with placement of individuals in the public or business sphere. Government, acting on behalf of the public, necessarily requires a more thorough evaluation of efforts in pursuit of the public good. Meaning well is important, but a provision of sign and symbolic value, or ineffective law and programs, is becoming an end in itself, in an era of thin resources and little patience.

Public consternation may result from a seeming inertia or apathy on the part of government, or otherwise, an arbitrariness, rooted in service of particular interests over wider designs of the public good. As shown in the preceding chapters, semiotic analysis can assist in uncovering the interplay of sign, symbol, and the construction of reality in public policy, and in the public sphere. Mindfulness of the nature of such processes and communication about the intent compared with the reality of policy processes and effects, if not resulting in a bit more empathy on both sides, may be helpful in spanning the gap between a skeptical public and governments keen to more effectively balance their values and technical capacities.

We must be cognizant of interactions that set forward illusions in a purposeful way, depending on the creation and perpetuation of falseness (Whitebook, 2004). Instead of rejoicing in a phony reconciliation, we might do better to recognize such ploys on our understanding for what they are – falsehoods that keep us from attaining enlightenment; everything is not what it seems, or what some would necessarily have us believe. In the public sphere, which can become a playground for the airing and attaining of individual desires above the larger interests of the public, it is essential to recognize where shortfalls in grasp may exist. Signaling abounds.

The hold some may have on reality may amount to transient states of awareness, readily altered by new information or interpretation, regardless of its authority or authenticity (Jay, 2004). The appearance is enough for limited purposes, even though the understanding of experience beyond oneself is necessary, for example, for a properly functioning public sphere. This is not to say that such an ideal can even be attained, but even some partial attainment of the ideal, in given instances, would be superior to tacit acceptance of civilization's failure, and an absolute belief in instrumental rationality as the unquestionable way forward. This leads to the potential for growth within the conception of a lifeworld.

Habermas and the Lifeworld

In the work of Habermas[1], the lifeworld is a network based on socialization conditions and social structures, and cultural traditions within a defined community. The lifeworld has the potential to encounter other lifeworlds within an open system, and rationally meet them midway. In the Habermasian view, the lifeworld is to be protected, even against the threat of market forces (Verovšek, 2012). The social is threatened by the systematic at a crisis point, through bureaucratic disempowerment and calls for loyalty; these aspects threaten the lifeworld, which ultimately undermines legitimacy. Legitimate decisions are made when consensus is genuine and passes from the margins to the center, from the informal to the formal, allowing the lifeworld to more effectively confront systems (Flynn, 2014).

Participation in the context-building of the lifeworld – including socialization and knowledge-sharing rather than an increasing default to marginalization and disadvantaging – can counteract a predisposition to instrumental rationality. Understanding comes from more meeting and interaction between individuals, not less. At some point, participation became inclined toward authoritative screaming into the void, rather than an opportunity for citizens to come to understand an issue thoroughly enough to comment on it judiciously. When only the loudest, most inflexible voices win, it may be that most of us lose. Statements in the Habermasian tradition would be assumed to be sincere, legitimate, coherent, and believable (Alvesson & Sköldberg, 2018); instead, some statements in popular discourse today make no such pretensions, and yet are accepted anyway. Sureness appears authentic, even though credibility in the form of meaningful change is lacking. Distortion is the rule and instability the result. Communication can be garbled, rather than clarified by technology. True dissent is not aired because competing modes of thought are cut down by sweet rhetoric; the decrease in trust between individuals and their groups in society approaches absurd if not destructive levels. There need not even be a perception that this clearing out of voice and debate is occurring, if the public is taken enough with technological tools. However, if the tools available to us do not result in desirable effects, from an individual or societal perspective, then we have a right to question the tools and responsibility to choose others.

Socialization and context for meaning are risked because, as Habermas suggested, this lifeworld is being colonized. Administration, politics, and money are removed from local contexts, torn from their referents, enduring as free ideals of their own, expansive and able to exist independently of support of any larger concern. Societies must be able to move beyond authoritarianism and dogma to achieve an opening up of the public sphere (Alvesson & Sköldberg, 2018): to make public participation in policy discussions anything beyond farcical signaling of concern for what citizens think, when choices have already been made.

In the public sphere of the Habermas conception, a speaker has in mind that their message will be accepted by their intended audience before it is communicated. This requires that the participants themselves be situated authentically – that they are who they appear or offer themselves to be. Further, we assume that individuals enter into the public sphere with the genuine will toward deliberation, harmony, and consensus. This requires efforts toward citizenship that are consequential. The other is often made an enemy, and it is expected that political rhetoric is eventually distilled into "facts and arguments...concrete policy proposals and justifications" (Selg, 2010).

Public policy is littered with claims of validity of varying degrees of authenticity. Habermas offered that validity involves the ability to be understood, truth in content, sincerity of the person conveying, and rightness/appropriateness of the speaking act itself (1975). The point is to create the conditions for understanding and allowance for social life, and to permit formation of individual identities. The self is created through interaction with others and so the larger society is developed from the totality of these interactions (Killion, 2010). Where the self and a richly formed identity are subsumed under administrative process, the larger society is injured as much if not more than the individuals themselves. Instead of creating a new, better lifeworld, there is some contentment in accepting what is seen to be unchanging and enshrined in law and policy.

Simon echoes Habermas by noting that modern society, and particularly Western civilization, sees a citizenry that "does not participate in democractic will-formation" and does not participate in the state's administration of the economy or of culture" (2000, p. 85). The focus is instead on ersatz legitimation filched from a preoccupied public. This soft legitimation effort rests in advertising technique and marketing of political movements in something akin to theater. Media occasionally eschews its responsibility to encourage a vigorous democratic debate, focusing instead on the support of consensus opinions that have already found normative backing amongst elite groups (Simon, 2000). While the public sphere, where citizens might participate and help guide government's efforts on their behalf, theoretically exists, in practice it exists as 'hope.' There may be little concern for any loss for the public sphere, as "prematurely foreclosing necessary social debate on the question of how we might learn to live together" (West & Davis, 2011, p. 239) may actually be seen as appealing, and not at all as a dangerous prospect.

The validity of claims figures heavily in the concept of the public sphere. Truth, in Habermas's view, transcends contexts where the original truth claim was made. Truth then is not "a correspondence between a subject and an object existing in a spatial and temporal continuum, but the intersubjective verification of a claim relative to rules recognized within a practical 'action context'" (p. 4). Habermas played upon Peirce's semiotic view by noting that the sign refers to a "past object and a future interpretant" (Habermas, quoted in Swindal, 1994, p. 4). Public policy aims for ideal ends to inquiry, but is unable to attain them, notably because the public is seldom ever able to agree upon specific definitions for public policy problems, prior to setting out for new lands of policy solutions to implement. Law and policy exist long after their creation, subject to new and changing interpretations, possibly from audiences not envisioned when the instruments of policy were devised.

Branding of public policy may encourage a bland thoughtlessness. Bringing in a policy that worked well in one locale may be thought to be a natural choice for another locale experiencing the same general (vaguely, even poorly defined) problem. However, a solution is heavily dependent on an organizational context – a larger framework of supporting structures and hierarchies, not to mention institutional actors and leaders that made it successful in the first place. Formal and informal aspects figure in success or failure as much as program names and language. The new context does not necessarily provide all that is needed to serve as a suitable host.

This speaks to larger organizational if not societal problems, and specifically those centering on the relationship between citizens and governments. If government merely gives the public a requested 'brand-name' public policy, then the public will be happy for the moment at least. Politicians will be reelected. Administrators will have their budgets and be able to provide services, and so on. There is little effort to make the answer reflect the community or its specific problems, and only a pretense to involvement. It is up to government to do what is right in order to 'do good.' It is up to government to know better than this.

Citizens and Administration – Expectations and Responsibilities

A goal of national union in the US was the protection of the public – of "the public good and the rights of other citizens" – from factions. Madison wrote in The Federalist No. 10 (1787) that "The diversity in the faculties of men, from which the rights of property originate, is not less an insuperable obstacle to a uniformity of interests. The protection of these faculties is the first object of government." Madison also noted that "the most frivolous and fanciful distinctions have been sufficient to kindle their unfriendly passions and excite their most violent conflicts." Madison saw a threat in the public speaking directly to the public good – instead offering that representatives in a republic might have a better chance of stating the public good more consistently. The people generally may approach the machinery of the public sphere, but they often do not actually involve themselves in it in an active meaningful way as direct participants. Keeping factions out of the public sphere effectively managed the problem of a policy issue burning out of control, threatening whole institutions, and setting alight the apparatus of governance for short-lived passions or misconceived beliefs.

On the other hand, keeping citizens from directly approaching and accessing the public sphere has not exactly worked out that well. There is confusion about the public interest. Frederickson (1991) offered that most administrators speak about the public and talk about the public interest but have only a vague understanding of what those terms might mean. To bridge this gap, he constructed a basis for understanding the public based on grand themes and purportedly commonly-held virtues, including: a reliance on the Constitution, a virtuous citizenry with strong beliefs, a sense of moral responsibility, civility, a system of processes that hears and responds to concerns of the public, and finally benevolence and love (pp. 409–410). To Frederickson, the public is an outward-searching concept, and by the same token, a legitimate government must make an effort to imbue its citizens with the virtues of civility, while endeavoring to hear and answer their concerns. This approaches an Augustinian prospect of instruction, persuasion, and appeal to the heart of the people (Manning, 2014).

Both approaches assume a lot. Even if self-interest played only a small role in the way people act and react, and it does not, this would likely not be enough to allow for an overhaul of human nature. One might argue that accounting for all the self-interests of the general population would require an utterly inhuman scheme in terms of public service: disinterested public servants of mythical, knightly quality. This is a far-fetched notion. And yet, somewhere between the ideals of a public-centered administrative state, an involved and knowledgeable citizenry, access to the machinery of government, and a need to stem the tide of intemperate, self-serving behavior, likely lies a decent balance of what government can and should be.

Responsibility and legitimacy are primary issues in public administration. Motivation for service aside, the practical realities of acting in a responsible way in a public job are not always so obvious. Views are in conflict, and actions may serve one perspective on professional responsibility while ignoring another. Is the goal to implement a policy as written, precisely as defined by legislation, to write rules that effect such outcomes on an administrative level, even when a public official knows the rules to create larger dilemmas of ethical importance? Are public officials limited in their action, to doing what they are told, so to speak, or engaging in that work while keeping in mind a personal and professional code of ethics?

Citizenship implies responsibility beyond what we want as individuals, or what we might do to help family members; the latter is only possible because of due attention to our societal bonds and obligations. If we have no regard for the common good – for people we may not even know, but have a responsibility for because they are also people and because caring about them is right – then our hold on self-government is weak. We cannot, in that instance, even govern ourselves effectively (Cooper, 1991). Cooper suggested that one of the roles of public administration was to "encourage citizens in their active pursuit of the common good" (1991, p. x). If we expect nothing more from others, and are willing to give nothing more of ourselves, then we are probably defeated.

Citizens have rights, but with those rights come responsibilities, even if those are not specifically enumerated in a constitution. In fact, it is a small-minded argument to suggest that a civil society can survive by only doing what is required specifically in a formal constitution. Constitutions are created by human minds, and thus are prone to bias, and failure to account for all potential views, interpretations, and uses of such a document. There are societal norms, too, but disagreement on what is right in any case, or appropriate action and behavior in the public space, is on the rise. Passivity in citizenship has gotten us nowhere positive, and in recent years, groundswells of dissent have occurred throwing more formalized political forces into a tailspin. Public administrators, rather than being trusted servants of the public, are seen with suspicion by a mostly passive, occasionally irritable and even rancorous, citizenry. As a result, the potential for community decreases (Cooper, 1991). What is worse, the potential we had for understanding one another and tackling some of the truly wicked policy problems of the day is also diminished. We might feel individually like we have accomplished something, in challenging the 'deep-state' or calling out some bureaucratic mistake, but in truth, this is all part of the problem – a problem that is getting worse.

Our cities and their social fabric are crumbling from pervasive jadedness and apparent need to differentiate this group from that group. There can be a sharing of values, toward positive ends, but increasingly factionalism undermines such efforts. Striving for consensus, through public participation, is still an ideal, but when faced with the possibility of following through on the will of a public that has voiced its desires, a government may wish it had never endeavored to ask what the public wanted in the first place. Government has gotten further away from its necessary focus – on serving our communities above ourselves; the public has failed to act in its revered role as citizens beyond the occasional call to legal requirements. We do because we have to, not because we are committed (Cooper, 1991).

Administrators have the position that their technical and subject-matter expertise have brought them to a position of responsibility in government administration, but the further separation of administration from the public through an elite professionalism, which may fall out of contact and favor with the public, is not appreciated by the larger population. The standoffish nature of some administrative departments is pointed to as exactly what is wrong with government. There is a lack of not only transparency but accountability. Why would a population bother to engage such a broken administrative system? If even the perception is that the system is broken beyond repair, the public might absolve themselves of the responsibility for working with it, or even bothering to fix it. To make matters more complex, there is some advantage in painting a structure that is not supposed to be overtly political, but rather expert in subject-matter and process-oriented, as bumbling and idiotic. It is theater and distraction. With power, there is the potential for an assumption that those that hold it are corrupt, or are about to become corrupted; it is just a matter of when they will be unethical and the circumstances, and it is down to the use of influence that is so associated with those holding power (Jurkiewicz, 2005). Public administrators are in a bind – do what is right, and have people hate one for it, or do what is wrong, and hate oneself for it, even if the public or administrative superiors like it. We may not even know precisely what is right and wrong, or 'more right' as the case may be, as public problems can be extremely difficult. Administrators are not likely to get much latitude for being wrong, whether the wrong is real or perceived, especially when absolute standards may be hard to identify. Still, people can and do aspire to great moral/ethical understanding and use that learning in public roles.

People may see government's excesses and want a champion to address those concerns, even if the public knows nothing of the subject matter, or the processes that are involved in government, regulation, and keeping right the ship of state. We need civic virtue on all sides, from elected officials, through a careful, thoughtful exercise of their power, to administrators, acting as citizens with special obligations, to the citizens generally. The risk of loss, absent such a mindset, is especially pronounced now, given the evolving shift to private-centeredness. Why bother? Because we have an *obligation* to bother, even if the project of reasserting civic virtue is a failure. Deliberative democracy may offer a positive way forward.

Deliberative Democracy

Deliberative democracy allows for expression and disagreement, and does not satisfy itself with the encouragement of consensus. As defined by Gutmann and Thompson, it is

> a form of government in which free and equal citizens (and their representatives), justify decisions in a process in which they give one another reasons that are mutually acceptable and generally accessible, with the aim of reaching conclusions that are binding in the present on all citizens but open to challenge in the future.
>
> (2004, p. 7)

In order for deliberative democracy to work, much has to occur. Citizens have to be educated – not only generally but on the issues involved in governance. Belief might trump fact in the court of public opinion – gleefully so – and some may fail to discern any difference. Government should be comfortable giving reasons for its actions to the public and it should give such reasons frequently. Information about government, its work, and performance, should be readily available and user-friendly (Cern, Juchacz, & Wojciechowski, 2012). As it is an ideal type, deliberative democracy perhaps bears little resemblance to reality. As a framework for aspiration, comparison of an ideal with reality shows how out of joint the public sphere is at present, or evidences the concept itself as out of phase with what is possible and even desirable in today's world, when aggregative approaches might be all that are within societal means. Compromising, on values, the meaning of law, or what is possible in policy, is more commonplace than insisting on ideal type.

If the goal of the public sphere is to encourage deliberative democracy, it is worth recognizing that consensus-seeking might well reduce the chances for it. It has been suggested that "the more an agreement approaches the ideal of a rational consensus, the worse the conditions will be ex-post for rational deliberation" (Friberg-Fernros & Schaffer, 2014, p. 113). If that is the case, perhaps agreement is not what we should be looking for at all; what might be desired is healthy disagreement. This would reduce the need for inauthentic statements and counterfeit claims of validity intended to secure a desired response in a message's recipient. Citizenship requires thought and effort. When this is put forward, the results are somewhat unpredictable. It is indeed possible that the reason many feel shut out of the public sphere in not only participation in the simplistic sense of the term, but ultimately involvement in deciding the direction for governance and public policy, is because consensus is far more desirable, and true deliberative democracy, with citizens acting as citizens, is not only unmanageable but possibly dangerous to the maintenance of elite interests. We do not have real citizenship because the elite 'we' has decided that 'we' do not want or need it. Involvement is therefore limited.

There is perhaps a general sentiment that public speech paints policy problems in overly dulcet tones, when immoderate speech and true deliberation are what is required. Feelings are hurt and discussion is shut down; we have no need of widening our ability to understand when it is easy enough to run to the internet to find others that agree with us. "Deliberating despite the pain of judgment," wrote Rob Goodman, "would seem to require a mode of political speech capable of modeling a constructive engagement with pain, and capable as well of pushing us to 'stretch and expand our minds" (2018, pp. 276–277). Rather than challenge the so-called 'prevailing wisdom,' the wisest among us withhold comment, and we are all the worse for it.

The threat of not engaging the public is that government may not appear as legitimate, possibly leading to a destabilization. This is not a sufficient answer for a lack of public engagement (Killion, 2010). Still, too much engagement and deliberation, and government will accomplish little else – the actual function of government and implementation of programs may fall to the wayside while the public expresses its feelings and dissent. This, too, is not a viable option, because the public, having been the source of the hindrance, would also be its primary cause. On some level, assuming genuine public participation were regularly and meaningfully possible, it is a question whether or not government (read as both politicians and administrators) would want that or be able to manage governmental processes in the face of it. Public participation works best on a community level, as increasing levels of complexity and accountability at higher levels in an intergovernmental system offer less of a chance of free-flowing discussion. But even on a local level, there may be a tendency to sweep dissent out when decisions, possibly favoring the connected few, have already been made. People may not be fully knowledgeable about government and its specializations, but maybe they know a sham in public participation when they see it.

Democracy has often had as a centering value the idea that competing interests would enter into a vigorous debate in an effort to reach some consensus. Dissent is healthy – as it takes an effort to craft an argument and an informed opinion, we should value dissent more highly. Morals and values in a diverse public are variable. The goal of law is to solve: to be helpful in removing doubt, where doubt may be removed. "Language indeterminacy, dogmatic concepts and value pluralism constitute the main elements that lead to alternative and conflicting interpretations of law in a democratic framework" (Izzo, 2012, p. 563). Because there is a lack of unifying principle for purposes of establishing compromise, it might be advisable to be comfortable with the ability of the legal tradition to deal effectively with disagreement in the public sphere (Izzo, 2012).

Mutual understanding is attainable, even if it is a difficult prospect. In a Habermasian viewpoint, validity claims are assessed – and to understand them, "an interpreter must have the ability to make clear to himself or herself the implicit reasons that enable participants to take the positions that they do take" (Bernstein, 1983, p. 182). If there is a hope to not put oneself in another's position, and see the world as they see it, then it will be very difficult to push forward the cause of active participation. A refusal to see others' perspectives is an opting-out of active participation in public discourse; unfortunately, this has become more commonplace as the public sphere has become a place for those with a loud voice to loudly air their grievances, rather to engage in a building of a moral/political understanding and common ground (Bernstein, 1983).

The forms of deliberative and participative forms of democracy themselves deserve notice. The venue for participation is one point – selection of place can send a message of inclusiveness for intended proceedings or an apparent desire for events to be limited, if not outright limiting of voice. Questions may be answered by government staff in a way that is welcoming or thoughtless. Even seating at events sends a message: the creation of an audience, potentially, rather than opening an opportunity for meaningful dialogue, or setting aside preferred seating instead of allowing members of the public to sit where they wish as the venue may accommodate. It becomes a question of whether the intent is for the public to interrelate in some purposeful way, or simply observe the proceedings and bear witness to what was going to occur anyway (Farrelly, 2009).

Deliberative democracy and an active lifeworld full of public participation is mostly a hopeful fiction – only occasionally do we get a peek at deliberative democracy, and usually only on a small scale, on the community level, where there exists mutual respect and education on the issues. Much stands in the way: That there is social inequality in today's world is obvious. It could be argued that the public sphere is not one sphere but a number of spheres depending on perspective and placement (Roberts &

Crossley, 2004). Opening up to what people really think and believe and having government act upon it, rather than allowing government to behave in its present manner, suggests a certain ominous turn-of-events. There is potentially a lack of trust, in society that has been allowed to spiral out of control, as people, not acting as citizens but rather as individual, autonomous consumers carrying on about their business. Prejudice masks itself as legitimate protected worldview and basis for public policy action. The unfortunate state of discourse makes schadenfreude common, but even in instances of disagreement and even domination of one group over another, there should be no delight in public misfortune. On various levels, public downfalls extend to all of us.

Arguments for and against even the simplest of issues carry a bombast or haughtiness that is disturbing and unnecessary for anything but ratings. Opinions voiced for their own sake, and arguments with no discernible positive end, are sometimes representative of the tempestuous public's contribution to public discourse. While free speech is defended and rightly so, some sense of self-restraint and patience could be helpful. Charity is lacking, and this limits unity. In this respect, it is fundamentally counter to some trends in society, which would seek to capitalize on separateness and individuality, and tend to accentuate a need for humility. Engaging in rhetorical dishonesty, essentially lacking control of one's will, prevents attention to intellectual morality. When one is selfish and partial to one's ends, greater truth such as the public interest is more difficult to attain. Wanting for oneself becomes a preoccupation and habit that further separates individual from seeking after truth (Huxley, 2004). An ideology assuming that people should take care of themselves, for example, absolves one of many constructive roles in the public sphere that such individuals rely upon for their wealth, safety, and quality of life. The mistaken assumption is that empathy is passé, and that we do not need to take care of one another; this devalues not only capacity but life (Kendzior, 2018). For the public sector to engage in such activity is an affront to the normative basis of high-quality public service, of and for the people.

Trust is often sorely missing in the public space; distrust has led to a point when some believe it does not matter whether they involve themselves in discussions of community importance. For public discourse to work and amount to anything, engagement is necessary, but trust is missing. Sins of the unpardonable sort are silence and indifference. Relationships and marriages die when apathy takes over and people stop trying, and society is no different. Elie Wiesel mentioned indifference and silence on several occasions, observing that this mundane sort of evil emboldens perpetrators and tormentors; he suggested "action is the only remedy to indifference, the most insidious danger of all." (2006, p. 120). Well before that, Hutchins observed "The death of democracy is not likely to be an assassination from ambush. It will be a slow extinction from apathy, indifference, and undernourishment" (1952, p. 80). Trust must be earned, but venturing no effort will result in no gain. Democracy and the public space die from shouting down of disagreement, pressing people into indifference, and from a citizenry that sees no reason to care anymore. Games, illusion, theater, and symbol take the place of discussion where understanding and growth can occur. The simple replaces the sublime, entertainment supplants obligation, and a lack of knowledge and critical thinking ensures it. We begin to find plausible the idea that we are all islands that can survive without one another, as long as we have our smartphones. We are fooling ourselves, and apparently happy with that prospect.

We are left with a public space defined by a need to portray achievement, with perspectives on public policy that seem more concerned with persuasion of the *potential* to fix a problem, than actually fixing it. The truth suffers and proof with it. There is a chance to turn from this reality – to refuse to further consent actively or passively to proxy development of views, and an absence of participation in an ersatz, hollowed-out public sphere. This might constitute a regaining of freedom already lost through atrophy. For now, we are far from creating a great community, and "free social inquiry…indissolubly wedded to the art of full and moving communication" (Dewey, 1954, orig. 1927, p. 184).

There is wisdom in recognizing that decisions have already been made, and that the airing of additional viewpoints would be superfluous. However, mere acceptance of those decisions continues to abdicate the right role of the public, and puts the public square at unacceptable risk. The cases in this book together paint an ominous view of dubious priorities and missed opportunities, and of illusion and reality. In this most likely of potential futures, the public remains ripe for the intellectual picking, and a tool for achievement of private successes in the guise of public benefit.

Note

1 See especially *The Theory of Communicative Action* (1984) and *Between Facts and Norms* (1996).

References

Alvesson, M., & Sköldberg, K. (2018). *Reflexive methodology: New vistas for qualitative research*, 3rd edition. London: SAGE Publications.

Bernstein, R. J. (1983). *Beyond objectivism and relativism: Science, hermeneutics, and praxis*. Philadelphia, PA: University of Pennsylvania Press.

Caron, J. E. (2016). The quantum paradox of truthiness: Satire, activism, and the postmodern condition. *Studies in American Humor, 2*(2), 153–181.

Cern, K. M., Juchacz, P. W., & Wojciechowski, B. (2012). Whose reason or reasons speak through the constitution? Introduction to the problematics. *International Journal for the Semiotics of Law, 25*, 455–463.

Claussen, D. (2008). *Theodor Adorno: One last genius* (R. Livingstone, Trans.). Cambridge, MA: Harvard University Press.

Cooper, T. L. (1991). *An ethic of citizenship for public administration.* Englewood Cliffs, NJ: Prentice Hall.

Dewey, J. (1954, orig. 1927). *The public and its problems.* Athens, OH: Swallow Press.

Edwards, J. (2008). Truthiness and consequences in the public use of reason: Useful lies, a noble lie, and a supposed right to lie. *Veritas Porto Alegre, 53*(1), 73–91.

Farrelly, M. (2009). Citizen participation and neighbourhood governance: Analysing democratic practice. *Local Government Studies, 35*(4), 387–400.

Flynn, J. (2014). System and lifeworld in Habermas' theory of democracy. *Philosophy and Social Criticism, 40*(2), 205–214.

Frederickson, H.G. (1991). Toward theory of the public for public administration. *Administration and Society, 22*(4), 395–417.

Friberg-Fernros, H., & Schaffer, J. K. (2014). The consensus paradox: Does deliberative agreement impede rational discourse? *Political Studies, 62*(S1), 99–116.

Goodman, R. (2018). The deliberative sublime: Edmund Burke on disruptive speech and imaginative judgment. *American Political Science Review, 112*(2), 267–279.

Grenberg, J. (1999). French feminist philosophy. In R. H. Popkin (Ed.), *Columbia history of western philosophy, 730–736.* New York: MJF Books.

Gutmann, A., & Thompson, D. (2004). *Why deliberative democracy?* Princeton, NJ: Princeton University Press.

Habermas, J. (1975). *Legitimation crisis (T. McCarthy, trans.).* Boston, MA: Beacon.

Habermas, J. (1984). *The theory of communicative action, 2 volumes (T. McCarthy, trans.).* Cambridge, MA: MIT.

Habermas, J. (1996). *Between facts and norms: Contributions to a discourse theory of law and democracy (W. Rehg, trans.).* Cambridge, MA: MIT.

Hutchins, R. M. (1952). *The great conversation: The substance of a liberal education.* Chicago: Encyclopedia Britannica.

Huxley, A. (2004, orig. 1945). *The perennial philosophy.* New York: Perennial Classics.

Izzo, V. N. (2012). Beyond consensus: Law, disagreement and democracy. *International Journal for the Semiotics of Law, 25*, 563–575.

Jay, M. (2004). Is experience still in crisis? Reflections on a Frankfurt school lament. In T. Huhn (Ed.), *The Cambridge companion to Adorno, 129–147.* Cambridge, UK: Cambridge University Press.

Jurkiewicz, C. L. (2005). Power and ethics: The communal language of effective leadership. In H. G. Frederickson & R. K. Ghere (Eds.), *Ethics in public management, 95–113.* Armonk, NY: M. E. Sharpe.

Kendzior, S. (2018). *The view from flyover country: Dispatches from the forgotten America.* New York: Flatiron.

Killion, M. U. (2010). The function of law in Habermas' modern society. *Global Jurist, 10*(2), 1–24.

Madison, J. (1787, November 22). The Federalist no. 10. The utility of the union as a safeguard against domestic faction and insurrection (continued). *Daily Advertiser.* Retrieved from http://www.constitution.org/fed/federa10.htm.

Manning, P. R. (2014). Truth and truthiness: What catholic catechists can learn from Stephen Colbert. *America, 210*(3), 26–28.

Roberts, J. M., & Crossley, N. (2004). Introduction. In N. Crossley & J. M. Roberts (Eds.), *After Habermas: New perspectives on the public sphere, 1–27.* Malden, MA: Blackwell.

Selg, P. (2010). Toward a semiotic model of democracy. *Applied Semiotics/Semiotique appliqué, 10*(25), 22–54.

Simon, J. (2000). Ideology, imagology, and critical thought: The impoverishment of politics. *Journal of Political Ideologies, 5*(1), 81–103.

Swindal, J. (1994). The problem of problematization in discourse ethics. *Philosophy & Social Criticism, 20*(3), 1–18.

Verovšek, P. J. (2012). Meeting principles and lifeworlds halfway: Jürgen Habermas on the future of Europe. *Political Studies, 60,* 363–380.

West, K., & Davis, P. (2011). What is the public value of government action? Towards a (new) pragmatic approach to values questions in public endeavours. *Public Administration, 89*(2), 226–241.

Wiesel, E. (2006). Nobel peace prize acceptance speech. In E. Wiesel (Ed.), *Night (M. Wiesel, trans.), 117–120.* New York: Hill and Wang.

Whitebook, J. (2004). Weighty objects: On Adorno's Kant-Freud interpretation. In T. Huhn (Ed.), *The Cambridge companion to Adorno, 51–78.* Cambridge, UK: Cambridge University Press.

Index